IMPENDING GLOBAL WATER CRISIS

IMPENDING GLOBAL WATER CRISIS

Edited by

Jeevan Nair

PENTAGON PRESS

Impending Global Water Crisis / Jeevan Nair, Ed.
Includes bibliographical references and index

ISBN 978-81-8274-397-7

First Published in 2009

Published by
PENTAGON PRESS
206, Peacock Lane, Shahpur Jat,
New Delhi-110049
Phones: 011-64706243, 26491568
Telefax: 011-26490600
email: rajan@pentagon-press.com
website: www.pentagon-press.com

Printed at
Syndicate Binders
A-20, Hosiery Complex, Noida Phase-II Extn., Noida-201305, U.P.

Preface

LET'S get it clear at the start: as of today there is no water insecurity. Certainly, there is a growing scarcity of water but the way we use that water—as if there's no tomorrow—will soon lead the world to internal conflicts, international confrontations and even wars and leave millions dead or dying earlier than they need to. Unless we do something and do it today.

This book makes a small attempt at describing the horrible future that faces the world as *usable* water is spread thin due to the growing number of users and sheer wastage. It also brings together the research conducted by scientists worldwide on measures that will allow us to spread this limited (and life-giving) resource, so that it is available at the right time at the right place. Because the problem is not that water is in short supply but that it is not available at the right place, at the right time.

We also need to be aware that when we talk of water for survival we refer to *freshwater*. The major portion of our earth is covered by oceans but, unfortunately, saline water cannot be consumed. Removing salinity is technologically possible—and is being done on a small scale in many places, particularly Israel—but the costs are so high that no country can afford to consider it as a major solution to the complex problem of water scarcity.

The amount of water in the world is finite. The number of people is growing fast and our water usage is growing even faster. A third of the world's population lives in water-stressed countries now. By 2025, this is expected to rise to two-thirds.

There is more than enough water available, in total, for everyone's basic needs. The UN recommends that people need a minimum of 50 litres of water a day for drinking, washing, cooking and sanitation. In 1990, over a billion people did not have even that. Providing universal access to that basic minimum worldwide by 2015 would take less than 1 per cent of the amount of water we use today. But we are a long way from achieving that.

Global water consumption rose six-fold between 1900 and 1995—more than double the rate of population growth—and goes on growing as farming, industry and domestic demands all increase.

As important as quantity is quality—with pollution increasing in some areas, the amount of useable water declines. More than five million people die from water-borne diseases each year—10 times the number killed in wars around the globe. And the wider effects of water shortages are just as chilling as the prospect of having too little to drink.

Seventy per cent of the water used worldwide goes to agriculture. Much more will be needed if we are to feed the world's growing population—predicted to rise from about six billion today to 8.9 billion by 2050. And consumption will soar further as more people convert to Western-style lifestyles and diets as urban surplus incomes keep increasing. China and India are already facing global accusations that these countries' growing prosperous middle class is responsible for pushing up the demand for luxury foods such as meat, which is the most water-intensive. A kilogram of meat uses up 13,000 litres of water, compared to just 1,000 litres for a kilo of wheat and 1,400 litres for a kilo of rice.

It is the poor who suffer the most from water scarcity. Water shortages can mean long walks to fetch water, high prices to buy it, food insecurity and disease from drinking dirty water. But the very thing needed to raise funds to tackle water problems in poor countries—economic development—requires yet more water to supply the agriculture and industries which drive it.

The UN-backed World Commission on Water estimated in 2000 that an additional $ 100 billion a year would be needed to tackle water scarcity worldwide. This dwarfs the $ 20 billion, which we need every year to tackle HIV and AIDS, and, according to the Commission, it is so much it could only be raised from the private sector. Even if the money can be found, spending it wisely is a further challenge. Dams and other large-scale projects now affect 60 per cent of the world's largest rivers and provide millions with water. But in many cases the costs in terms of population displacement and irreversible changes in the nearby ecosystems have been considerable.

Using underground supplies is another widely used solution, but it means living on capital accumulated over millennia and depleting it faster than what the interest can cover up. As groundwater is exploited, water tables in parts of China, India, West Asia, the former Soviet Union and the western United States are dropping—in India by as much as 3 meters a year.

New technology can help, however, especially by cleaning up pollution and so making more water useable; and in agriculture, where water use can be made far more efficient. Drought-resistant plants can also help. Drip irrigation drastically cuts the amount of water needed, low-pressure sprinklers are an improvement, and even building simple earth walls to trap rainfall is helpful.

Some countries are now treating wastewater so that it can be used—and drunk—several times over. Desalinisation makes seawater available, but takes huge quantities of energy and leaves vast amounts of brine. The optimists say 'virtual water' may save the day—the water contained in crops, which can be exported from water-rich countries to arid ones. But the amounts involved would be immense, and the energy needed to transport them gargantuan. And affordable, useable energy will probably soon be a bigger problem than water itself. In any case, it is not just we who need water, but also every other species that shares the planet with us—as well as all the ecosystems on which we, and they, rely. Climate change will also have an impact. Some areas will probably benefit from increased rainfall, but others are likely to be losers.

We have to rethink how much water we really need if we are to learn how to share the Earth's supply. While dams and other large-scale schemes play a big role worldwide, there is also a growing recognition of the value of using the water we already have more efficiently rather than harvesting ever more from our rivers and aquifers.

For millions of people around the world, getting it right is a matter of life and death.

New Delhi, India

Jeevan Nair

Contents

1

Introduction

'WATER crisis' is a term that refers to the status of the world's water resources relative to human demand. The term has been applied to the worldwide water situation by the United Nations and other world organizations. The major aspects of the water crisis are overall scarcity of usable water and water pollution.

The Earth has a finite supply of fresh water, stored in aquifers, surface waters and the atmosphere. Sometimes, oceans are mistaken for available water, but the amount of energy needed to convert saline water to potable water is prohibitive today, explaining why only a very small fraction of the world's water supply is derived from desalination.

There are several principal manifestations of the water crisis.

- Inadequate access to safe drinking water for about 1.1 billion people.
- Groundwater over-drawal leading to diminished agricultural yields.
- Over-use and pollution of water resources harming biodiversity.
- Regional conflicts over scarce water resources sometimes resulting in warfare.

Water-borne diseases and the absence of sanitary domestic water are one of the leading causes of death worldwide. For children under age five, water-borne diseases are the leading cause of death. At any given time, half of the world's hospital beds are occupied by patients suffering from water-borne diseases. According to the World Bank, 88 per cent of all diseases are caused by unsafe drinking water, inadequate sanitation and poor hygiene.

Historically, the manifestations of water crisis have been less pronounced, but 20th century levels of human overpopulation have emphasized the limited quantity of fresh water. Drought dramatizes the underlying tenuous balance of safe water supply, but it is the imprudent actions of people that have rendered the human population vulnerable to the devastation of major droughts.

Not only are there 1.1 billion people without adequate drinking water, but the United Nations acknowledges 2.6 billion people are without adequate water for sanitation (for example, wastewater disposal). The issues are magnified, since, without water for sewage disposal, cross-contamination of drinking water by untreated sewage is the chief adverse outcome of inadequate safe water supply. Consequently, disease and significant increase in deaths arise from people using contaminated water supplies; these effects are particularly pronounced for children in underdeveloped countries, where 3,900 children per day die of diarrhoea alone.

While these deaths are generally considered preventable, the situation is considerably more complex, since the Earth is beyond its carrying capacity with respect to available fresh water. Often technology is advanced as a panacea, but the costs of technology presently exclude a number of countries from availing these solutions. If lesser-developed countries acquire more wealth, partial mitigation will occur, but sustainable solutions must involve each region in balancing population to water resources and in managing water resources more optimally. In any case, the finite nature of water resources must be acknowledged if the world is to achieve a better balance.

Damage to Biodiversity

Vegetation and wildlife are fundamentally dependent upon adequate freshwater resources. Marshes, bogs and riparian zones are more obviously dependent upon sustainable water supply, but forests and other upland ecosystems are equally at risk of significant productivity changes as water availability is diminished. In the case of wetlands, considerable area has been taken from wildlife use to feed and house the expanding human population. Other areas have suffered reduced productivity from gradual diminishing of freshwater inflow, as upstream sources are diverted for human use. In seven states of the U.S.A. over 80 per cent of all historic wetlands were filled by the 1980s, when Congress acted to create a 'no net-loss' policy for wetlands.

In Europe, extensive loss of wetlands has also occurred with resulting loss of biodiversity. For example, many bogs in Scotland have been drained or developed through human population expansion. One example is the Portlethen Moss in Aberdeenshire, where the area has been halved and a number of species which inhabited this moss, such as the great crested newt, have disappeared.

On Madagascar's central highland plateau, a massive transformation occurred that eliminated virtually all the heavily forested vegetation in the period 1970 to 2000. Slash-and-burn agriculture eliminated about 10 per cent of the country's total native biomass and converted it into a barren wasteland. These effects were from overpopulation and the necessity to feed poor indigenous peoples, but the adverse effects included widespread gully erosion that in turn produced heavily silted rivers that 'run red' decades after the deforestation. This eliminated a large amount of usable fresh water and also destroyed much of the riverine ecosystems of several large west-flowing rivers. Several fish species have been driven to the edge of extinction and some coral reef formations in the Indian Ocean are effectively lost.

Water Politics

There are approximately 260 different river systems worldwide, where conflicts exist which cross national boundaries. While the Helsinki Rules help to interpret intrinsic water rights among countries, there are some conflicts so bitter or so related to basic survival that strife and even warfare are inevitable. In many cases, water use disputes are merely an added dimension to underlying border tensions based on other reasons.

The Tigris-Euphrates river system is one example where differing national interests and withdrawal rights have been in conflict. The countries of Iran, Iraq and Syria, each present valid claims of certain water use, but the total demands on the riverine system surpass the physical constraints of water availability. As early as 1974, Iraq massed troops on the Syrian border and threatened to destroy Syria's al-Thawra dam on the Euphrates.

In 1992, Hungary and Czechoslovakia took a dispute over the Danube river water diversion and dam construction to the International Court of Justice. This case represents a very few of the disputes where logic and jurisprudence could be the path of dispute resolution. Other conflicts involving North and South Korea, Israel and Palestine and Egypt and Ethiopia, may prove more difficult tests of negotiation.

Overview of Regions Suffering Crisis Impacts

There are many other countries of the world that are severely stressed because of human health problems and inadequate drinking water. The following is a partial list of some of the countries with significant affected populations whose only source of consumption is of contaminated water:

Country	Population Affected by Polluted Water
Sudan	12.3 million
Iran	5.6 million
Venezuela	5.0 million
Syria	3.8 million
Zimbabwe	2.7 million
Tunisia	2.1 million
Cuba	1.2 million

In the U.S.A., according to the California Department of Water Resources, if more supplies are not found by 2020, the region will face a shortfall nearly as great as the amount consumed today. Los Angeles is a coastal desert able to support at most 1 million people on its own water; the Los Angeles basin now is the core of a megacity that spans 220 miles (350 km) from Santa Barbara to the Mexican border. The region's population is expected to reach 22 million by 2020. The population of California continues to grow by more than a half million a year and is expected to reach 48 million in 2030. However, the problem of water shortage is likely to surface well before then.

Water deficits, which are already spurring heavy grain imports in numerous smaller countries, may soon become unsupportable in countries such as China and India. Water tables are falling in scores of countries (including Northern China, the U.S.A. and India) due to widespread over-pumping using powerful diesel and electric pumps. Other countries affected include Pakistan, Iran, and Mexico. This will eventually lead to drastic water scarcity and cutbacks in the grain harvest. Even with the over-pumping of its aquifers, China is developing a grain deficit. When this happens, it will almost certainly drive grain prices upward.

Most of the 3 billion people projected to be added worldwide by the mid-21st century will be born in countries already experiencing water shortages. Unless population growth can be slowed down quickly by investing heavily in female literacy and family planning services, there may not be a non-violent and humane solution to the emerging world water shortage.

After China and India, there is a second tier of smaller countries with large water deficits—Algeria, Egypt, Iran, Mexico and Pakistan. Four of these already import a large share of their grain. Only Pakistan remains self-sufficient. However, with a population expanding by 4 million a year it is also likely to soon turn to the world market for grain.

According to a U.N. climate report, the Himalayan glaciers that are the sources of Asia's biggest rivers—Ganga, Indus, Brahmaputra, Yangtze, Mekong, Salween and Yellow—could disappear by 2035 as temperatures rise.

Approximately 2.4 billion people live in the drainage basin of the Himalayan rivers. India, China, Pakistan, Bangladesh, Nepal and Myanmar could experience floods followed by droughts in the coming decades. In India alone, the Ganga provides water for drinking and farming for more than 500 million people.

Outlook

Forecasts for the year 2025 state that two-thirds of the world's population will be without safe drinking water and basic sanitation services. Construction of wastewater treatment plants and reduction of groundwater over-drafting appear to be obvious solutions to the worldwide problem; however, a deeper look reveals more fundamental issues at play. Wastewater treatment is highly capital intensive, restricting access to this technology in some regions; furthermore, the rapid increase in the population of many countries makes this a race that is difficult to win. As if those factors are not daunting enough, one must consider the enormous costs and skill sets involved to maintain wastewater treatment plants even if they are successfully developed.

Reduction in groundwater over-drafting is usually politically very unpopular and has major economic impacts on farmers; moreover, this strategy will necessarily reduce crop output, which is something the world can ill afford, given the population level at present.

At more realistic levels, developing countries can strive to achieve primary wastewater treatment or secure septic systems, and carefully analyse wastewater outfall design to minimise impacts on drinking water and ecosystems. Developed countries can not only share technology better, including cost-effective wastewater and water treatment systems but also hydrological transport modelling. At the individual level, people in developed countries can look inward and reduce over-consumption, which further strains worldwide water availability. Both developed and developing countries can increase protection of ecosystems, especially wetlands and riparian zones. These measures will not only conserve biota, but also render more effective the natural water cycle flushing and transport that make water systems more healthy for humans.

Desalination

As new technological innovations continue to reduce the capital cost of desalination, more countries are considering desalination plants in their strategy to find a solution to their water crises. However, the costs of such plants are still comparatively on the higher side and not every country will be able to afford them.

- Israel desalinizes water for a cost of 53 cents per cubic metre.
- Singapore desalinizes water for 49 cents per cubic metre and also treats sewage with reverse osmosis for industrial and potable use.
- China and India, the world's two most populous countries, are turning to desalination to meet a small part of their water needs.
- In 2007, Pakistan announced plans to take recourse to desalination.
- Australia has introduced desalination.
- In 2007, Bermuda signed a contract to purchase a desalination plant.
- In the United States, California, Arizona, Texas and Florida use desalination to meet a very small part of their water needs.

Nuclear power may be practicable to meet the large energy requirement for desalination. However, given the energy intensive nature of desalination, with associated economic and environmental costs, desalination is generally considered a last resort after all water conservation measures are exhausted.

Global Experiences in Managing Water Crisis

It is alleged that the likelihood of conflict rises if the rate of change within the basin exceeds the capacity of the institution to absorb that change. Although water crisis is closely related to regional tensions, history shows that the 37 records of acute conflict over water are far below the number of cooperative ventures. In the last 50 years, 157 treaties were signed, and 1,288 crises turned out to be cooperative opportunities.

The key lies in strong institutions and cooperation. The Indus River Commission and the Indus Water Treaty survived two wars between India and Pakistan and proved to be a successful mechanism in resolving conflicts by providing a framework for consultation, inspection and exchange of data. The Mekong Committee has also functioned since 1957 and it survived the Vietnam War. In contrast, regional instability resulted when there was an absence of institutions to cooperate and build regional collaboration, like Egypt's plan for a high dam on the Nile. However, there is currently no global institution in place for the management and management of trans-boundary water sources, and international cooperation has happened through *ad hoc* collaborations between agencies, such as the Mekong Committee, formed due to an alliance between UNECAFE and the U.S. Bureau of Reclamation. The formation of strong international institutions seem to be a way forward: they allow early intervention and management, preventing a costly dispute resolution process.

One common feature of almost all disputes resolved is that the negotiations had a 'need-based' instead of a 'right-based' paradigm. Irrigable lands, populations, technicalities of projects define 'needs'. The success of a need-based paradigm is reflected in the only water agreement ever negotiated in the Jordan River Basin; it focuses on needs, not on the rights of riparian populations. In the Indian subcontinent, the irrigation requirements of Bangladesh determine water allocations of the Ganga river. A need-based, regional approach focuses on providing individuals water, ensuring that minimum quantitative needs are being met. It removes the conflict that arises when countries view the treaty from a national interest point of view and move away from the zero-sum approach to a positive sum, integrative approach that equitably allocates available water and its benefits.

2

Overview: Causes, Impacts and Solutions

EXCEPT in a few areas, water scarcity has not yet resulted in internal violence or cross-border conflicts. Thankfully, bi- or multi-lateral cooperation has paved the way to much mutual relief between bordering nations. However, the present 'water scarcity' may soon shape into a 'water crisis.' The reasons for such an expectation are simple:

- The amount of water in the world is finite. The population is growing fast and water use is growing even faster.
- A third of the world's population lives in water-stressed countries. By 2025, this is expected to rise to two thirds.

Today, there is more than enough water for humanity's basic needs but the growing requirement of the global agricultural and industrial sectors could seriously deflate this availability for human use.

The UN recommends that people need a minimum of 50 litres of water a day for drinking, washing, cooking and sanitation. In 1990, over a billion people did not have even that. Providing universal access to that basic minimum worldwide by 2015 would take less than 1 per cent of the amount of water we use today. However, we are a long way from achieving that.

Pollution and Disease

Global water consumption rose six-fold between 1900 and 1995—more than double the rate of population growth—and goes on growing as farming, industry and domestic demands keep increasing. As important as quantity is quality – with pollution increasing in some areas, the amount of useable water is declining.

More than five million people die from water-borne diseases each year – 10 times the number killed in wars around the globe. And the wider effects of water shortages are just as chilling as the prospect of having too little to drink.

Seventy per cent of the water used worldwide is used for agriculture. Much more will be needed if we are to feed the world's growing population – slated to rise from about six billion today to 8.9 billion by 2050. Consumption will soar further as more people adopt Western lifestyles and diets – one kilogram of grain-fed beef needs at least 15 cubic metres of water, while a kilo of cereals needs only up to three cubic metres.

Poverty and Water

The poor are the ones who suffer the most. Water shortages can mean long walks to fetch water, high prices to buy it, food insecurity and diseases inflicted by drinking dirty water. But the prime requirement to raise funds to tackle water problems in poor countries – economic development – requires yet more water to supply the agriculture and industries which drive it.

The UN-backed World Commission on Water estimated in 2000 that an additional $ 100 billion a year would be needed to tackle the water scarcity worldwide.

This dwarfs the $ 20 billion that was needed in 2007 to tackle HIV and AIDS and, according to the Commission, such large funding cannot be raised by the public sector alone – the private sector must also be involved. Even if the money can be found, spending it wisely is a further challenge. Dams and other large-scale projects now affect 60 per cent of the world's largest rivers and provide millions with water. But in many cases the costs in terms of population displacement and irreversible changes in the nearby ecosystems have been considerable.

Using underground supplies is another widely used solution, but it means living on capital accumulated over millennia and depleting it faster than the interest can recharge it. As groundwater is exploited, water tables in parts of China, India, West Asia, the former Soviet Union and the western United States are dropping – in India by as much as 3 metres a year.

Technical Solutions

New technology can help, however, especially by cleaning up pollution and thus making more water useable; and in agriculture, where water use can be made far more efficient. Drought-resistant plants can also help. Drip irrigation drastically cuts the amount of water needed, low-pressure sprinklers are an improvement and even building simple earth walls to trap rainfall is helpful. Some countries are now treating wastewater so that it can be used—and drunk—several times over. Desalinization makes seawater available, but takes huge quantities of energy and leaves vast amounts of brine.

The optimists say 'virtual water' may save the day—the water contained in crops, which can be exported from water-rich countries to arid ones. However, the amounts involved would be immense, and the energy needed to transport them gargantuan. Moreover, affordable, useable energy will probably soon be a bigger problem than water itself.

Climate Change

In any case, it is not just we who need water, but also every other species that shares the planet with us—as well as all the ecosystems on which we, and they, rely. Climate change will also have an impact. Some areas will probably benefit from increased rainfall, but others are likely to be losers. We have to rethink how much water we really need if we are to learn how to share the Earth's supply.

While dams and other large-scale schemes play a big role worldwide, there is also a growing recognition of the value of using the water we already have more efficiently rather than harvesting even more from our rivers and aquifers. For millions of people around the world, getting it right is a matter of life and death.

While the world's population tripled in the 20th century, the use of renewable water resources has grown six fold. Within the next 50 years, the world population will increase by another 40 to 50 per cent. This population growth—coupled with industrialization and urbanization—will result in an increasing demand for water and will have serious consequences on the environment.

There is more wastewater generated and dispersed today than at any other time in the history of our planet: still more than one out of six people lack access to safe drinking water, namely 1.1 billion people and more than two out of six lack adequate sanitation, namely 2.6 billion people. Nearly 4,000 children die every day from water-borne diseases. These figures represent only people in poor conditions and the reality could be much higher.

Agricultural Crisis

Withdrawals of water for irrigation represent 66 per cent of the total withdrawals (up to 90 per cent in arid regions), the other 34 per cent being used by domestic households (10 per cent), industry (20 per cent), or lost in evaporation from reservoirs (4 per cent).

As the per capita use of water increases due to changes in lifestyle and as population increases as well, the proportion of water for human use is increasing. This, coupled with spatial and temporal variations in water availability, means that the water to produce food for human consumption, industrial processes and all the other uses is becoming scarcer.

Environmental Crisis

Increased water use by humans not only reduces the amount of water available for industrial and agricultural development but also has a profound effect on aquatic ecosystems and their dependent species. Environmental balances are disturbed and cannot play their regulating role any more.

The Concept of Water Stress

Water stress results from an imbalance between water use and water resources. The water stress indicator is the proportion of water withdrawal with respect to total renewable resources. It is a criticality ratio, which implies that water stress depends on the variability of resources.

Water stress causes deterioration of freshwater resources in terms of quantity (aquifer over-exploitation, dry rivers, etc.) and quality (eutrophication, organic matter pollution, saline intrusion, etc.).

The value of this criticality ratio that indicates high water stress is based on expert judgement and experience. It ranges between 20 per cent for basins with highly variable runoff and 60 per cent for temperate zone basins.

Increasing Tensions

As the resource is becoming scarce, tensions among different water users may intensify, both at the national and international level. Over 260 river basins are shared by two or more countries. In the absence of strong institutions and agreements, changes within a basin can lead to trans-boundary tensions.

When major projects proceed without regional collaboration, they can become a point of conflict, heightening regional instability. The Parana La Plata, the Aral Sea, the Jordan and the Danube are examples. Due to the pressure on the Aral Sea, half of its capacity has disappeared, representing two-thirds of its volume. Over 36,000 km^2 of marine grounds are now covered by salt.

Improving the Situation

> There is a water crisis today. But the crisis is not about having too little water to satisfy our needs. It is a crisis of managing water so badly that billions of people—and the environment—suffer badly.
>
> —*World Water Vision Report*

Despite the current state of affairs, corrective measures still can be taken to prevent the crisis worsening. There is an increasing awareness that our freshwater resources are limited and need to be protected in terms of both quantity and quality.

This water challenge affects not only the water community, but also decision-makers and every human being. 'Water is everybody's business' was one of the key messages of the 2nd World Water Forum.

Saving Water Resources

Whatever the use of freshwater (agriculture, industry, domestic), huge savings of water and improvements in water management are possible.

Almost everywhere, water is wasted and as long as people are not facing water scarcity, they believe access to water is natural and never-ending. With urbanization and changes in lifestyle, water consumption is bound to increase.

However, changes in food habits, for example, may reduce the problem, knowing that growing 1 kg of potatoes requires only 100 litres of water, whereas 1 kg of beef requires 13,000 litres.

Improving Drinking Water Supply

Water should be recognized as a great priority. One of the main objectives of the World Water Council is to increase awareness of the water issue. Decision-makers at all levels must be implicated. One of the Millennium Development Goals is to halve, by 2015, the proportion of people without sustainable access to safe drinking water and sanitation. To that aim, several measures need to be taken, such as:

- guarantee the right to water;
- decentralise the responsibility for water;
- develop know-how at the local level;
- increase and improve financing;
- evaluate and monitor water resources.

Improving Trans-Boundary Cooperation

As far as trans-boundary conflicts are concerned, regional economic development and cultural preservation can all be strengthened by states cooperating on water. Instead of a trend towards war, water management can be viewed as a trend towards cooperation and peace. Many initiatives have been and can be launched to avoid crises. Institutional commitments as in the Senegal River are created. In 2001, UNESCO and Green Cross International joined forces in response to the growing threat of conflicts linked to water. They launched the joint 'From Potential Conflicts to Co-Operation Potential' programme to promote peace in the use of trans-boundary watercourses by addressing conflicts and fostering co-operation among states and stakeholders.

3

2025: A Future Perspective

FOR some time, experts have argued about the Earth's capacity to support ever larger human populations. Can the Earth produce enough food to feed 8 billion people? 10 billion? It now appears that one of the main factors limiting future food production will be water.

This scarce resource is facing heavy and unsustainable demand from users of all kinds, and farmers have to compete increasingly for water with urban residents and industries. Environmental uses of water, which may be the key to ensuring the sustainability of the Earth's water supply in the long run, often get short shrift.

Based on a global model of supply and demand for food and water, a report shows that if current water policies continue, farmers will indeed find it difficult to meet the world's food needs. The hardest hit will be the world's poorest people.

The results from the model used in this report also show the consequences of changing the course of the water policy. Further inattention to water-related investments and policies will produce a severe water crisis, which will lead in turn to a food crisis.

A commitment to sustainable use of water, through appropriate policies and investments, however, will lead to a more water- and food-secure world. Water may be a scarce resource, but humans have developed many ways of using it more efficiently—that is, getting more from each unit of water. However, water-saving policies, practices and technologies are of no help if they are not used. Inappropriate incentives and institutions often hinder the effective use of water. This report spells out the future results of our current choices.

Demand for the world's increasingly scarce water supply is rising rapidly, challenging its availability for food production and putting global food security at risk. Agriculture, upon which a burgeoning population depends for food, is competing with industrial, household, and environmental uses for this scarce water supply. Even as demand for water by all users grows, groundwater is being depleted, other water ecosystems are becoming polluted and degraded and developing new sources of water is becoming more costly.

Will there be enough water to grow food for the almost 8 billion people expected to populate the Earth by 2025? It is impossible to answer this question without an understanding of the evolving relationship between water availability and food production. This understanding will allow decision makers to look squarely at the consequences of the choices they make to balance water supply and demand among all users in the years to come.

To spell out these consequences, a global model was developed of water and food supply and demand to address the following questions:

- How are water availability and water demand likely to evolve by the year 2025?
- What impact will various water policies and investments have on water availability for the environment, domestic and industrial uses, and irrigation?
- What steps can policymakers take to ensure a sustainable use of water that meets the world's food needs?

The Outlook up to 2025

Water development underpins food security, people's livelihoods, industrial growth and environmental sustainability throughout the world. In 1995, the world withdrew 3,906 cubic kilometres (km^3) of water for these purposes.

By 2025, water withdrawal for most uses (domestic, industrial, and livestock) is projected to increase by at least 50 per cent. This will severely limit irrigation water withdrawal, which will increase by only 4 per cent, constraining food production in turn.

Growing Thirst

About 250 million hectares are irrigated worldwide today, nearly five times more than at the beginning of the 20th century. Irrigation has helped boost agricultural yields and outputs and stabilize food production and prices. But growth in population and income will only increase the demand for irrigation water to meet food production requirements.

Although the achievements of irrigation have been impressive, in many regions poor irrigation management has markedly lowered groundwater tables, damaged soils and reduced water quality.

Water is also essential for drinking and household uses and for industrial production. Access to safe drinking water and sanitation is critical to maintain health, particularly for children.

However, more than 1 billion people across the globe lack enough safe water to meet the minimum levels of health and income. Although the domestic and industrial sectors use far less water than agriculture, the growth in water consumption in these sectors has been rapid.

Globally, withdrawals for domestic and industrial uses quadrupled between 1950 and 1995, compared with agricultural uses, for which withdrawals slightly more than doubled.

Water is integrally linked to the health of the environment. Water is vital to the survival of ecosystems and the plants and animals that live in them and, in turn, ecosystems help to regulate the quantity and quality of water.

Wetlands retain water during high rainfall, release it during dry periods and purify it of many contaminants. Forests reduce erosion and sedimentation of rivers and recharge groundwater.

The importance of reserving water for environmental purposes has only recently been recognized: during the 20th century, more than half of the world's wetlands were lost.

Three scenarios have been developed in regard to the availability and demand of water up to 2025. They are:

1. Business as Usual
2. Water Crisis
3. Sustainable Water.

Business as Usual Scenario

In the 'business as usual scenario', current trends in water and food policy, management and investment remain as they are. International donors and national governments, complacent about agriculture and irrigation, cut their investments in these sectors. Governments and water users implement institutional and management reforms in a limited and piecemeal fashion. These conditions leave the world ill prepared to meet major challenges to the water and food sectors.

Over the coming decades, the area of land devoted to cultivating food crops will grow slowly in most of the world because of urbanization, soil degradation and slow growth in irrigation investment and because a high proportion of arable land is already cultivated. Moreover, steady or declining real prices for cereals will make it unprofitable for farmers to expand harvested area.

As a result, greater food production will depend primarily on increases in yield. Yet growth in crop yields will also diminish because of falling public investment in agricultural research and rural infrastructure.

Moreover, many of the actions that produced yield gains in recent decades, such as increasing the density of crop planting, introducing strains that are more responsive to fertilizer and improving management practices, cannot easily be repeated.

In the water sector, the management of river basin and irrigation water will become more efficient, but slowly. Governments will continue to transfer management of irrigation systems to farmer organizations and water-user associations. Such transfers will increase water efficiency when they are built upon existing patterns of cooperation and backed by a supportive policy and legal environment. However, these conditions are often lacking.

In some regions, farmers will adopt more efficient irrigation practices. Economic incentives to induce more efficient water management, however, will still face political opposition from those concerned about the impact of higher water prices on farmers' income and from entrenched interests that benefit from existing systems of allocating water.

Water management will also improve slowly in rainfed agriculture as a result of small advances in water harvesting, better on-farm management techniques and the development of crop varieties with shorter growing seasons.

Public investment in expanding irrigation systems and reservoir storage will decline as the financial, environmental and social costs of building new irrigation systems escalate and the prices of cereals and other irrigated crops drop.

The future of water and food is highly uncertain. Some of this uncertainty is due to relatively uncontrollable factors such as weather. However, other critical factors can be influenced by the choices made collectively by the world's people. These factors include income and population growth, investment in water infrastructure, allocation of water to various uses, reform in water management and technological changes in agriculture. Policy decisions—and the actions of billions of individuals—determine these fundamental, long-term drivers of water and food supply and demand.

To show the very different outcomes that policy choices produce, there are three alternative futures that have been envisaged for global water and food, followed by an assessment of specific policy options.

Alternative Futures for Water

Where benefits outweigh costs, many governments will construct dams and reservoir water for irrigation will increase moderately.

With slow growth in irrigation from surface water, farmers will expand pumping from groundwater, which is subject to low prices and little regulation. Regions that currently pump groundwater faster than aquifers can recharge, are the western United States, northern China, northern and western India, Egypt, and West Asia and North Africa. They will continue to do so.

The cost of supplying water to domestic and industrial users will rise dramatically. Better delivery and more efficient home water use will lead to some increase in the proportion of households connected to piped water. Many households, however, will remain unconnected. Small price increases for industrial water, improvements in pollution control regulation and enforcement and new industrial technologies will cut industrial water use intensity (water demand per $ 1,000 of gross domestic product). Yet, industrial water prices will remain relatively low and pollution regulations will often be poorly enforced. Thus, significant potential gains will be lost.

Environmental and other interest groups will press to increase the amount of water allocated to preserving wetlands, diluting pollutants,

TABLE 3.1

Rainfed and Irrigated Cereal Yield by Region for Three Scenarios (2021-2025):

1. Business as Usual (BAU)

2. Lower Irrigation Investment and Higher Rainfed Area and Yield (LINV-HRF)

3. Lower Irrigation Investment and Higher Effective Rainfall Use (LINV-HIER)

Region	Rainfed Yield (metric tons/hectare)			Irrigated Yield (metric tons/hectare)		
Region	**BAU**	**LINV-HRF**	**LINV-HIER**	**BAU**	**LINV-HRF**	**LINV-HIER**
Asia	2.46	2.96	2.49	4.50	4.05	4.13
Latin America	2.92	3.13	3.08	5.46	4.85	4.92
Sub-Saharan Africa	1.19	1.22	1.30	3.08	2.95	2.99
West Asia/North Africa	1.75	1.93	1.89	4.86	4.55	4.61
Developed Countries	3.89	4.24	3.95	5.97	5.54	5.59
Developing Countries	2.08	2.36	2.18	4.53	4.09	4.16
World	**2.77**	**3.07**	**2.86**	**4.80**	**4.37**	**4.43**

Source: IMPACT-WATER Projections, 2002.

maintaining riparian flora and other aquatic species, and supporting tourism and recreation. Yet because of competition for water for other uses, the share of water devoted to environmental uses will not increase.

The Water Situation

Almost all users will place heavy demands on the world's water supply under the 'business as usual scenario.'

Total global water withdrawals in 2025 are projected to increase by 22 per cent above 1995 withdrawals, to 4,772 km^3. Projected withdrawals in developing countries will increase 27 per cent over the 30-year period, while developed-country withdrawals will increase by 11 per cent.

Together, consumption of water for domestic, industrial, and livestock uses—that is, all non-irrigation uses—will increase dramatically, rising by 62 per cent from 1995 to 2025.

Because of rapid population growth and rising per capita water use, total domestic consumption will increase by 71 per cent, of which more than 90 per cent will be in developing countries. Conservation and technological improvements will lower per capita domestic water use in developed countries with the highest per capita water consumption.

Industrial water use will grow much faster in developing countries than in developed countries. In 1995, industries in developed countries consumed much more water than industries in the developing world. By 2025, however, developing world industrial water demand is projected to increase to 121 km^3, 7 km^3 greater than in the developed world.

The intensity of industrial water use will decrease worldwide, especially in developing countries (where initial intensity levels are very high), thanks to improvements in water-saving technology and demand policy. Nonetheless, the sheer size of the increase in the world's industrial production will still lead to an increase in total industrial water demand.

Direct water consumption by livestock is very small compared with other sectors. However, the rapid increase of livestock production, particularly in developing countries, means that livestock water demand is projected to increase 71 per cent between 1995 and 2025.

Whereas livestock water demand will increase only 19 per cent in the developed world between 1995 and 2025, it is projected to more than double in the developing world, from 22 to 45 km^3.

Although irrigation is by far the largest user of the world's water, use of irrigation water is projected to rise much more slowly than other sectors. For irrigation water, both potential demand and actual consumption have been computed. Potential demand is the demand for irrigation water in the absence of any water supply constraints, whereas actual consumption of irrigation water is the realized water demand, given the limitations of water supply for irrigation.

The proportion of potential demand that is realized in actual consumption is the 'irrigation water supply reliability index' (IWSR). An IWSR of 1.0 would mean that all potential demand is being met. Potential irrigation demand will grow by 12 per cent in developing countries, while it will actually decline in developed countries by 1.5 per cent. The fastest growth in potential demand for irrigation water will occur in Sub-Saharan Africa, with an increase of 27 per cent, and in Latin America, with an increase of 21 per cent.

Each of these regions has a high percentage increase in irrigated area from a relatively low 1995 level. India is projected to have the highest absolute growth in potential irrigation water demand, 66 km^3 (17 per cent), owing to relatively rapid growth in irrigated area from an already high level in 1995. West Asia and North Africa will increase by 18 per cent (28 km^3, mainly in Turkey), while China will experience a much smaller increase of 4 per cent (12 km^3).

In Asia as a region, potential irrigation water demand will increase by 8 per cent (100 km^3). Water scarcity for irrigation will intensify, with actual consumption of irrigation water worldwide projected to grow more slowly than potential consumption, increasing only 4 per cent between 1995 and 2025. In developing countries, a declining fraction of potential demand will be met over time.

The IWSR for developing countries will decline from 0.81 in 1995 to 0.75 in 2025, and in dry river basins the decline will be steeper (Table 3.2). For example, in the Haihe River Basin in China, which is an important wheat and maize producer and serves major metropolitan areas, the IWSR is projected to decline from 0.78 to 0.62, and in the Ganga of India, the IWSR will decline from 0.83 to 0.67.

In the developed world, the situation is the reverse: the supply of irrigation water is projected to grow faster than potential demand (although certain basins will face increasing water scarcity). Increases in river basin efficiency will more than offset the very small increase in irrigated area.

As a result, after initially declining from 0.87 to 0.85 in 2010, the IWSR will improve to 0.90 in 2025 thanks to the slowing growth of domestic and industrial demand (and actual declines in total domestic and industrial water use in the United States and Europe) and more efficient use of irrigation water.

TABLE 3.2
Irrigation Water Supply Reliability by Region
1995 and 2025

	Irrigation Water Supply Reliability Index	
Region	**1995**	**2025**
Asia	0.81	0.76
Latin America	0.83	0.75
Sub-Saharan Africa	0.78	0.72
West Asia/North Africa	0.78	0.74
Developed Countries	0.87	0.90
Developing Countries	0.81	0.75
World	**0.82**	**0.78**

Source: IMPACT-WATER Projections, 2002.
Note: Projections for 2025 are for the 'business as usual' scenario.

The Food Situation

Water scarcity under 'business as usual' will lead to slower growth of food production and substantial shifts where the world's food is grown. Farmers will find themselves unable to raise crop yields as quickly as in the past in the face of a decline in relative water supply. The global yield growth rate for all cereals is projected to decline from 1.5 per cent per year from 1982 to 1995 to 1.0 per cent per year from 1995 to 2025. In developing countries, average crop yield growth will decline from 1.9 per cent per year to 1.2 per cent. The projected relative crop yields for irrigated cereals show that scarce water is a significant cause of the slowdown in cereal yield growth in developing countries.

Relative crop yield is the ratio of the actual projected crop yield to the economically attainable yields at given crop and input prices under conditions of zero water stress. The relative crop yield for cereals in irrigated areas in developing countries is projected to decline from 0.86 in 1995 to 0.75 in 2025. This fall in the relative crop yield represents an annual loss in crop yields forgone due to increased water stress of 0.68 metric tons per hectare in 2025, or an annual loss of cereal production of 130 million metric tons, equivalent to the annual rice crop in China in the late 1990s and double the U.S. wheat crop in the same period.

Crop-harvested area is expected to grow even more slowly than crop yield in the coming decades. Cereal-harvested area will rise by only 64 million hectares by 2025, from 687 million hectares in 1995. All of this growth is projected to occur in developing countries, with a slight decline in cereal-harvested area in developed countries.

Growth in food demand will be concentrated in developing countries, where rising incomes and rapid urbanization will also cause people to change the kinds of food they demand. Consumers will shift from maize and coarse grains to wheat and rice, livestock products and fruits and vegetables. In much of Asia, an additional shift will occur from rice to wheat. The projected strong growth in meat consumption, in turn, will substantially increase cereal consumption in the form of animal feed, particularly maize. The total world cereal demand is projected to grow by 828 million tons, or 47 per cent. With slowing production growth, the prices of most food commodities are projected to decline, but far more slowly than in the past two decades. Maize prices will increase slightly, while rice, wheat, and other cereals will all decline in price.

Rice prices show the biggest decline, a drop of $ 64 per ton, or 22 per cent, between 1995 and 2025, but this is still far below the rate of decline in the past three decades. Real world prices of wheat, rice, and maize fell by 47, 59, and 61 per cent, respectively, between 1970 and 2000.

Under the 'business as usual scenario,' irrigated and rainfed production will each account for about one-half the increase in production between 1995 and 2025. The large contribution to production from rainfed areas may surprise some observers. However, more than 80 per cent of cereal area in developed countries is rainfed, and much of this area is highly productive maize and wheat land.

The average rainfed cereal yield in developed countries was 3.2 tons per hectare in 1995, virtually as high as irrigated cereal yields in developing countries and is projected to grow to 4.0 tons per hectare by 2025. Moreover, whereas rainfed cereal yields in developing countries are projected to increase only from 1.5 tons per hectare to 2.1 tons per hectare by 2025, the rainfed area in developing countries will account for 62 per cent of the total cereal area in developing countries. By substituting cereal and other food imports for irrigated agricultural production (so-called imports of virtual water), countries can effectively reduce their agricultural water use.

Under the 'business as usual scenario', developing countries will dramatically increase their reliance on food imports from 107 million tons in 1995 to 245 million tons in 2025. The increase in developing-country cereal imports by 138 million tons between 1995 and 2025 is the equivalent of saving 147 km^3 of water at 2025 water productivity levels, or 8 per cent of total water consumption and 12 per cent of irrigation water consumption in developing countries in 2025.

The water (and land) savings from the projected large increases of food imports by the developing countries are particularly beneficial if they are the result of strong economic growth that generates the necessary foreign exchange to pay for the food imports. However, even when rapidly growing food imports are primarily a result of rapid income growth, national policymakers concerned about heavy reliance on world markets often see them as a signal to set trade restrictions that can slow growth and food security in the longer term.

More serious food security problems arise when high food imports are the result of slow agricultural and economic development that fails to keep pace with basic food demand driven by population and income growth. Under these conditions, countries may find it impossible to finance the required imports on a continuing basis, causing a further deterioration in the ability to bridge the gap between food consumption and the food required for basic livelihood.

'Hot spots' for food trade gaps are Sub-Saharan Africa, where cereal imports are projected to more than triple by 2025 to 35 million tons and West Asia and North Africa, where cereal imports are projected to increase from 38 million tons in 1995 to 83 million tons in 2025. The reliance on water-saving cereal imports in West Asia and North Africa makes economic and environmental sense, but it must be supported by faster non-agricultural growth.

It is highly unlikely that Sub-Saharan Africa could finance the projected level of imports internally; instead, international financial or food aid would be required. Failure to finance these imports would further increase food insecurity and pressure on water resources in this region.

The Water Crisis Scenario

A moderate worsening of many of the current trends in water and food policy and in investment could build up to a genuine water crisis. In the 'water crisis scenario,' government budget problems worsen. Governments further cut their spending on irrigation systems and accelerate the turnover of irrigation systems to farmers and farmer groups but without the necessary reforms in water rights.

Attempts to fund operations and maintenance in the main water system, still operated by public agencies, cause water prices to irrigators to rise. Water users fight price increases and conflict spills over to local management and cost-sharing arrangements. Spending on the operation and maintenance of secondary and tertiary systems falls dramatically and deteriorating infrastructure and poor management lead to falling water use efficiency. Likewise, attempts to organize river basin organizations to coordinate water management fail because of inadequate funding and high levels of conflict among water stakeholders within the basin.

National governments and international donors will reduce their investments in crop breeding for rainfed agriculture in developing countries, especially for staple crops such as rice, wheat, maize, other coarse grains, potatoes, cassava, yams and sweet potatoes. Private agricultural research will fail to fill the investment gap for these commodities. This loss of research funding will lead to further declines in productivity growth in rainfed crop areas, particularly in more marginal areas. In search of improved incomes, people will turn to slash-and-burn agriculture, thereby deforesting the upper watersheds of many basins.

Erosion and sediment loads in rivers will rise, in turn causing faster sedimentation of reservoir storage. People will increasingly encroach on wetlands for both land and water and the integrity and health of aquatic ecosystems will be compromised.

The amount of water reserved for environmental purposes will decline as unregulated and illegal withdrawals increase. The cost of building new dams will soar, discouraging new investment in many proposed dam sites. At other sites, indigenous groups and non-governmental organizations (NGOs) will mount opposition, often violent, over the environmental and human impacts of new dams. These protests and high costs will virtually halt new investment in medium and large dams and storage reservoirs. Net reservoir storage will decline in developing countries and remain constant in developed countries.

In an attempt to get enough water to grow their crops, farmers will extract increasing amounts of groundwater for several years, driving down water tables. Nevertheless, because of the accelerated pumping, after 2010, key aquifers in northern China, northern and north-western India and West Asia and North Africa will begin to fail. With declining water tables, farmers will find the cost of extracting water too high and a big drop in groundwater extraction from these regions will further reduce water availability for all uses.

As in the 'business as usual scenario,' the rapid increase in urban populations will quickly raise demand for domestic water. However, governments will lack the funds to extend piped water and sewage disposal to newcomers. Governments will respond by privatizing urban water and sanitation services in a rushed and poorly planned fashion.

The new private water and sanitation firms will be undercapitalized and able to do little to connect additional populations to piped water. An increasing number and percentage of the urban population must rely on high-priced water from vendors or spend many hours fetching often-dirty water from standpipes and wells.

The Water Situation

The developing world will pay the highest price for the 'water crisis scenario.' Total worldwide water consumption in 2025 will be 261 km^3 higher than under the 'business as usual scenario' – a 13 per cent increase – but much of this water will be wasted, of no benefit to anyone.

Virtually all of the increase will go to irrigation, mainly because farmers will use water less efficiently and withdraw more water to compensate for water losses. The supply of irrigation water will be less reliable, except in regions where so much water is diverted from environmental uses to irrigation that it compensates for the lower water use efficiency.

For most regions, per capita demand for domestic water will be significantly lower than under the 'business as usual scenario,' in both rural and urban areas. The result is that people will not have access to the water they need for drinking and sanitation. The total domestic demand under the 'water crisis scenario' will be 162 km^3 in developing countries, 28 per cent less than under 'business as usual;' 64 km^3 in developed countries, 7 per cent less than under 'business as usual'; and 226 km^3 in the world, 23 per cent less than under 'business as usual'.

Demand for industrial water, on the other hand, will increase, owing to failed technological improvements and economic measures. In 2025, the total industrial water demand worldwide will be 80 km^3 higher than under the 'business as usual scenario'—a 33 per cent rise—without generating additional industrial production.

With water diverted to make up for less efficient water use, the 'water crisis scenario' will hit environmental uses particularly hard. Compared with 'business as usual,' environmental flows will drop significantly by 2025, with 380 km^3 less environmental flow in the developing world, 80 km^3 less in the developed world, and 460 km^3 less globally.

The Food Situation

The 'water crisis scenario' will have severe consequences for food production. Total cereal production under water crisis, for example, will be 249 million metric tons, or 10 per cent, less than the 'business as usual scenario'—the result of declines in both cultivated area and yields. This reduction is the equivalent of annually losing the entire cereal crop of India, or the combined annual harvest of Sub-Saharan Africa and West Asia and North Africa.

Compared with the 'business as usual scenario,' the total cereal-harvested area under the 'water crisis scenario' is 17.7 million hectares, or 3 per cent lower than 'business as usual' in the developing world, 8.9 million hectares, or 4 per cent lower in the developed world, and 26.6 million hectares, or 4 per cent, lower globally. Yields will fall for both irrigated and rainfed crops. The average total cereal yield in 2025 is 216 kilograms per hectare, or 6 per cent, lower under the 'water crisis scenario' than under 'business as usual.' Because the supply of irrigation water in most regions is less reliable under the 'water crisis scenario,' the average yield of irrigated cereals will be lower for developing and developed countries and the world as a whole in 2025. Globally, irrigated cereal yields will be 4 per cent lower under 'water crisis' than under 'business as usual.'

Since farmers fail to harvest more rainfall and crop research cutbacks slow yield growth, rainfed crops will yield 191 kilograms per hectare less than 'business as usual,' a 7 per cent decrease from 1995 to 2025. The decline in food production will help push up food prices sharply under the 'water crisis scenario.' The price of rice will rise by 40 per cent, wheat by 80 per cent, maize by 120 per cent, other coarse grains by 85 per cent, soybeans by

70 and potatoes, sweet potatoes and other roots and tubers by 50 to 70 per cent. Crop prices under the 'water crisis scenario' in 2025 are 1.8 times that of 'business as usual' for rice, 1.7 times for potatoes, 1.6 times for soybeans, and more than double for all other crops.

These high prices will dampen food demand. Under the 'water crisis scenario,' cereal demand in 2025 will decline by 55 million tons, or 7 per cent, compared with the 'business as usual scenario' in the developed world, and 192 million tons, or 11 per cent, in the developing world. Compared with 'business as usual,' net trade will decline in the 'water crisis scenario.'

Developing countries will import 58 million tons, or 23 per cent, less cereal than under 'business as usual.' This decline implies that high prices dampen crop demand and thus lead to trade reductions. The ultimate result of this scenario is growing food insecurity, especially in developing countries. Per capita cereal consumption in 2025 in the developing world is 2 per cent lower than 1995 levels.

This scenario makes it clear that increasing water scarcity, combined with poor water policies and inadequate investment in water, has the potential to generate sharp increases in cereal food prices over the coming decades. Price increases of this magnitude will take a significant bite out of the real income of poor consumers. Malnutrition will increase substantially, given that the poorest people in low-income developing countries spend more than half their income on food. Sharp price increases can also fuel inflation, place severe pressure on foreign exchange reserves, and have adverse impacts on macroeconomic stability and investment in developing countries.

Sustainable Water Scenario

A 'sustainable water scenario' would dramatically increase the amount of water allocated to environmental uses, connect all urban households to piped water and achieve a higher per capita domestic water consumption, while maintaining food production at the levels described in the 'business as usual scenario.' It would achieve greater social equity and environmental protection through both careful reform in the water sector and sound government action.

Governments and international donors will increase their investments in crop research, technological change and reform of water management to boost water productivity and the growth of crop yields in rainfed agriculture. Accumulating evidence shows that even drought-prone and high temperature rainfed environments have the potential for dramatic increases in yield. Breeding strategies will directly target these rainfed areas. Improved policies and increased investment in rural infrastructure will help link remote farmers to markets and reduce the risks of rainfed farming.

To stimulate water conservation and free agricultural water for environmental, domestic, and industrial uses, the effective price of water to the agricultural sector will be gradually increased. Agricultural water price increases will be implemented through incentive programmes that provide farmers income for the water that they save, such as charge-subsidy schemes that pay farmers for reducing water use and through the establishment, purchase and trading of water use rights. By 2025, agricultural water prices will be twice as high in developed countries and three times as high in developing countries as in the 'business as usual scenario.'

The government will simultaneously transfer water rights and the responsibility for operation and management of irrigation systems to communities and water user associations in many countries and regions. The transfer of rights and systems will be facilitated with an improved legal and institutional environment for preventing and eliminating conflict and with technical and organizational training and support. As a result, farmers will increase their on-farm investments in irrigation and water management technology and the efficiency of irrigation systems and basin water use will improve significantly.

River basin organizations will be established in many water-scarce basins to allocate mainstream water among stakeholder interests. Higher funding and reduced conflict over water, thanks to better water management, will facilitate effective stakeholder participation in these organizations. Farmers will be able to make more effective use of rainfall in crop production, thanks to breakthroughs in water harvesting systems and the adoption of advanced farming techniques like precision agriculture, contour ploughing, precision land levelling and minimum-till and no-till technologies.

These technologies will increase the share of rainfall that goes to infiltration and evapotranspiration. Spurred by the rapidly escalating costs of building new dams and the increasingly apparent environmental and human resettlement costs, developing and developed countries will reassess their reservoir construction plans, with comprehensive analysis of the costs and benefits, including environmental and social effects, of proposed projects. As a result, many planned storage projects will be cancelled, but others will proceed with support from civil society groups.

Yet, new storage capacity will be less necessary because rapid growth in rainfed crop yields will help reduce rates of reservoir sedimentation from erosion due to slash-and-burn cultivation. The policy towards groundwater extraction will change significantly. Market-based approaches will assign rights to groundwater based on both annual withdrawals and the renewable stock of groundwater. This step will be combined with stricter regulations and better enforcement of these regulations. Groundwater overdrafts will be phased out in countries and regions that previously pumped groundwater unsustainably.

Domestic and industrial water use will also be subject to reforms in pricing and regulation. Water prices for connected households will double, with targeted subsidies for low-income households. Revenues from price increases will be invested to reduce water losses in existing systems and to extend piped water to previously unconnected households. By 2025, all households will be connected. Industries will respond to higher prices, particularly in developing countries, by increasing in-plant recycling of water, which reduces consumption of water.

With strong societal pressure for improved environmental quality, allocations for environmental uses of water will increase. Moreover, the reforms in the agricultural and non-agricultural water sectors will reduce pressure on wetlands and other environmental uses of water. Greater investments and better water management will improve the efficiency of water use, leaving more water instream for environmental purposes. All reductions in domestic and urban water use, due to higher water prices, will be allocated to instream environmental uses.

The Water Situation

In the 'sustainable water scenario', the world consumes less water but reaps greater benefits than under 'business as usual,' especially in developing countries. In 2025, total worldwide water consumption will be 408 km^3, or 20 per cent, lower than under the 'sustainable scenario' and under the 'business as usual' scenario. This reduction in consumption frees water for environmental uses. Higher water prices and higher water use efficiency reduces consumption of irrigation water by 296 km^3

compared with 'business as usual.' The reliability of irrigation water supply is reduced slightly in the sustainable scenario compared with 'business as usual', because this scenario places a high priority on environmental flows. Over time, however, more efficient water use in this scenario counterbalances the transfer of water to the environment and results in an improvement in the reliability of supply of irrigation water by 2025.

This scenario will improve the domestic water supply through universal access to piped water for rural and urban households. Globally, potential domestic water demand under the sustainable water scenario will decrease 9 per cent compared with 'business as usual,' owing to higher water prices. However, potential per capita domestic demand for connected households in rural areas will be 12 per cent higher than that under 'business as usual' in the developing world, and 5 per cent higher in the developed world.

This increase is accomplished by expanding universal access to piped water in rural areas even with higher prices for water. In urban areas, potential per capita water consumption for poor households sharply improves through connection to piped water, while the initially connected households reduce consumption in response to higher prices and improved water-saving technology.

Through technological improvements and effective economic incentives, the sustainable water scenario will reduce industrial water demand. In 2025, the total industrial water demand worldwide under the 'sustainable scenario' will be 85 km^3, or 35 per cent, lower than under 'business as usual.' The environment is a major beneficiary of the sustainable water scenario, with large increases in the amount of water reserved for wetlands, instream flows, and other environmental purposes. Compared with the 'business as usual scenario', the 'sustainable scenario' will also result in an increase in the environmental flow of 850 km^3 in the developing world, 180 km^3 in the developed world, and 1,030 km^3 globally. This is the equivalent of transferring 22 per cent of global water withdrawals under 'business as usual' to environmental purposes.

The Food Situation

The 'sustainable water scenario' can raise food production slightly over the 'business as usual scenario,' while achieving much greater gains for domestic water use and the environment. The total harvested area under the 'sustainable water scenario' in 2025 will be slightly lower than under 'business as usual' owing to less water for irrigation and barely lower crop prices. Because the supply of irrigation water will be less reliable under the 'sustainable water scenario' than under 'business as usual,' the yield of irrigated cereals will be 2 per cent lower for the world as a whole in 2025. On the other hand, global rainfed yields under the 'sustainable water scenario' will be 7 per cent higher than 'business as usual,' owing to higher agricultural research investment and a larger improvement in rainfall harvesting. With the faster growth in rainfed yields making up for slower growth in harvested area and irrigated yields, total cereal production in 2025 will be 19 million tons, or 1 per cent, more under the 'sustainable scenario' than under 'business as usual.'

Crop prices under this scenario will decline slowly from 1995 to 2025 except for slight increases for maize and soybeans due to heavy demand for livestock feeds. As in the 'water crisis scenario,' net trade in the 'sustainable scenario' is lower than that under 'business as usual,' with cereal imports from the developing world declining by 14 million tons, or 6 per cent. This decline reflects the different rates of adjustment of food production between food importing and exporting countries. Cereal production under the 'sustainable water scenario' is 10 million tons less in developed countries and 29 million tons more in developing countries than under the 'business as usual scenario.'

The 'sustainable scenario' shows that with improved water policies, investments and rainfed cereal crop management and technology, growth in food production can be maintained while universal access to piped water is achieved and environmental flows are increased dramatically. Compared with the 'water crisis scenario,' the increase in environmental flows under the 'sustainable water scenario' is about 1,490 km^3, equivalent to five times the annual flow of the Mississippi River, 20 times the annual flow of the Yellow River and four times the annual flow of the Ganga River.

Raising Water Prices

Raising water prices seems to make sense for several reasons. Higher water prices not only encourage all users to use water more efficiently, but also could generate funds to maintain existing water infrastructure and to build new infrastructure. Yet, because of perceived political risks and concern that higher prices would hurt poor farmers and consumers, there have been few attempts to implement higher water prices. In fact, in most instances, the poor suffer from current subsidized water prices because water subsidies in most countries go disproportionately to the better off urban water users connected to the public system and irrigated farmers. Well-designed price hikes for water can create incentives for people to use water efficiently and recover at least operation and maintenance costs, while protecting and even increasing farm incomes. However, would such water price increases save significant amounts of water that could be left instream for environmental purposes without reducing food production?

To address this question, we examine two scenarios with higher water pricing. One implements higher water prices but with water use efficiency remaining the same as under the 'business as usual scenario.' The other scenario assumes higher water prices but also assumes that higher water prices induce improvements in basin efficiency through better crop water management and investments in new irrigation technology compared with the 'business as usual scenario.'

Under both scenarios, water prices for agriculture, industry, and connected households are assumed to increase gradually over the period from 2000 to 2025. By 2025, water prices for industrial water use are 1.75 times higher than prices under the 'business as usual scenario' in developed countries and 2.25 times higher in developing countries. For domestic water users, water prices are 1.5 times higher in developed countries and double in developing countries. For agricultural water users, prices double by 2025 in developed countries and triple in developing countries compared with the 'business as usual' prices.

The higher-price scenarios result in a reduction of water withdrawals of 839 km^3 (18 per cent) and of total water consumption of 287 km^3 (14 per cent) compared with 'business as usual,' with more than half of the reduction occurring in developing countries. Withdrawals and consumption are the same in the two scenarios; higher efficiency influences the proportion of withdrawals and consumption that are used beneficially. The impact on water withdrawal is even greater in some regions, with reductions of more than 20 per cent in China, Southeast Asia, Latin America, West Asia and North Africa, and between 14 and 20 per cent in other countries and regions. The reduction in withdrawals and consumption thus represents a major benefit for the environment, dramatically increasing environmental flows.

Demand for water for all non-irrigation uses—that is, for industrial, domestic and livestock use—falls dramatically under the 'higher-price scenarios' compared with 'business as usual.' Total non-irrigation consumption of water falls from 599 km^3 under the 'business as usual' scenario to 449 km^3 globally, from 395 km^3 to 285 km^3 in developing countries, and from 204 km^3 to 164 km^3 in developed countries. Water withdrawals for these purposes also fall significantly. Total consumption of irrigation water under both the 'higher-price' and the 'higher-price/ higher efficiency scenarios' is about 100 km^3 less than under the 'business as usual scenario.' Yet, because of more efficient water use in the 'higher price/higher-efficiency scenario,' more of the irrigation water is consumed beneficially by crops. Whereas cereal production declines by about 5 per cent in the 'higher-price' scenario compared with 'business as usual,' under the 'higher-price/higher-efficiency scenario' the change in cereal production is slight.

With the decline in production under the 'higher-price scenario,' world food prices increase, with the greatest increase for rice (10 per cent) and price increases of 4 to 8 per cent for other cereals. When water prices induce higher basin efficiency, however, food prices are the same or lower.

These results show that higher water prices for industry, domestic, and agricultural sectors would result in large water savings that can be used for environmental purposes. Making water use more efficient in conjunction with higher prices is critical to maintaining or increasing the reliability of irrigation water supply and food production compared with 'business as usual.'

Shifting to Sustainable Groundwater Use

A number of basins and countries are pumping groundwater in excess of natural recharge rates. These include the Rio Grande and Colorado River Basins in the western United States, the Yellow and Haihe River Basins in northern China, and several river basins in northern and western India, Egypt, West Asia and North Africa. What would happen to water and food if these regions stopped overpumping and returned to sustainable water use?

The 'low-groundwater-pumping scenario' assumes that all countries and regions will phase out unsustainable groundwater overdraft over the next 25 years. Areas with more plentiful groundwater will increase their pumping almost as much as in the 'business as usual' scenario. Total global groundwater pumping will fall to 753 km^3 in 2021–25, a decline from the 1995 value of 817 km^3 and from the 2025 'business as usual' value of 922 km^3. Compared with 'business as usual,' global consumptive water use will decline 5.6 per cent in the irrigation sector, 0.5 per cent in the livestock sector, 0.1 per cent in the domestic sector and 0.1 per cent in the industrial sector, with most of this change occurring in developing countries. Virtually no change in consumption will occur in other sectors.

In 2021–25, the total area planted to cereals will be 730,000 hectares less under the 'low-groundwater scenario' than under 'business as usual.' Although rainfed area will increase, it will not be enough to offset the large decline in irrigated area. Most of the change in irrigated area will occur in developing countries, especially in China. In most regions, yields for irrigated cereals will fall and yields for rainfed cereals will rise slightly. Total cereal production will decline by an annual average of 18 million tons from 'business as usual' projections in 2021–25.

The fall in irrigated cereal production will lead to price increases that stimulate increased rainfed production, but, once again, the increase will not be enough to overcome the decline in irrigated cereal production. Crop prices under the 'low groundwater scenario' are projected to be 5-10 per cent higher in 2021–25 than under 'business as usual' projections. Although total developing country cereal production will decline in the 'low groundwater scenario' compared with business as usual in 2021-25, these price rises will actually cause farmers in developed countries to produce more cereals and thus lead to an overall increase in cereal production there compared with 'business as usual.'

Not surprisingly, the low-groundwater scenario projects the biggest drop in cereal production to be concentrated in the basins that currently experience large overdrafts, especially China and India. As a result, the developing world as a whole will increase its net imports, with major increases concentrated in China and India, and developed countries will increase their net exports.

These country-level shortfalls in demand and increases in imports could be serious, but they may be a worthwhile trade-off for restoring sustainable groundwater supplies. More important, countries must combine a phase-out of groundwater overdrafting with policies to mitigate the impacts on the overdrafting regions in order to maintain income growth. Countries should increase their agricultural research investments and, particularly in the hardest-hit river basins, make investments and implement policy reforms to increase basin efficiency and encourage diversification from irrigated cereals to crops that give more value per unit of water.

Exploiting the Potential of Rainfed Agriculture

Could more rapid growth in rainfed cereal production—through either research and technology-driven growth in cereal yield and area or through increased rainfall harvesting—compensate for significant reductions in irrigation and water supply investment compared with 'business as usual?' We explore these questions in two alternative scenarios.

The 'low-investment scenario' assumes that basin efficiency will not increase above 1995 levels, that the rate of increase in potential irrigated area will be about one-third of the rate under the 'business as usual scenario,' that the increase in reservoir storage will be 40 per cent of 'business as usual,' and that increases in maximum allowable water withdrawals will be 30 per cent as high. This reduction in investment in infrastructure and management seriously constrains growth in food production, causing an annual drop in irrigated cereal production of 120 million tons (11 per cent) in 2021–2025 and driving cereal prices up by 25–35 per cent.

We then estimate the required rainfed area and yield increases to offset the reduction of irrigated production and maintain essentially the same international trade prices. A larger increase is assigned to rainfed yield than area (because of limited potential for area expansion), and a larger increase is assigned to those basins, countries or regions where irrigation effects are greater. Under this scenario, the international price will maintain approximately the same level as the 'business as usual scenario' for all cereal crops except rice.

It proved impossible to fully compensate for the loss of rice production, which has a high proportion of irrigated area. Compared with 'business as usual,' this scenario results in a decline in global irrigation water consumption of 240 km^3, or 16 per cent and a decline in irrigated cereal production of 153 million tons. Rainfed area, however, increases by 10 million hectares, mostly in developing countries.

Rainfed yields increase by 11 per cent and rainfed production increases by 187 million tons compared with 'business as usual.' The share of the world's cereal produced on rainfed lands will increase significantly, to 62 per cent globally, 51per cent in developing countries, and 78 per cent in developed countries, compared with 56, 43, and 74 per cent, respectively, under 'business as usual.'

The second scenario looks at the possibility of increasing effective rainfall use through water harvesting, conservation tillage and precision farming to counteract the reduction of irrigated production due to low investment in irrigation development and water supply. Effective rainfall use increases by 10 to 15 per cent above 1995 levels from 1995 to 2025 in those basins and countries with rainwater shortages for crop production, including river basins in the western United States, northern and western China, northern and western India and countries in West Asia and North Africa. An increase ranging from 5 to 10 per cent is projected for other regions. These rates compare to 3–5 per cent increases under 'business as usual.'

Under this scenario, world cereal prices (especially for rice) are higher than those under 'business as usual.' The projected increase in effective rainfall water use cannot fully compensate for the irrigation decline. Although the global production of rainfed cereals is 126 million tons more than under 'business as usual,' irrigated production is 131 million tons lower.

Developing countries are harder hit, with a shortfall in total cereal production of 42 million tons (2.8 per cent) that causes a reduction in demand of 26 million tons and an increase in imports of 16 million tons. Nevertheless, the results show significant benefits from better management that generates higher effective rainfall.

These scenarios show that there is significant potential for increasing rainfed production to compensate for lower investment in irrigation. Appropriate investments and policy reforms, however, will be required to enhance the contribution of rainfed agriculture. In some regions, water harvesting has the potential to improve rainfed crop yields. However, crop breeding for rainfed environments is crucial to future cereal yield growth. Strong progress has been made in breeding for enhanced crop yields in rainfed areas, even in the less favourable environments.

The continued application of conventional breeding and the recent developments in non-conventional breeding offer considerable potential for improving cereal yield growth in rainfed environments. Progress could be hastened by extending research to farmers and by using tools derived from biotechnology to assist conventional breeding (Table 3.3).

Governments must also combine crop research targeted to rainfed areas with increased investment in rural infrastructure and policies to close the gap between potential and actual yields in rainfed areas. Important policies include higher priority for rainfed areas in agricultural extension services and access to markets, credit and input supplies.

TABLE 3.3
Water Consumption
Total and Irrigation Water (km³)

Region/Country	Total Water Consumption			Irrigation Water Consumption		
	1995	2010	2025	1995	2010	2025
Ohio and Tennessee	9.3	100.0	10.0	1.1	1.0	1.3
Rio Grande	4.8	4.8	4.8	3.2	2.9	2.9
Columbia	16.9	16.9	17.1	15.2	14.8	15.0
Colorado	16.8	15.9	16.0	13.5	11.9	11.9
Great Basin	7.2	7.7	7.8	5.8	6.0	6.1
California	29.7	30.4	31.0	25.1	25.2	25.4
White-Red	16.5	16.0	17.1	12.5	10.4	10.5
Mid Atlantic	9.3	10.2	9.9	1.1	1.1	1.3
Mississippi downstream	8.2	8.7	9.1	5.8	5.9	6.2
Mississipi upstream	5.3	5.6	5.5	1.4	1.4	1.4
Great Lakes-Red	6.6	7.1	6.9	0.9	1.0	1.0
South Atlantic-Gulf	14.7	16.0	16.8	6.4	6.5	6.9
Texas-Gulf	14.1	14.4	14.9	9.3	8.9	9.0
Missouri	25.7	24.6	24.3	22.6	21.2	20.8
U.S. Total	**185.1**	**188.3**	**191.2**	**123.8**	**118.3**	**119.8**
Huaihi	30.2	32.9	36.6	24.4	22.3	22.4
Haihe	25.4	24.4	23.9	22.1	19.3	17.9
Huanghe	25.0	26.1	28.7	21.3	20.7	22.3
Changjian	101.7	107.9	115.8	82.5	75.7	77.4
Songliao	23.4	25.5	28.6	18.9	18.7	20.2
Inland	32.7	32.7	34.9	31.8	31.2	32.7
Zhujiang	32.9	34.1	38.1	26.6	23.1	23.3
Southeast	16.6	16.5	18.4	14.4	12.4	12.4
China Total	**290.7**	**203.2**	**328.8**	**244.2**	**225.5**	**230.9**
Sahyadri Ghats	7.6	9.3	10.1	5.0	5.3	5.3
Eastern Ghats	5.4	7.4	5.7	5.0	6.4	5.0
Cauvery	6.3	6.5	6.5	5.7	5.5	5.2
Godavari	15.8	16.5	18.8	13.9	13.2	14.3
Krishna	24.3	25.7	28.3	22.6	22.7	24.5
Indian-Coastal-Drain	17.9	23.9	21.6	15.8	20.8	18.0

Continued...

...Continued

Region/Country	Total Water Consumption			Irrigation Water Consumption		
	1995	2010	2025	1995	2010	2025
Chotanagpur	3.2	4.8	6.2	0.7	0.7	0.8
Brahmani	13.0	13.3	15.1	12.0	11.6	13.3
Luni River Basin	19.9	20.1	23.6	19.2	19.1	22.4
Mahi-Tapti-Narmada	17.0	17.8	18.5	15.9	16.0	16.4
Brahmaputra	2.5	3.2	4.0	0.6	0.5	0.4
Indus	79.2	84.1	90.9	77.3	81.1	86.8
Ganges	140.5	140.9	147.0	127.5	118.7	119.5
India Total	**352.8**	**372.9**	**396.3**	**321.3**	**321.6**	**331.7**
European Union	86.4	93.4	96.8	48.4	50.2	51.7
Japan	29.9	29.9	29.0	16.7	15.0	14.8
Australia	12.8	13.5	14.6	10.2	10.4	11.0
Other developed countries	28.4	29.8	31.6	13.7	13.0	14.0
Eastern Europe	33.9	39.2	41.9	20.6	21.7	24.8
Central Asia	82.1	84.6	87.3	77.9	79.2	80.9
Rest of former Soviet Union	63.8	67.3	72.5	38.2	38.4	40.8
Mexico	38.9	40.2	43.1	31.3	29.9	31.1
Brazil	27.8	34.5	39.0	13.6	14.9	15.3
Argentina	19.8	22.1	24.2	15.2	15.7	16.9
Colombia	3.6	4.7	5.8	0.7	0.8	0.9
Other Latin America	41.3	47.9	57.7	27.5	28.3	32.8
Nigeria	5.6	8.6	11.8	3.5	5.0	6.7
Northern Sub-Saharan Africa	30.8	33.7	37.5	27.7	28.6	29.7
Central & Western Sub-Saharan Arica	5.4	8.1	11.3	2.6	3.1	3.6
Southern Sub-Saharan Africa	16.0	18.8	24.2	14.0	15.7	19.6
Eastern Sub-Saharan Africa	4.6	6.4	8.5	2.6	2.9	3.2
Egypt	27.9	30.0	31.9	25.4	26.4	27.2
Turkey	22.8	28.6	34.4	18.1	21.7	25.8

Continued...

...Continued

Region/Country	Total Water Consumption			Irrigation Water Consumption		
	1995	2010	2025	1995	2010	2025
Other West Asia/ North Africa	84.4	88.9	95.9	78.1	79.9	84.2
Pakistan	123.7	129.2	133.1	118.0	119.9	120.1
Bangladesh	20.8	23.5	25.1	18.0	19.1	19.2
Other South Asia	29.3	32.8	35.8	27.2	29.1	30.0
Indonesia	40.5	46.4	52.2	29.5	30.3	30.3
Thailand	27.4	28.4	32.0	24.1	22.9	24.7
Malaysia	4.8	6.4	7.2	2.8	3.2	3.3
Philippines	20.1	23.7	27.7	15.9	16.4	17.1
VietNam	14.7	16.2	19.7	10.2	11.9	13.1
Myanmar	3.3	4.3	5.6	2.2	2.3	2.6
Other Southeast Asia	1.5	2.0	2.8	0.9	0.9	1.0
South Korea	9.4	12.5	12.9	4.9	5.7	6.2
Other East Asia	8.5	9.6	10.6	6.7	7.4	7.5
Rest of the World	0.2	0.2	0.3	0.1	0.0	0.0
Developed countries	440.3	461.3	477.5	271.7	267.1	276.9
Developing countries	1,358.3	1,468.2	1,603.0	1,163.8	1,168.3	1,215.5
World	**1,798.6**	**1,929.5**	**2,080.6**	**1,435.5**	**1,435.5**	**1,492.3**

Source: 1995 data, Estimates based on Shiklomanov (1999), Gleick (1993).
2010, 2025 data, IMPACT-WATER Projections, 2002.

Water scarcity can lead to declining food demand and increasing food prices. As shown in the 'water crisis scenario,' major cereal crop prices may be more than double the projections under the 'business as usual scenario,' and at the same time food demand may be significantly reduced, especially in developing countries. Moreover, price increases can have an even larger impact on low income consumers.

Excessive diversion of water flows and overdraft of groundwater have already caused environmental problems in many regions around the world. The analysis shows that the problems, from a local to a worldwide scale, will likely be even more serious in the future. If current investment plans and recent trends in the water and food sectors continue, expanding the environmental uses of water would require reducing the consumption of irrigation water or domestic and municipal water or both. Thus, in the absence of policy and investment reform, competition over water between households and industries and between farmers and environmental uses will increase in many parts of the world.

With water becoming increasingly scarce, continued high flow diversions would become self-defeating. Excess extraction speeds the recession of ecological systems and lowers water quality, finally reducing the qualified water supply for human uses. This has already occurred in the Aral Sea Basin in Central Asia. Groundwater overdraft can likewise lead to the loss of an important water source for human uses, as is already happening in many regions.

However, the analysis also reveals cause for hope. The scenarios explored in this report point to three broad strategies that can address the challenge posed by water scarcity for food production:

1. Invest in infrastructure to increase the supply of water for irrigation, domestic and industrial purposes;
2. Conserve water and improve the efficiency of water use in existing systems through reforms in water management and policy; and
3. Improve crop productivity per unit of water and land through integrated water management and agricultural research and policy efforts, including crop breeding and water management for rainfed agriculture.

Although the financial, environmental and social costs of new water supply projects are high, in some regions, especially in developing countries, it is still crucial to selectively expand water supply, storage and withdrawal capacities.

Storage and water distribution systems (such as water lift projects and canals) are particularly needed for Sub-Saharan Africa, some countries in South and Southeast Asia (such as Bangladesh, India and Vietnam) and some countries in Latin America.

These countries must consider not only the full social, economic and environmental costs of development, but also the costs of failure to develop new water sources. Projects must be designed to account for full costs and benefits, including not only irrigation benefits, but also health, household water use and catchment improvement benefits. It is also essential to improve compensation programmes for those who are displaced or negatively affected by water projects.

TABLE 3.4
Water Consumption: Non-Irrigation

Region/Country	Domestic (km^3)			Industry (km^3)			Livestock (km^3)			Total Non-Irrigation (km^3)		
	1995	2010	2025	1995	2010	2025	1995	2010	2025	1995	2010	2025
Ohio and Tennessee	1.3	1.3	1.3	6.7	7.4	7.0	0.3	0.3	0.4	8.2	9.0	8.7
Rio Grande	0.7	0.8	0.8	0.8	0.9	0.9	0.1	0.1	0.1	1.6	1.8	1.9
Columbia	1.0	1.2	1.3	0.7	0.9	0.7	0.1	0.1	0.1	1.8	2.1	2.1
Colorado	1.7	1.9	2.1	1.4	1.8	1.7	0.2	0.2	0.2	3.3	3.9	4.1
Grand Basin	0.7	0.8	0.9	0.6	0.8	0.8	0.1	0.1	0.1	1.3	1.6	1.7
California	3.0	3.3	3.6	1.2	1.4	1.5	0.4	0.4	0.5	4.5	5.2	5.6
White-Red	1.8	2.9	3.5	1.5	1.9	2.2	0.7	0.8	0.9	4.1	5.6	6.6
Mid Atlantic	2.6	2.6	2.7	5.4	6.3	5.7	0.2	0.2	0.2	8.1	9.1	8.6
Mississippi-Downstream	1.1	1.1	1.2	0.9	1.0	1.0	0.5	0.6	0.7	2.5	2.8	2.9
Mississippi-Upstream	1.2	1.2	1.2	2.5	2.7	2.5	0.3	0.4	0.4	3.9	4.3	4.1
Great Lakes-Red	1.4	1.4	1.4	4.1	4.6	4.2	0.1	0.2	0.2	5.7	6.2	5.9
South Atlantic-Gulf	3.9	4.3	4.8	3.6	4.2	4.1	0.8	0.9	1.0	8.3	9.5	10.0
Texas-Gulf	2.4	2.6	2.7	2.3	2.8	3.0	0.1	0.1	0.1	4.8	5.5	5.9
Missouri	1.5	1.6	1.7	1.2	1.2	1.1	0.5	0.6	0.7	3.1	3.4	3.5
USA Total	**24.2**	**27.0**	**29.4**	**32.6**	**37.9**	**36.4**	**4.4**	**5.1**	**5.7**	**61.3**	**69.9**	**71.5**
Huaihe	4.0	6.9	7.9	1.2	2.9	5.2	0.5	0.8	1.0	5.7	10.5	14.2
Haihe	1.9	2.8	3.6	1.1	2.0	1.8	0.3	0.4	0.6	3.3	5.2	6.0
Huanghe	2.4	3.4	4.0	1.0	1.5	1.8	0.3	0.5	0.7	3.7	5.4	6.5
Changjian	12.3	20.3	24.3	5.7	10.0	11.3	1.2	2.0	2.8	19.2	32.2	38.4
Songliao	2.2	3.2	3.5	2.0	2.9	4.1	0.4	0.6	0.8	4.5	6.7	8.4
Inland	0.7	1.2	1.5	0.1	0.2	0.4	0.1	0.2	0.2	0.9	1.5	2.2

Continued...

...Continued

Region/Country	Domestic (km^3)			Industry (km^3)			Livestock (km^3)			Total Non-Irrigation (km^3)		
	1995	2010	2025	1995	2010	2025	1995	2010	2025	1995	2010	2025
Southwest	0.4	0.6	0.8	0.1	0.3	0.7	0.0	0.1	0.1	0.5	1.0	1.6
ZhuJiang	4.3	6.9	10.3	1.6	3.4	3.5	0.4	0.7	1.0	6.4	11.0	14.7
Southeast	1.9	2.8	3.5	0.3	1.1	2.2	0.1	0.2	0.3	2.3	4.1	6.0
China Total	**30.0**	**48.0**	**59.4**	**13.1**	**24.4**	**31.1**	**3.4**	**5.3**	**7.4**	**46.5**	**77.7**	**97.9**
Sahyadri Ghats	1.3	1.8	2.3	0.8	1.5	1.6	0.4	0.6	0.9	2.5	3.9	4.5
Eastern Ghats	0.3	0.4	0.5	0.1	0.1	0.1	0.1	0.1	0.2	0.4	0.6	0.7
Cauvery	0.4	0.6	0.9	0.1	0.2	0.3	0.1	0.1	0.1	0.6	1.0	1.3
Godavari	1.4	2.2	3.0	0.2	0.6	0.9	0.3	0.4	0.7	1.8	3.0	3.8
Krishna	1.2	1.9	2.5	0.3	0.7	0.6	0.3	0.5	0.7	1.8	3.0	3.8
Indian-Coastal-Drain	1.1	1.3	1.5	0.8	1.4	1.5	0.3	0.4	0.6	2.1	3.2	3.7
Chotanagpur	1.9	2.8	3.4	0.6	1.3	2.0	0.0	0.0	0.0	2.5	4.0	5.4
Brahmani	0.9	1.2	1.5	0.2	0.3	0.3	0.1	0.1	0.1	1.1	1.6	1.9
Luni River Basin	0.9	0.8	1.0	0.1	0.1	0.1	0.0	0.0	0.0	0.8	1.0	1.1
Mahi-Tapti-Narmada	0.9	1.3	1.5	0.2	0.4	0.6	0.1	0.1	0.1	1.1	1.6	2.1
Brahmaputra	0.6	0.8	1.0	0.4	0.5	0.6	0.8	1.3	2.1	1.9	2.7	3.6
Indus	0.9	1.4	1.8	0.4	0.6	0.7	0.6	2.0	2.6	1.9	3.0	4.1
Ganga	9.6	15.6	20.1	3.0	6.0	6.5	0.4	0.6	1.0	13.1	22.2	27.6
India Total	**21.0**	**32.1**	**40.9**	**7.2**	**13.8**	**15.7**	**3.3**	**5.1**	**8.1**	**31.5**	**51.3**	**64.7**
European Union	12.5	13.1	13.3	21.0	25.2	26.8	4.6	4.9	5.0	38.0	43.2	45.1
Japan	3.4	3.6	3.6	9.5	10.9	10.3	0.3	0.3	0.3	13.2	14.8	14.2
Australia	0.5	0.6	0.7	1.2	1.4	1.5	0.9	1.1	1.3	2.6	3.1	3.6

Continued...

...Continued

Region/Country	Domestic (km³)			Industry (km³)			Livestock (km³)			Total Non-Irrigation (km³)		
	1995	2010	2025	1995	2010	2025	1995	2010	2025	1995	2010	2025
Other developed countries	6.0	6.8	7.2	7.0	8.1	8.4	1.7	1.9	2.0	14.7	16.7	17.6
Eastern Europe	2.9	3.3	3.6	9.0	12.7	11.9	1.4	1.5	1.6	13.3	17.5	17.0
Central Asia	1.6	2.1	2.6	1.7	2.2	2.5	0.9	1.1	1.3	4.2	5.4	6.4
Rest of former Soviet Union	9.1	10.1	10.9	14.4	16.7	18.6	2.1	2.1	2.2	25.6	28.9	31.6
Mexico	3.1	4.2	4.9	3.5	4.8	5.4	0.9	1.3	1.8	7.5	10.3	12.1
Brazil	5.7	7.8	9.6	6.1	8.5	9.7	2.5	3.4	4.4	14.2	19.6	23.7
Argentina	1.1	1.5	1.7	2.0	3.1	3.3	1.4	1.8	2.2	4.6	6.4	7.3
Colombia	1.5	2.1	2.6	0.5	0.7	0.9	0.8	1.1	1.4	2.9	3.9	4.9
Other Latin America	6.7	9.5	11.8	5.7	8.2	10.5	1.3	1.9	2.6	13.7	19.5	25.0
Nigeria	1.7	2.8	3.8	0.2	0.4	0.7	0.2	0.4	0.6	2.1	3.6	5.1
Northern Sub-Saharan Africa	2.4	3.9	5.9	0.2	0.3	0.5	0.5	0.9	1.3	3.1	5.1	7.8
Central and Western Sub-Saharan Africa	2.4	4.2	6.4	0.2	0.4	0.6	0.2	0.4	0.6	2.8	5.0	7.7
Southern Sub-Saharan Africa	1.5	2.3	3.4	0.2	0.3	0.5	0.3	0.5	0.7	2.0	3.1	4.6
Eastern Sub-Saharan Africa	1.6	4.8	4.3	0.1	0.1	0.2	0.3	0.5	0.8	2.0	3.5	5.3
Egypt	1.6	2.3	2.9	0.7	1.1	1.5	0.2	0.2	0.3	2.5	3.6	4.7
Turkey	2.1	3.1	4.0	1.9	2.9	3.6	0.7	0.9	1.1	4.7	6.9	8.7
Other West Asia/North	3.4	4.8	6.3	2.0	2.9	3.5	0.9	1.3	1.9	6.2	9.0	11.7

Continued...

...Continued

Region/Country	Domestic (km^3)			Industry (km^3)			Livestock (km^3)			Total Non-Irrigation (km^3)		
	1995	**2010**	**2025**	**1995**	**2010**	**2025**	**1995**	**2010**	**2025**	**1995**	**2010**	**2025**
Africa (WANA)												
Pakistan	3.1	5.1	7.0	1.6	2.7	3.9	0.9	1.4	2.1	5.7	9.2	13.0
Bangladesh	2.3	3.6	4.7	0.2	0.3	0.5	0.3	0.5	0.8	2.8	4.4	5.9
Other South Asia	1.6	2.8	4.6	0.1	0.2	0.3	0.5	0.7	1.0	2.2	3.7	5.8
Indonesia	6.9	9.5	13.5	3.6	5.7	7.1	0.6	0.9	1.3	11.0	16.1	22.0
Thailand	1.9	3.1	4.3	1.1	1.9	2.5	0.2	0.4	0.6	3.3	5.4	7.3
Malaysia	1.0	1.5	2.0	0.9	1.6	1.9	0.1	0.1	0.1	1.9	3.2	4.0
Philippines	1.3	2.1	3.0	2.8	4.9	7.3	0.2	0.3	0.4	4.2	7.3	10.7
Viet Nam	1.8	3.2	4.5	2.5	0.7	1.4	0.3	0.4	0.6	4.6	4.3	6.6
Myanmar	0.7	1.4	2.1	0.1	0.1	0.2	0.3	0.5	0.7	1.1	2.0	3.0
Other Southeast Asia	0.4	0.6	1.0	0.2	0.3	0.5	0.1	0.2	0.3	0.7	1.1	1.8
South Korea	1.6	2.0	2.3	2.7	4.5	4.2	0.2	0.2	0.3	4.5	6.8	6.8
Other East Asia	0.7	1.1	1.4	0.9	0.9	1.4	0.2	0.2	0.3	1.8	2.2	3.0
Rest of the World	0.1	0.1	0.2	0.0	0.0	0.0	0.0	0.1	0.1	0.1	0.2	0.3
Developed countries	58.7	64.5	68.6	94.7	112.8	113.8	15.3	16.9	18.2	168.6	194.2	200.6
Developing countries	110.6	169.5	221.0	62.2	98.3	121.4	21.8	32.1	45.2	194.5	299.9	387.6
World	**169.2**	**234.0**	**289.6**	**156.9**	**211.0**	**235.2**	**37.0**	**49.0**	**63.4**	**363.1**	**494.1**	**588.2**

Source: 1995 data, Estimates based on Shiklomanov (1999); Gleick (1993).
2010, 2025 data, IMPACT-WATER Projections, 2002.

Expanding water supplies can help alleviate water scarcity, but the results show that the most promising avenue is likely to be water management reforms, incentive policies and investments in infrastructure and technology to enhance efficiency in existing uses.

Throughout this report, it has been shown that feasible improvements in the efficiency of basin-scale irrigation water use can, on a global scale, compensate for irrigation reduction resulting from :

1. the phasing out of groundwater overdraft worldwide;
2. increased committed environmental flows;
3. higher prices for agricultural water use (which themselves encourage investments in improved efficiency); and
4. low irrigated area development.

It has also been shown that improving irrigation water use efficiency is an effective way to increase water productivity.

In severely water-scarce basins, however, relatively little room exists for improving water use efficiency and food production and farm incomes could fall significantly if water for irrigation is transferred to other uses.

In these basins, governments will need to compensate for the negative impact of growing water scarcity on agriculture by alternative means, such as investing in agriculture to obtain more rapid growth in crop yields, promoting the diversification of farming into less water-intensive crops and diversifying the economy to reduce the economic role of agriculture over time.

Making big improvements in river basin efficiency in specific river basins will require site-specific analysis and implementation. Basin efficiency depends on improvements both in water-saving technologies and in the institutions governing water allocation, water rights and water quality. Industrial water recycling, such as recirculation of cooling water, can be a major source of water savings in many countries.

Much potential also exists for improving the efficiency of domestic water use. Steps may include anything from detecting and repairing leaks in municipal systems to installing low-flow showerheads and low-water or waterless toilets. Treated wastewater can be used for a variety of non-potable purposes including landscape and recreational irrigation, maintenance of urban stream flows and wetlands, wastewater-fed aquaculture, and toilet flushing.

To encourage water-saving innovation, domestic and industrial water prices should be increased. Generalized subsidies should be replaced with subsidies targeted to the poor. Water providers should charge low prices for a basic entitlement of water, with increasing prices for greater amounts of water.

Improvements in the irrigation sector can be made at the technical, managerial and institutional levels. Technical improvements include advanced irrigation systems such as drip irrigation, sprinklers, conjunctive use of surface and groundwater, and precision agriculture, including computer monitoring of crop water demand.

Managerial improvements include the adoption of demand-based irrigation scheduling systems and improved equipment maintenance. Institutional improvements involve the establishment of effective water user associations and water rights, the creation of a better legal environment for water allocation and the introduction of higher water prices.

Great care must be taken in designing a water pricing system for agriculture. Direct water price increases are likely to be punitive to farmers because water plays such a large role in their cost of production.

Better alternatives would be pricing schemes that pay farmers for reducing water use and water rights and water trading arrangements that provide farmers or water user associations with incentives to reduce wasteful water use.

Rainfed agriculture emerges from the analysis as a potential key to sustainable development of water and food. Rainfed agriculture still produces about 60 per cent of total cereals and its role remains very important in both the 'business as usual' and the 'sustainable water scenarios.'

Improved water management and crop productivity in rainfed areas would relieve considerable pressure on irrigated agriculture and on water resources.

Exploiting the full potential of rainfed agriculture, however, will require investing in water harvesting technologies, crop breeding targeted to rainfed environments, agricultural extension services and access to markets, credit and input supplies in rainfed areas.

A large part of the world is facing severe water scarcity, but the impending water crisis can be averted. The precise mix of water policy and management reforms and investments, and the feasible institutional arrangements and policy instruments to be used, must be tailored to specific countries and basins. They will vary based on the level of development, agroclimatic conditions, relative water scarcity, level of agricultural intensification and degree of competition for water. However, these solutions are not easy and they take time, political commitment and money. The fundamental reform of the water sector must start now.

4

Freshwater Scarcity and Solutions

FRESHWATER availability, as we have seen, is static and the world has almost reached the limits of discovering new sources of freshwater at its present state of technology development. New—and reasonably priced—sources may come up in the future; for instance, desalinisation of seawater at a cost which makes it affordable or extraction of water from hydrogen. However, we do not have the time to wait for these and other developments. The world is already in the throes of the water scarcity phase but if the problem is not managed it will soon deteriorate into a water crisis phase. The only avenues left to us to avoid the crisis phase is to ensure that existing freshwater is used economically and that pollution is eliminated.

Overuse and pollution of the world's freshwater resources are a recent development. Their long-term consequences are unknown. Already, however, they have taken a heavy toll on the environment, and they pose increasing risks for many species. Polluted water and lack of sanitation also are fostering a human health tragedy. Moreover, the sad state of freshwater resources contributes to the deterioration of coastal waters and seas.

In 1996, the world's human population was using an estimated 54 per cent of all the accessible freshwater contained in rivers, lakes and underground aquifers. This percentage is conservatively projected to climb to at least 70 per cent by 2025, reflecting population growth alone and by much more if per capita consumption continues to rise at its current pace.

As humankind withdraws a growing share of all water, less remains to maintain the vital ecosystems on which we also depend. A substantial portion of the total freshwater available in the hydrological cycle is needed to sustain natural aquatic ecosystems—marshes, rivers, coastal wetlands—and the millions of species that they shelter. Healthy natural ecosystems are indispensable regulators of water quality and quantity. For example, wetlands soak up and store water when rivers flood their banks, reducing downstream damage.

The value of these environmental services to humankind is immense. One estimate, made by Robert Costanza, director of the Institute of Ecological Economics at the University of Maryland, puts the global value of wetlands at close to US$ 5 trillion a year, based on their value as flood regulators, waste treatment plants and wildlife habitats, as well as for fisheries production and recreation, among other uses. New York City is spending US$ 1 billion to conserve and protect water catchment areas in upstate New York—the source of the city's drinking water. The alternative would be to spend $ 5 billion on a state-of-the-art water filtration plant that would cost an additional $ 300 million a year to operate.

In virtually all regions of the world, careless use of water resources is harming the natural environment. Globally, over 20 per cent of all freshwater fish species are either endangered or vulnerable or recently have been made extinct. As the following examples demonstrate, overusing and misusing freshwater resources carries serious consequences for natural species as well as for human populations:

- Diverting water from the Nile River, along with build-up of sediments trapped behind dams and barrages, has caused the fertile Nile delta to shrink. Of 47 commercial species of fish, about 30 have become extinct or virtually extinct. Delta fisheries that once supported over a million people have been wiped out.
- Lake Chad, in Africa's Sahel region, has shrunk from 25,000 square kilometres to just 2,000 square kilometres in the last three decades from periodic droughts and massive diversions of water for irrigation. The lake's once rich fisheries have entirely collapsed.
- Despite cleanup efforts, the Rhine River, which runs through the industrial heartland of Western Europe, is so polluted that it has lost eight of its 44 species of fish. Another 25 species have become rare or are endangered.
- In Colombia, fish production in the Magdalena River plunged from 72,000 metric tons to 23,000 metric tons—a two-thirds drop in

15 years—as a result of agricultural, urban and industrial development and deforestation in the river's watershed.

- Southeast Asia's Mekong River has had a two-thirds drop in fisheries production due to dams, deforestation and conversion of 1,000 square kilometres of mangrove swamps into rice paddies and fish ponds.
- The US state of California has lost over 90 per cent of its wetlands. As a result, nearly two-thirds of the state's native fish are extinct, endangered, threatened, or in decline.

In many countries, ever-increasing demand for forest products and agricultural land, fuelled by rapid population growth and development, is putting environmental resources and the water supply itself increasingly in jeopardy. Forests are important water regulators. Their root structures act as nature's sponges, soaking up water and releasing it slowly throughout the year, thus contributing to reliable river flow, replenishing groundwater supplies, reducing soil erosion, and releasing moisture into the atmosphere. Take away forests and croplands erode, waterways silt up, floods become more frequent, groundwater reserves disappear and the climate changes.

The Pollution Problem

Pollution is pervasive. Few countries, whether developing or industrialized, have adequately safeguarded water quality and controlled water pollution. Many countries do not have standards to control water pollution adequately, while others cannot enforce water quality standards.

Increasingly, international development agencies are urging that developing countries devote more attention to protecting and improving water quality. The developed world also must spend more and do more to clean up degraded waterways, or economic development will stall and the quality of life will fall.

Agriculture is the biggest polluter, even more so than industries and municipalities. In virtually every country where agricultural fertilizers and pesticides are used, they have contaminated groundwater aquifers and surface waters. Animal wastes are another source of persistent pollution in some areas. The water that goes back into rivers and streams after being used for irrigation is often severely degraded by excess nutrients, salinity, pathogens and sediments that render it unfit for any further use, unless cleaned typically at great expense—by water purification plants.

In the U.S.A., agricultural chemicals, eroded sediment and animal wastes have fouled over 173,000 miles of waterways. Farming is said to be

TABLE 4.1
Growing Water Shortages
Population Size and Growth and Renewable Freshwater Availability in Water-Short Countries, 1995 and 2025

Country	Population 1995 (millions)	Water per Capita 1995*	Population 2025	Water per Capita 2025 (millions)	TFR 1998	% Growth Rate 1988
Water Scarcity in 1995 and/or 2025						
Algeria	28.1	**527**	47.3	**313**	4.4	2.4
Bahrain	0.6	**161**	0.9	**104**	3.2	2.0
Barbados	0.3	**192**	0.3	**169**	1.7	0.5
Burundi	6.1	**594**	12.3	**292**	6.6	2.5
Cape Verde	0.4	777	0.7	**442**	5.3	2.9
Comoros	0.6	*1.667*	1.3	**760**	5.1	2.7
Cyprus	0.7	*1,208*	1.0	**947**	2.1	0.7
Egypt	62.1	**936**	95.8	**607**	3.6	2.2
Ethiopia	56.4	1,950	136.3	**807**	7.0	2.5
Haiti	7.1	*1,544*	12.5	**879**	4.8	2.1
Iran	68.4	1,719	128.3	**916**	3.0	1.8
Israel	5.5	**389**	8.0	**270**	2.9	1.5
Jordan	5.4	**318**	11.9	**144**	4.4	2.5
Kenya	27.2	*1,112*	50.2	**602**	4.5	2.0
Kuwait	1.7	**95**	2.9	**55**	3.2	2.3
Libya	5.4	**111**	12.9	**47**	6.3	3.7
Malawi	9.7	1,933	20.4	**917**	5.9	1.7
Malta	0.4	**82**	0.4	**71**	2.1	0.6
Morocco	26.5	*1,131*	39.9	**751**	3.3	1.8
Oman	2.2	**874**	6.5	**295**	7.1	3.9
Qatar	0.5	**91**	0.8	**64**	4.1	1.7
Rwanda	5.2	*1,215*	13.0	**485**	6.0	2.1
Saudi Arabia	18.3	**249**	42.4	**107**	6.4	3.1
Singapore	3.3	**180**	4.2	**142**	1.7	1.1
Somalia	9.5	*1,422*	23.7	**570**	7.0	3.2
South Africa	41.5	*1,206*	71.6	**698**	3.3	1.6

Continued...

...Continued

Country	Population 1995 (millions)	Water per Capita 1995*	Population 2025	Water per Capita 2025 (millions)	TFR 1998	% Growth Rate 1988
Tunisia	9.0	**434**	13.5	**288**	3.2	1.9
U.A.E.	2.2	**902**	3.3	**604**	4.9	2.2
Yemen	15.0	**346**	39.6	**131**	7.3	3.3
Water Stress in 1995 and/or 2025						
Afghanistan	19.7	2,543	45.3	*1,105*	6.1	2.5
Belgium	10.1	*1,234*	10.3	*1,217*	1.6	0.1
Burkino Faso	10.5	2,672	23.5	*1,194*	6.9	2.9
Eritrea	3.2	2;775	6.5	*1,353*	6.1	3.0
Ghana	17.3	3,068	36.3	*1,464*	5.5	2.9
India	929.0	2,244	1,330.2	*1,567*	3.4	1.9
Lebanon	3.0	1,854	4.4	*1,261*	2.3	1.6
Lesotho	2.0	2,565	4.0	*1,290*	4.3	2.1
Mauritius	1.1	1,970	1.5	*1,485*	2.0	1.0
Niger	9.2	3,552	22.4	*1,452*	7.4	3.4
Nigeria	111.7	2,506	238.4	*1,175*	6.5	3.0
Peru	23.5	*1,700*	35.5	*1,126*	3.5	2.2
Poland	38.6	*1,458*	40.0	*1,406*	1.6	0.1
S. Korea	44.9	*1,472*	52.5	*1,258*	1.7	1.0
Tanzania	30.7	2,964	62.4	*1,425*	5.7	2.5
Togo	4.1	2,938	8.8	*1,370*	6.8	3.6
Uganda	19.7	3,352	45.0	*1,467*	6.9	2.7
U.K.	58.1	*1,222*	59.5	*1,193*	1.7	0.2
Zimbabwe	11.2	1,787	19.3	*1,034*	4.4	1.5

Water-stressed countries are those with annual water resources of between 1,000 and 1,700 cubic metres per person, shown in italics. Countries suffering from water scarcity are those with annual supplies of less than 1,000 cubic metres per person, shown in **dark type.**

TFR = Total Fertility Rate.

* In cubic metres per year.

responsible for 70 per cent of current water pollution in the U.S.A. In India, which depends on irrigated agriculture for food supplies, more than 4 million hectares of high-quality land have been abandoned because of salinization and waterlogging caused by too much irrigation.

The world's tremendous output of pollutants challenges the capacity of waterways to assimilate or flush away pollution. A saying among water engineers is 'the solution to pollution is dilution.' This truism is taking on frightening dimensions. Each year roughly 450 cubic kilometres of waste water are discharged into rivers, streams and lakes. To dilute and transport this dirty water before it can be used again, another 6,000 cubic kilometres of clean water are needed—an amount equal to about two-thirds of the world's total annual useable fresh water runoff. If current trends were to continue, the world's entire stable river flow would be needed just for pollutant transport and dilution by the middle of the 21st century, according to an estimate by the UN Food and Agriculture Organization.

Industrialized Countries

Europe and North America confront enormous water pollution problems. Over 90 per cent of Europe's rivers have high nitrate concentrations, mostly from agrochemicals and 5 per cent of them have concentrations at least 200 times greater than nitrate levels naturally occurring in unpolluted rivers. In Poland, three-quarters of the country's river water is too polluted even for industrial use.

Over half of Europe's lakes are eutrophied from a glut of agricultural and municipal nutrients. Eutrophication is a process that occurs when excess nutrients stimulate the growth of algae which, when they die and decay, rob the water of oxygen. In Europe, eutrophication has become one of the most serious problems affecting freshwater and near-shore marine environments.

Groundwater pollution in Europe is worsening. Within 50 years, some 60,000 square kilometres of groundwater aquifers in western and central Europe are likely to be contaminated with pesticides and fertilizers. Of Hungary's 1,600 wells tapping groundwater, 600 of them are already contaminated, mostly with agricultural chemicals. In the Czech Republic, 70 per cent of all surface waters are heavily polluted, mostly with municipal and industrial wastes. Some 30 per cent of the country's rivers are so fouled with pollutants that no fish survive. In the U.S.A., 40 per cent of all surface waters are unfit for bathing or fishing and 48 per cent of all lakes are eutrophied.

Developing Countries

Pollution is a vexing problem in countries where the population is growing rapidly, development demands are great and governments have other investment priorities.

In developing countries, on an average, 90 to 95 per cent of all domestic sewage and 75 per cent of all industrial wastes are discharged into surface waters without any treatment whatsoever. Consider these examples:

- All of India's 14 major rivers are badly polluted. Together they transport 50 million cubic metres of untreated sewage into India's coastal waters every year. The city of New Delhi dumps 200 million litres of raw sewage and 20 million litres of industrial wastes into the Yamuna River every day as the river passes through the city on its way to the Ganga.

- In Thailand and Malaysia, water pollution is so heavy that rivers often contain 30 to 100 times more pathogens, heavy metals and poisons from industry and agriculture than is permitted by government health standards.

- Over three quarters of China's 50,000 kilometres of major rivers are so filled with pollution and sediment that they no longer support fish life. In 1992, China's industries discharged 36 billion metric tons of untreated or partially treated effluents into rivers, streams and coastal waters. In 1986, along sections of the Liao River, which flows through a heavily industrialized part of northern China, almost every aquatic organism within 100 kilometres was killed when over 1 billion tons of industrial wastes were dumped into the river in a period of three months.

- In Greater São Paulo, Brazil, 300 metric tons of untreated effluents from 1,200 industries are dumped into the Tiete River every day as it flows through the city. As a result, the river contains high concentrations of lead, cadmium and other heavy metals. The city also dumps some 1,000 metric tons of sewage into the river each day, of which only 12 per cent gets any treatment whatsoever.

- Karachi, Pakistan's largest city, has completely overwhelmed the capacity of its outdated sewage treatment plants. Because of frequent breakdowns and clogged sewage pipes, these plants often operate at no more than 15 per cent of capacity. The great majority of all sewage water leaks out into the surrounding soil, contaminating the wells used by city residents for drinking water.

Industrial and Municipal Pollutants

While agriculture remains the biggest source of water pollution, wastes from industries and municipalities have increased enormously in recent decades. Between 200 and 400 major chemicals are estimated to contaminate the world's rivers.

Industrial pollutants, such as wastes from chemical plants, are often dumped directly into waterways. Oils and salts are washed off city streets. Heavy metals and organochlorines are leached from municipal and industrial dump sites.

Furthermore, pollutants such as sulphur dioxide and oxides of nitrogen, which combine in the atmosphere to form acid rain, have had pervasive effects on both freshwater and land ecosystems. Acid rain lowers the pH of rivers and streams.

Unless buffered by calcium (as contained in limestone), acidified waters kill many acid-sensitive fish, including salmon and trout. In the soil, acids can release heavy metals, such as lead, mercury and cadmium, that then percolate into waterways.

Some of the worst pollutants are synthetic chemicals. Some 70,000 different chemical substances are in regular use throughout the world. Every year, an estimated 1,000 new compounds are introduced.

Many of them find their way into rivers, lakes and groundwater aquifers. In the U.S.A. alone, more than 700 chemicals have been detected in drinking water, 129 of them considered highly toxic.

A number of synthetic chemicals, particularly the group known as persistent organic pollutants (POPs), which includes halogenated hydrocarbons, dioxins and organochlorines such as DDT and PCBs, are long-lived and highly toxic in the environment.

They do not break down easily under natural processes and thus tend to accumulate and travel up the biological food chain, until they pose risks to human health.

For example, Beluga whales swimming in the highly polluted St. Lawrence River, which connects the Atlantic Ocean to North America's Great Lakes, have such high levels of PCBs in their blubber that, under Canadian law, they now qualify as 'toxic waste dumps.' Indigenous communities that once hunted these whales no longer are permitted to do so because of the health risks.

The Health Dimension

Water-related diseases are a human tragedy, killing millions of people each year, preventing millions more from leading healthy lives, and undermining development efforts. About 2.3 billion people in the world suffer from diseases that are linked to water.

Some 60 per cent of all infant mortality is linked to infectious and parasitic diseases, most of them water-related. In some countries, water-related diseases make up a high proportion of all illnesses among both adults and children. In Bangladesh, for example, an estimated three-quarters of all diseases are related to unsafe water and inadequate sanitation facilities. In Pakistan, aquarter of all people attending hospitals are ill from water-related diseases. Providing clean supplies of water and ensuring proper sanitation facilities would save millions of lives by reducing the prevalence of water-related diseases. Thus, finding solutions to these problems should become a high priority for developing countries and assistance agencies.

While water-related diseases vary substantially in their nature, transmission, effects and management, adverse health effects related to water can be organized into three categories: water-borne diseases, including those caused by both faecal-oral organisms and those caused by toxic substances; water-based diseases; and water-related vector diseases (see Table 4.2)

Water-Borne Diseases

Water-borne diseases are 'dirty-water' diseases—those caused by water that has been contaminated by human, animal or chemical wastes. Worldwide, the lack of sanitary waste disposal and of clean water for drinking, cooking and washing is to blame for over 12 million deaths a year.

Water-borne diseases include cholera, typhoid, shigellosis, polio, meningitis and hepatitis A and E. Human beings and animals can act as hosts to the bacterial, viral, or protozoan organisms that cause these diseases. Millions of people have little access to sanitary waste disposal or to clean water for personal hygiene. An estimated 3 billion people lack a sanitary toilet, for example. Over 1.2 billion people are at risk because they lack access to safe freshwater.

Where proper sanitation facilities are lacking, water-borne diseases can spread rapidly. Untreated excreta carrying disease organisms wash or

TABLE 4.2
Major Water-Related Diseases

Disease	Cause and Root of Transmission	Geographic Extent of Cases[a]	Number per Year	Deaths
Major Water-Borne Diseases				
Amoebic dysentery	Protozoa travel the faecal-oral route via contaminated water, food, person-to-person contact	Worldwide	500 million per year	*
Bacillary dysentery	Bacteria travel the faecal-oral route via contaminated water, food, person-to-person contact	Worldwide	*	*
Diarrhoeal disease (including amoebic and bacillary dysentery)	Various bacteria travel the fecal-oral route via contaminated water, food, person-to-person contact	Worldwide	4 billion currently 3–4 million	3–4 million
Cholera	Bacteria travel the faecal-oral route via contaminated water, food, person-to-person contact	South America, Africa, Asia	384,000 per year	20,000
Hepatitis A	Virus travels the faecal-oral route via contaminated water, food, person-to-person contact	Worldwide	600,000 to 3 million per year	2,400 to 12,000
Paratyphoid and typhoid	Bacteria travel the faecal-oral route via contaminated water, food, person-to-person contact	80% in Asia, 20% in Latin America, Africa	16 million currently	9,000

Continued...

...*Continued*

Disease	Cause and Root of Transmission	Geographic Extent of Cases[a]	Number per Year	Deaths
Polio	Virus travels the faecal-oral route via contaminated water, food, person-to person	66% in India; 34% in Near East, Asia, Africa	82,000 currently	9,000
Major Water-Based Diseases				
Ascariasis	Fertilised eggs are passed out in human faeces. Larvae in eggs develop in warm soil. Humans ingest soil in food. Hatched larvae penetrate intestinal wall, where they mature	Africa, Asia, Latin America	250 million currently	60,000
Clonorchiasis	Worms reproduce in gastropod snails, then are swallowed by freshwater fish or other snails. When humans eat raw or undercooked fish, the worms migrate to the bile ducts and lay eggs	Southeast Asia	28 million currently	None reported
Dracunculiasis (guinea worm)	Worm Dracunculus ingested by Cyclops (a crustacean). When humans digest Cyclops, worm larvae are released into the stomach. Larvae penetrate intestinal wall, then develop into worms, migrating through tissues. After a year, adult worm reaches skin surface of lower extremities. Female comes in contact with water, then discharges larvae into water	78% in Sudan; 22% in other sub-Saharan African countries and a few cases in India and Yemen	153,000 currently	None reported

Continued...

...Continued

Disease	Cause and Root of Transmission	Geographic Extent of Cases[a]	Number per Year	Deaths
Paragonimiasis	Worms living in pulmonary cysts lay eggs in human lungs, which are coughed up and then swallowed. Worm eggs are passed out in faeces and break when in fresh water. Larvae find snail host in which to replicate, then move into freshwater crab or crayfish. Humans eat uncooked seafood. Worms migrate in pairs from stomach through intestinal wall and diaphragm to lungs, where they mate	Far East, Latin America	5 million currently	None reported
Schistosomiasis (bilharzia)	Eggs of the schistosome worm are passed out in human faeces. Eggs hatch on contact with water, releasing the parasite miracidium. Parasite moves into a fresh water snail, where it replicates. It is released back into the water, then penetrates human skin within seconds and moves into blood vessels. Within 30 to 45 days miracidium grows into worm, which can lay 200 to 2000 eggs per day for an average of 5 years	Africa, Near East, rain forest belt in Central Africa, Western Pacific, Kampuchea, Laos	200 million currently	20,000

Continued...

...Continued

Disease	Cause and Root of Transmission	Geographic Extent of Cases[a]	Number per Year	Deaths
Major Water-Related Vector Diseases				
Dengue	Virus is picked up by a mosquito from an infected human or animal. The virus incubates for 8 to 12 days and replicates. The next time the mosquito takes a blood meal, the virus is injected into a human's blood	All tropical environments; concentrated in Asia, Central and South Ameria	50–100 million per year	24,000
Filiarisis (includes elephantiasis)	Worm larvae are ingested by a mosquito and develop. When the infected mosquito bites a human, the larvae penetrate the puncture and reach the lymhatics, where they reproduce.	Africa, Eastern Mediterranean, Asia, South America	120 million currently	None reported
Malaria	Protozoa develop in gut of a mosquito and are passed on in its saliva each time it takes a new blood meal. Parasites are then carried by the blood to the human's liver, where they invade the cells and multiply	Africa, Southeast Asia, India, South America	300–500 million per year (clinical)	2 million
Onchocerciasis	Worm embryos are ingested by black flies. Embryos then develop into larvae within the black flies, and the flies inject the larvae into humans when they bite	Sub-Saharan Africa, Latin America	18 million currently	None reported**

Continued...

...Continued

Disease	Cause and Root of Transmission	Geographic Extent of Cases[a]	Number per Year	Deaths
Rift Valley fever	Virus usually exists in animal hosts. Virus is picked up by mosquitos and other blood-sucking insects and injected into the blood of humans. Humans also are infected while working with body fluids of dead animals	Sub-Saharan Africa	NA	1% of cases

a Number of cases are reported as incidence ('per year')—the number of new cases occurring in a year—or as prevalence ('currently')—the number of cases existing at a point in time.

* Included in diarrhoeal disease.

** No deaths but causes 270,000 reported cases of blindness annually.

NA not available.

Source: WHO 1996.

leach into freshwater sources, contaminating drinking water and food. The extent to which disease organisms occur in specific freshwater sources depends on the amount of human and animal excreta that they contain.

Diarrhoeal disease, the major water-borne disease, is prevalent in many countries where sewage treatment is inadequate. Instead, human wastes are disposed of in open latrines, ditches, canals and water courses, or they are spread on cropland. An estimated 4 billion cases of diarrhoeal disease occur every year, causing 3 to 4 million deaths, mostly among children.

Using contaminated sewage for fertilizer can result in epidemics of such diseases as cholera. These diseases can even become chronic where clean water supplies are lacking. In the early 1990s, for example, raw sewage water that was used to fertilize vegetable fields caused outbreaks of cholera in Chile and Peru. In Buenos Aires, Argentina, a slum neighbourhood faced continual outbreaks of cholera, hepatitis and meningitis because only 4 per cent of homes had either water mains or proper toilets, while poor diets and little access to medical services aggravated health problems.

Toxic substances that find their way into freshwater are another cause of water-borne diseases. Increasingly, agricultural chemicals, fertilizers, pesticides and industrial wastes are being found in freshwater supplies. Such chemicals, even in low concentrations, can build up over time and, eventually, can cause chronic diseases such as cancers among people who use the water.

Health problems from nitrates in water sources are becoming a serious problem almost everywhere. In over 150 countries, nitrates from fertilizers have seeped into water wells, fouling the drinking water. Excessive concentrations of nitrates cause blood disorders. Also, high levels of nitrates and phosphates in water encourage growth of blue-green algae, leading to de-oxygenation (eutrophication).

Oxygen is required for metabolism by the organisms that serve as purifiers, breaking down organic matter such as human wastes that pollute the water. Therefore, the amount of oxygen contained in water is a key indicator of water quality.

Pesticides such as DDT and heptachlor, which are used in agriculture, often wash off in irrigation water. Their presence in water and food products has alarming implications for human health because they are known to cause cancer and also may cause low sperm counts and neurological disease. In Dhaka, Bangladesh, heptachlor residues in water sources have reached levels as high as .789 micrograms per litre—more than 25 times the WHO-recommended maximum of .03 micrograms per litre. Also, in Venezuela, a study of irrigation water collected during the rainy season found that the water was contaminated with a number of pesticides. Examination of pregnant women in the area found that they all had breast milk containing DDT residues—toxins that can be passed to an infant.

The seepage of toxic pollutants into ground and surface water reservoirs used for drinking and household use causes health problems in industrialized countries as well. In Europe and Russia, the health of some 500 million people is at risk from water pollution. For example, in northern Russia half a million people on the Kola Peninsula drink water contaminated with heavy metals, a practice that helps to explain high infant mortality rates and endemic diarrhoeal and intestinal diseases reported there.

Prevention and Solutions

Improving public sanitation and providing a clean water supply are the two steps needed to prevent most water-borne diseases and deaths. In particular, constructing sanitary latrines and treating waste water to allow for biodegradation of human wastes will help curb diseases caused by pollution. At the least, solids should be settled out of waste water so that it is less contaminated. It is important that a clean water supply and the construction of proper sanitary facilities be provided together because they reinforce each other to limit the spread of infection.

Many studies link improvements in sanitation and provision of potable water with dramatic reductions in water-related morbidity and mortality. A review of over 100 studies of the effects of clean water and sanitation on human health found that the median reduction in deaths from water-related diseases was 69 per cent among people with access to potable water and proper sanitation (see Table 4.3).

Providing clean water and sanitation greatly reduces child mortality. According to a review of 144 studies from the 1980s, infant and child deaths fell by an average of 55 per cent as a result of providing clean water and sanitation. In a study of countries where infant mortality rates dropped dramatically—as in Costa Rica, where the decline was from 68 deaths per 1,000 live births in the 1970s to just 20 per 1,000 in the 1980s—researchers

TABLE 4.3
Reducing Water-Related Diseases
Impact of Improved Water Infrastructure, Selected Studies

Place	Type of Facilities or Improvement	Type of Study	Diseases	Difference in Incidence After Improvement
Teknaf, Bangladesh	Hand pumps and health education	Case control	Diarrhoeal diseases	17% difference between groups
Northeast, Brazil	Latrines, communal taps, laundry facilities, showers, hand pumps	Case control	Schistosomiasis	77% difference between groups
Khuzestan, Iran	Courtyard latrines and public standpipes	Case control	Ascariasis	16% difference between groups
Uttar Pradesh, India	Piped water	Before and after	Dysentery	76% reduction
Peninsular Malaysia	Toilets and running water	Case control	Diarrhoeal diseases	82% difference in infant mortality between groups
Kwara State, Nigeria	Boreholes, hand pumps and health education	Before and after	Dracunculosis	81% reduction
Cebu, Philippines	Private, sanitary latrines	Before and after	Diarrhoeal diseases	42% reduction
St. Lucia	Household water and latrines	Case control	Ascariasis	31% difference between groups
Lusaka, Zambia	Extension of piped water supply	Before and after	Typhoid	37% reduction

attributed three-quarters of the mortality decline to water and sanitation projects provided as part of rural community health programmes.

While the cost of building freshwater supply systems and sanitation facilities is high, the costs of not doing so can become staggering. In Karachi, Pakistan, for example, a study found that poor people living in areas without any sanitation or hygiene education spent six times more on medical care than people who lived in areas with access to sanitation and who had a basic knowledge of household hygiene.

Water-Based Diseases

Water-based diseases are caused by aquatic organisms that spend part of their life cycle in the water and another part as parasites of animals. These organisms can thrive in either polluted or unpolluted water. As parasites, they usually take the form of worms, using intermediate animal vectors such as snails to thrive, and then directly infecting humans either by boring through the skin or by being swallowed.

Water-based diseases include guinea worm (dracunculiasis), paragonimiasis, clonorchiasis, and schistosomiasis (bilharzias). These diseases are caused by a variety of flukes, tapeworms, roundworms and tissue nematodes, often collectively referred to as helminths, that infect humans. Although these diseases usually are not fatal, they can be extremely painful, preventing people from working and sometimes even making movement impossible.

The prevalence of water-based diseases often increases when dams are constructed, because the stagnant water behind dams is ideal for snails, the intermediary host for many types of worms. For example, the Akosombo Dam on the Volta Lake in Ghana and the Aswan High Dam on the Nile in Egypt, have resulted in huge increases of schistosomiasis in these areas. Also, in Mali, a survey conducted in 225 villages in different ecological settings found that the prevalence of urinary schistosomiasis was five times greater in villages with small dams (67 per cent) than in the drier savannah villages (13 per cent).

Prevention and Solutions

Individuals can prevent infection from water-based diseases by washing vegetables in clean water and thoroughly cooking food. They can refrain from entering infected rivers because many parasites bore through the feet and legs. In areas where guinea worm is endemic, people can use a piece of cloth or nylon gauze to filter out guinea worm larvae, if clean water is unavailable. As with water-washed diseases, providing hygienic disposal of human wastes helps control water-based diseases. Also, for irrigation channels and other constructed waterways, building fast-flowing streams makes it more difficult for snails to survive, thus eliminating the intermediary host.

Some water-development schemes have started disease control programmes along with construction of facilities. In the Philippines, for example, where the development of water resources is a high priority, the National Irrigation System Improvement Project in Layte, begun in 1979, included specific provisions and funding to control schistosomiasis. As a result of these measures, the prevalence of water-based diseases fell from 24 per cent in 1979 to 9 per cent in 1985. Because fewer people fell ill, the average increase in productivity was an estimated 19 days of work per person per year, worth an additional US $ 1 million in wages.

Water-Related Vector Diseases

Millions of people suffer from infections that are transmitted by vectors – insects or other animals capable of transmitting an infection, such as mosquitoes and tsetse flies – that breed and live in or near both polluted and unpolluted water. Such vectors infect humans with malaria, yellow fever, dengue fever, sleeping sickness and filariasis. Malaria, the most widespread, is endemic in about 100 developing countries, putting some 2 billion people at risk. In sub-Saharan Africa, malaria costs an estimated US$ 1.7 billion annually in treatment and lost productivity.

The incidence of water-related vector diseases appears to be increasing. There are many reasons: people are developing resistance to anti-malarial drugs; mosquitoes are developing resistance to DDT, the major insecticide used; environmental changes are creating new breeding sites; migration, climate change and creation of new habitats mean that fewer people build up natural immunity to the disease; and many malaria control programmes have slowed or been abandoned.

Lack of appropriate water management, along with failure to take preventive measures, contributes to the rising incidence of malaria, filariasis and onchocerciasis. Construction projects often increase the mosquito population, as pools of stagnant water, even if they exist only briefly, become breeding grounds. For example, in West Africa an epidemic of Rift Valley fever in 1987 has been linked to the Senegal River Project. The project, which flooded the lower Senegal River area, enabled the type of mosquito that carries the virus to expand so much that the virus was transmitted to humans rather than remaining in the usual animal hosts.

Prevention and Solutions

The solution to water-related vector diseases would appear to be clear—eliminate the insects that transmit the diseases. This is easier said than done, however, as pesticides themselves may be harmful to health if they get into drinking water or irrigation water. Also, many insects develop resistance to pesticides and diseases can emerge again in new forms.

Alternative techniques to control these diseases include the use of bed-nets and introducing natural predators and sterile insects. In Gujarat, India, for example, an important part of an integrated project to control disease vectors was breeding guppies—fish that eat mosquito larvae—in bodies of water, while eliminating the use of insecticides altogether. An inexpensive approach to controlling insect vectors involves the use of polystyrene spheres floating on the top of bodies of static water. Because the spheres cover the surface of the water, the mosquito larvae die from lack of air.

Another way to control the vectors is species sanitation—using biological methods and habitat management to reduce or eliminate the natural breeding grounds of the disease vectors. Such methods can include: filling and draining unneeded bodies of stagnant water; covering water storage containers; eliminating mosquito breeding sites by periodically clearing canals, reservoirs and fish ponds of weeds; installing sprinkler and trickle irrigation instead of canals; and lining canals to prevent silt deposits from forming and impeding the flow of water. Also, integrating education about disease prevention into health services and encouraging community discussion of prevention would help people to control vectors and to identify and eliminate inconspicuous breeding sites.

Water-Scarce Diseases

Many other diseases—including trachoma, leprosy, tuberculosis, whooping cough, tetanus, and diphtheria—are considered water-scarce (also known as water-washed) in that they thrive in conditions where freshwater is scarce and sanitation is poor. Infections are transmitted when too little fresh water is available for washing hands. These diseases, which are rampant throughout most of the world, can be effectively controlled with better hygiene, for which adequate freshwater is necessary.

Some parasitic diseases not usually considered water-related and previously limited in their reach have been rapidly expanding as populations grow and water supplies become more polluted. For example, cysticercosis, a disease usually produced by tapeworms found in undercooked pork and limited to rural areas, expanded rapidly in Mexico City in the early 1980s. As the city's population soared, the parasite multiplied in the highly polluted water of the Tula River, which supplies much of the drinking water for the makeshift settlements on the city's outskirts. Tens of thousands of people downstream from the city sewage system were infected.

Cooperation among Sectors

Conquering the variety of water-related health risks requires a perspective that links freshwater management to public health in development projects. Primary health care projects need to take into account the key role that adequate supplies of clean freshwater play in preventing disease and in promoting good health. Development projects need to pay more attention to water management. Also, water management efforts can cooperate more with health care and development agencies.

Addressing problems of water supply and sanitation can be part of improving maternal and child health care. If such problems are not addressed, they can undercut other health measures. For example, a study in Nigeria found that even though guinea worm was prevalent and known to affect many mothers and small children, primary health care providers did not focus on provision of safe water as a health measure.

In general, public health and disease control programmes have not been concerns of water resources development projects, which typically focus on potential economic benefits. Nor have most municipal planners taken into account the community health benefits to be achieved from water-related projects, in addition to such benefits as power generation, irrigation, flood control and water supply. So strong are the links between clean water provision, sanitation and good health that better coordination among health care providers, development agencies, and water management agencies should become a major concern in all of these sectors.

Water Conservation and Management

No matter how freshwater is used—whether for agriculture, industry, or municipalities—there is great potential for better conservation and management. Water is wasted nearly everywhere. Until actual scarcity hits, most countries and most people take access to freshwater for granted.

"We have to stop living as if we had unlimited water supplies and start recognizing that we must deal with serious water constraints," Falkenmark and colleagues have warned. The relevant question about freshwater is not 'how much water do we need and where do we get it?' Rather, it is 'how much water is there and how can we best benefit from it?' That is, we must do better at managing the demand for water rather than continuing to focus on 'supply-oriented' water management.

On the demand side, a variety of economic, administrative and community-based measures can help conserve water immediately. In the long run, slowing population growth will slow the increase in demand for water and help buy more time to develop better water conservation and management strategies.

Agriculture: Producing More from Less

Since agriculture accounts for nearly 70 per cent of all water withdrawn from rivers, lakes, and underground aquifers for human use, the greatest potential for conservation lies with increasing irrigation efficiencies. For example, increasing irrigation efficiency on the Indus Plains of Pakistan by just 10 per cent would allow an estimated 2 million more hectares of farm land to be irrigated.

Most irrigation systems waste water. Typically, only between 35 per cent and 50 per cent of water withdrawn for irrigated agriculture ever reaches the crops. Most soaks into unlined canals, leaks out of pipes, or evaporates before reaching the fields. Although some of the water 'lost' in inefficient irrigation systems returns to streams or aquifers, where it can be tapped again, water quality is invariably degraded by pesticides, fertilizers and salts that run off the land. Poorly planned and poorly built irrigation systems have limited the yields on one-half of all irrigated land.

Paradoxically, even when sufficient irrigation water reaches agricultural fields, it can spoil much of the land unless drained properly. Particularly, in many arid areas, salts that occur naturally in the soil must be drained away with irrigation runoff. If left to accumulate in the soil, they eventually work their way to the surface, poisoning the land. Also, poorly drained irrigation water can raise the groundwater table until it reaches the root zone, waterlogging and drowning crops. Globally, some

80 million hectares of farmland have been degraded by a combination of salinization and waterlogging.

Improving Irrigation Efficiency

A number of countries are working to improve irrigation efficiencies, thus saving water and protecting the land. Drip irrigation is one technique. Drip irrigation consists of a network of porous or perforated piping, usually installed on the surface or below ground, which delivers water directly to the root zones of the crops. This technique keeps evaporation losses low, at an efficiency rate of 95 per cent. Drip irrigation systems cut water use by an estimated 40 per cent to 60 per cent compared with gravity systems.

In the 1970s, drip irrigation systems were used on only 56,000 hectares worldwide, mostly to supply water for vegetables and fruit orchards in Australia, Israel, Mexico, New Zealand, South Africa and the U.S.A. This figure has grown to 1.6 million hectares. Although this area constitutes less than 1 per cent of all irrigated land worldwide, drip irrigation is widely used in some countries. Israel, for instance, uses drip irrigation on 50 per cent of its total irrigated area.

Another promising conservation method—low-energy precision application (LEPA)—offers substantial improvements over conventional sprinkler systems that spray water into the air. Instead, the LEPA method delivers water to the crops from drop tubes that extend from the sprinkler's arm.

When applied together with appropriate water-saving farming techniques, this method also can achieve efficiencies as high as 95 per cent. Since this method operates at low pressure, energy costs drop by 20 per cent to 50 per cent compared with conventional systems. Farmers in Texas who have retrofitted conventional sprinkler systems with LEPA have reported that their yields have increased by as much as 20 per cent and that their investment costs have been recouped within one or two years.

Irrigation Options for the Rural Poor

Many developing countries cannot afford to invest in such techniques as drip irrigation and LEPA. Yet, pressures to feed rapidly growing rural populations require making better use of scarce freshwater resources. In many regions that face acute seasonal water shortages, conservation projects are working with rural farmers to build small reservoirs that collect and store water from the rainy season for use in the dry season.

Also, in parts of East Africa, subsistence farmers use 'water harvesting' – ancient techniques that consist mainly of digging deep holes near each plant to collect and store water from the wet season for use during the dry season. Another traditional method involves placing long lines of stones along the contours of gently sloping ground to slow runoff and spread the water across a wider area. Developed in the Yatenga region of Burkina Faso, this method is now being used on over 8,000 hectares in 400 villages throughout the country. It is also used in Kenya and Niger. Combined with the practice of deep-hole water harvesting, this practice has increased crop production by about 50 per cent.

Re-Using Urban Wastewater

A number of countries channel treated urban wastewater from towns and cities onto nearby farms growing vegetables and fruits. Today at least half a million hectares in 15 countries are being irrigated with treated urban wastewater, often referred to as 'brown water.' Israel has the most ambitious brown-water programme of any country. Most of Israel's sewage is purified and re-used to irrigate 20,000 hectares of farm land.

Some developing countries also use this technique:

- In Mexico City treated urban wastewater irrigates and fertilizes alfalfa fields. The alfalfa in turn is sold as feed to small-scale farmers who raise guinea pigs and rabbits.
- One-third of the vegetables grown in Asmara, Eritrea, are irrigated with treated urban wastewater.
- In Lusaka, Zambia, one of the city's biggest squatter settlements irrigates its vegetable crops with sewage water from nearby settling ponds.

Some places apply the same concept differently. For example, Kolkata, India, channels much of its raw sewage into a system of natural lagoons, where fish are raised. The city's 3,000 hectares of lagoons produce about 6,000 metric tons of fish a year for urban consumers. The fish are safe to eat because the lagoons soak up and clean the sewage. Unless urban wastewater receives some pre-treatment, either from natural wetlands or sewage treatment plants, however, it can transfer disease organisms to vegetables and fruits and endanger human health.

Such natural water treatment technologies as using wetlands often can be an alternative to modern water treatment systems that are too costly for poor urban areas of developing countries. Recycling waste for agricultural purposes by using oxidation ponds and aerated lagoons does not require as much land as is often assumed. Moreover, it decreases pollution, reduces the need for fertilizers, and often can be accomplished with 'small-scale, low-cost technology that is based in local traditions, decentralized, and ecologically sound,' according to water resource engineer Janus Niemczynowicz.

Saving Water in Industry

Industry is water-intensive. For example, making one ton of steel can consume as much as 300 tons of water. In developed countries industries use from one-half to three-quarters of all water withdrawals compared with about one-quarter as the global average.

Driven by stiffer regulations and the need to cut costs, such water-intensive industries as chemicals, iron and steel, and pulp and paper have made impressive strides in reducing the amount of water needed for production. In some countries these industries are both re-using and recycling water in current production processes and also redesigning production processes to require less water per unit of production. Consider these examples:

- In the U.S.A., industrial water use fell by over one-third between 1950 and 1990, while industrial output nearly quadrupled.
- In the former West Germany, the total amount of water used in industry today is the same as in 1975, while industrial output has risen by nearly 45 per cent.
- In Sweden, strict pollution control measures have cut water use in half in the pulp and paper industry, while production has doubled in little more than a decade.

In developing countries, however, there is tremendous scope for saving water in industry. Take China, for instance: The amount of water needed to produce a ton of steel ranges from 23 to 56 cubic metres, whereas in the U.S.A., Japan, and Germany, the average is less than 6 cubic metres. Similarly, a ton of paper produced in China requires around 450 cubic metres of water, twice as much as is used in European countries.

Municipal Conservation

Conserving water for personal use in cities (including use by households and municipalities) requires managing both the supply of and demand for water. Much of the municipal water supply is lost before it can reach consumers, leaking out of water mains, pipes and faucets, or disappearing through illegal taps. Moreover, when they have convenient access to running water, consumers often use much more water than they actually need. For instance, in the U.S.A. average personal water use is nearly 600 litres per day compared with about 50 litres per day in India.

Supply

Municipal water supply faces problems almost everywhere. A 1986 survey of 15 Latin American cities found that municipal systems lost between 40 per cent and 70 per cent of their water. In India, over 40 per cent of the total municipal water supply is lost in transit, before it can reach consumers. Even in Malta, one of the world's most water-stressed countries, 30 per cent of the water intended for consumers leaks out of the system instead.

Municipal supply systems do not have to lose so much of their water. For example, Geneva, Switzerland, loses only 13 per cent of its water on the way from source to consumer.

In most cities tightening the joints in the water pipes and fixing leaky community standpipes and household connections would save more than one-third of the water that is currently wasted. Jakarta, Indonesia, for instance, could cut its water losses an estimated 20 per cent by fixing leaky distribution pipes and thus save nearly 12 billion gallons of water a year, enough to provide an extra 800,000 people with tap water.

Many cities could manage their water supply better if they could eliminate illegal water taps. In the Philippines, for example, the Water Regulatory Board has estimated that there are about 20,000 illegal connections to Manila's water supply system, both domestic and commercial, which siphon off more than 200,000 cubic metres of water per day. Under the terms of the Water Crisis Act of 1995, anyone caught stealing water can be fined or sent to prison.

Demand

"Slowly the idea is spreading that managing demand rather than continuously striving to meet it is a surer path to water security," water expert Sandra Postel has observed. Demand management consists of several approaches to conserve water, including: economic policies, notably pricing water; laws and regulations, such as restrictions on certain types of water use; technical solutions, such as installing water flow constrictors; and public and community participation.

For example, at the 1998 meeting of the United Nations Commission for Sustainable Development, many delegates argued for an economic approach in countries with adequate water distribution systems. In these countries water could be treated as a commodity and sold to consumers at rates that reflect its value in order to encourage conservation. Other examples of measures that could reduce municipal demand include:

- More use of water-saving household appliances;
- Building codes that require installation of low-flush toilets in new construction; and
- Low-water-use landscaping—known as xeriscaping—in arid and semi-arid areas.

Such measures could be adopted in both developed and developing countries. Mexico City provides an example: This megacity relies on groundwater for more than 80 per cent of its municipal water supply. The pumping of groundwater exceeds the natural recharge of the aquifer by 50 to 80 per cent. As a result, groundwater levels have fallen, not only reducing the future water supply but also causing land to sink, damaging buildings. The city has had to import water from increasingly longer distances.

Mexico City has responded to this challenge with a multi-faceted water conservation strategy. In 1989, the municipal government adopted strict efficiency standards for all new household plumbing fixtures and appliances. A year later, it raised water rates, thus encouraging residents to install more water-efficient faucets and appliances.

In addition, the city required that all new toilets installed must use no more than 6 litres per flush compared with conventional toilets that average 16 litres per flush. By 1991, more than 350,000 low-flush toilets had been installed, saving 28 million cubic metres of water a year—enough to meet the annual household needs of an additional 250,000 people. The city's water woes are far from over, but progress has been made in reducing the heavy demand on the water supply system.

In most cases introducing a pricing structure that values water properly can make a significant difference. For example, when the water utility of Bogor, Indonesia, tripled, and in some cases quadrupled, water prices, average monthly household water consumption dropped by 30 per cent in less than one year. The utility was able to connect more houses to the existing water supply system and avoided having to build a new system.

The Need for Better Policies

Freshwater is the liquid that lubricates development. It is as much an economic input as are infrastructure, energy and human know-how. Without better management of scarce water supplies, sustainable development is impossible. Four principal policy weaknesses, in general, underscore the world's inability to manage freshwater supplies for sustainable development, according to Ismail Serageldin, Vice President for Environmentally Sustainable Development at the World Bank:

1. Water management is fragmented among sectors and institutions. There are too many agencies with their fingers on the water tap and virtually no coordination of policies between sectors of the economy. Issues of water quality and health often go entirely unaddressed because they do not fit within the mandate of any single government agency.

2. Governments depend too much on centralized administration to develop, operate and maintain water systems. Agencies charged with managing water supplies often are already overextended and lack technical competence. At the same time, there is little stakeholder involvement and community participation in setting water policies and regulating use, so projects often do not meet people's needs.

3. Most countries undervalue freshwater as a resource and do not price it at its economic value. Many heavy users of water, such as farmers, receive government subsidies and in effect are encouraged to waste water that they otherwise probably would not waste. Most governments have found it politically more palatable to develop new water supplies than to charge heavy users the full costs of water.

4. Water management policies do not link the quality of water to human and environmental health. In most cases, water is viewed as a resource to be pumped around and used as often and as much as needed for any purpose. Without adequate consideration of water's key role in human and environmental health, it is little wonder that water resources are degraded nearly everywhere.

Freshwater is the universal necessity – providing all forms of life with sustenance, nurturing natural ecosystems, and transporting and diluting wastes. Without assured supplies of freshwater, living standards decline, people suffer, and development becomes more difficult.

Ensuring sustainable development increasingly will require wise policies and effective strategies that not only conserve and protect freshwater sources but also manage them equitably to meet the needs of consumers, industry and agriculture.

The Need to Slow Population Growth

While the links between population and freshwater resources are complex, there is no doubt that population growth increases the demand for freshwater. While new approaches to managing water supply and demand can help in the short term, reducing population growth is necessary to avoid catastrophe in the long term. There is an urgent need, therefore, to slow population growth and to stabilize population size as soon as possible.

While water scarcity affects countries in all regions of the world, it is particularly a problem in developing countries. Nearly three-quarters of the world's population of 6 billion plus live in developing countries. Moreover, close to 95 per cent of population growth is taking place in the developing world.

At current fertility rates, populations in sub-Saharan Africa, the Near East and parts of South Asia would double in another 20 to 40 years. At projected growth rates, by the year 2050, the global population is expected to be 9.4 billion, of whom 8 billion will live in developing countries.

How can population growth be slowed? Providing widespread access to family planning has already helped millions of couples who want to space and limit births. Family planning programmes have helped lower fertility rates worldwide over the past 30 years, particularly in developing countries. Nevertheless, in the developing countries alone there are at least 100 million married women and probably millions more unmarried people, who want to avoid pregnancy but are not using any contraception, according to surveys. Meeting this unmet need for family planning would avoid about one-third of the projected population increase in developing countries over the next half century.

Also, family planning and reproductive health services need to be extended and improved to serve the millions of more people who are coming of reproductive age. As the world's population grows by 80 million each year, these young people's future decisions about family size and resource use will have a powerful impact on world conditions. About half of the projected population increase over the next 50 years will result from the fact that some 3 billion people will enter their reproductive years over the next 25 years. This number equals the entire world population in 1960.

Providing these young couples with family planning information and services on a voluntary basis is essential. Even if each decided to have only two children apiece—replacement-level fertility—the world's population would still grow by nearly 2 billion over the next 50 years. For some countries, this fact makes a water crisis inevitable. For many others, it signals the need to address water demand and water supply issues immediately.

Towards a Blue Revolution

The world needs a Blue Revolution in water management, just as we need another Green Revolution in agriculture. Time is the essence. Dwindling freshwater supplies per capita are threatening the health and living standards of millions of people in a growing number of countries, as well as undermining agricultural productivity and industrial development. Achieving a blue revolution will require coordinated policies and responses to problems at international, national, and local levels.

International Responses

Countries have agreed to numerous recommendations at international conferences on water over the past 30 years. For the most part, however, the international development community and national governments have yet to turn these words into action.

The first international conference to draw attention to the coming water crisis was in 1977—the United Nations Water Conference held in Mar del Plata, Argentina. Several others have followed, including the Global Consultation on Safe Water and Sanitation for the 1990s, held in New Delhi in 1990, and the International Conference on Water and the Environment, held in Dublin in 1992.

The Dublin Water Principles, agreed to at the 1992 conference, summarize the principles of sustainable water management:

- Principle No. 1: Freshwater is a finite and vulnerable resource, essential to sustain life, development, and the environment.
- Principle No. 2: Water development and management should be based on a participatory approach, involving users, planners, and policy-makers at all levels.
- Principle No. 3: Women play a central part in the provision, management and safeguarding of water.
- Principle No. 4: Water has an economic value in all its uses and should be recognized as an economic good.

In 1997, a comprehensive assessment of global freshwater resources, based on a series of expert background analyses, was prepared for the fifth session of the UN Commission on Sustainable Development. As a 1998 report of the Secretary-General states,

> "The assessment concludes that water shortages and pollution are causing widespread public health problems, limiting economic and agricultural development and harming a wide range of ecosystems. Those problems may threaten global food supplies and lead to economic stagnation in many areas of the world. The result could be a series of local and regional water crises, with serious global implications."

Making Needed Investments

Turning principles into practice will be difficult. Most countries need massive investments in sanitation and water supply infrastructure. In the developed world, for example, the United Kingdom must spend close to US$ 60 billion building wastewater treatment plants over the next decade in order to meet new European water quality standards. This amounts to about $ 1,000 for every person in the country.

Hungary faces similar problems. One-fifth of the country's population is not connected to a functioning sewer system. Hungary will need to invest about US$ 3.5 billion over the next two decades to connect all of its citizens to wastewater treatment plants.

In developing countries, one of the most pressing problems is the overwhelming need to invest heavily in sanitation facilities and the provision of clean water.

The World Bank has estimated that over the next decade between

US$ 600 billion and US$ 800 billion will be required to meet the total demand for freshwater, including for sanitation, irrigation and power generation.

Of this huge amount, the World Bank will be able to lend only US$ 35 to 40 billion at most. The remainder will have to come from a combination of public funding and private investment. It will be difficult, if not impossible, for most developing countries to finance the remainder, however.

In Latin America alone, for instance, it is estimated that investments in water resources management and infrastructure will require $ 100 billion over the course of the next two decades.

Avoiding International Conflicts

An important part of any international water-management strategy is to help countries that share river basins fashion workable policies to manage water resources more equitably. A water-short world is an inherently unstable world. Nearly 100 countries share just 13 major rivers and lakes. More than 200 river systems cross international borders. Conflicts can arise, especially where countries with rapidly growing populations and limited arable land collide over access to shared freshwater resources.

The case of India and Bangladesh demonstrates how international river basins can be managed to meet demand in the face of scarce water supplies. The Ganga, the subcontinent's largest and most important river, rises in Nepal and flows 1,400 miles through three densely populated Indian states – Uttar Pradesh, Bihar and West Bengal – before entering Bangladesh and flowing into the Bay of Bengal. The river affects the lives of half a billion people, many of whom depend on the river for subsistence agriculture and fishing. After half a century of bitter rivalry over access to the waters of the Ganga, India and Bangladesh signed a new 30-year water-sharing agreement in December 1996. Both countries have proclaimed a new era of water management.

The agreement, if implemented fully, will provide Bangladesh with a guaranteed minimum amount of water during the dry season, especially the three driest months of March, April and May. The new treaty sets 10-day periods during these three months when India and Bangladesh will alternately have access to an agreed-upon amount of the water reaching the Farakka Barrage, a huge dam built by India in 1974 in an effort to claim as much of the water for its own use as possible before the Ganga enters

Bangladesh. In order to ensure implementation of the agreement, a team of inspectors from the two countries will monitor the flow rate at the Farakka Barrage during the dry months.

Critics argue that if the agreement is to work over the long term, India must begin to manage the Ganga watershed much better than it does now. Deforestation in Nepal and northern India has greatly increased the amount of sediment washed from the hills into the river during the monsoon season, clogging waterways and increasing the incidence of damaging floods. Unless ways can be found to capture more stable runoff during the wet season for use during the dry season, Indian farmers might be tempted to take all the water they can get from the river during the driest months, putting the agreement in jeopardy.

Despite such caveats, the fact that two neighbouring countries have successfully negotiated and reached a comprehensive agreement over such a contentious issue is a positive sign. It promises to permit downstream Bangladesh a more equitable supply of water from the Ganga and to foster better water management practices in upstream India.

National Responses

In water-short countries national governments need to give water resources management their highest priority. Crafting and implementing a national water strategy is essential to sustainable development. Such a strategy should include four elements:

1. Adopting a watershed or river-basin management perspective, especially in water-short regions (also appropriate as an international response, since watersheds frequently cross national boundaries);
2. Instituting a workable water infrastructure so that national, regional and local water needs can be met within the context of a national water policy;
3. Enacting and enforcing water legislation and regulations that conserve water and value the resource properly according to type of use; and
4. Connecting water management to the needs of agriculture, industry and municipalities and meeting public health requirements for proper sanitation and disease prevention.

1. A Watershed Management Perspective

Watershed management refers to managing an entire land area

served by all the rivers and aquifers that drain into a particular body of water (such as a semi-enclosed bay). River basin management is essentially the same concept applied to one river system, although the two terms are used interchangeably.

The U.S.A. defines a watershed as the entire area drained by a river system or one of its major tributaries. The U.K. defines a watershed as the divide between river basins, a potentially much larger area.

No matter how it is defined, "we need to see a river or lake, along with its entire watershed and all its physical, chemical, and biological elements, as part of a complex, integrated system," according to Janet Abramovitz of the Worldwatch Institute.

Everyone has a watershed address: we all live in basins that drain rainwater into streams and rivers that eventually send the water back to the sea or into inland lakes.

The people living in most of these addresses have radically altered the natural drainage systems around them. Tampering with watersheds has proved ruinous for many developing countries, where hillsides denuded of vegetation empty tons of soil into water courses every year, causing floods during the wet seasons and suffocating aquatic life during the dry seasons.

Deforestation has ruined land and altered climates, causing less rain to fall in some areas. In others, rainwater runs off so fast that little can be collected for use. In sub-Saharan Africa, for example, the albedo effect—the drying of the landscape as a result of the wholesale clearance of tropical forests and poor farming practices—has resulted in below-average rainfall over the past 40 years compared with the century as a whole.

Watershed or river basin management pays multiple benefits. The economic value of ecosystem maintenance is high. The value of an intact floodplain, for instance—including its fisheries, wildlife, recreation and natural flood control effects—has been calculated at close to US$ 2,000 per acre. Another estimate puts the value of one hectare of wetland at US$ 15,000.

Ideally, a comprehensive watershed management plan mobilizes communities and individuals and gains broad public acceptance at the national level. Watershed management is not easy to accomplish, however. It is a complex and contentious process that involves many stakeholders with competing views about water use.

Not many countries have been able to initiate workable watershed management strategies. In fact, the Chesapeake Bay, the largest brackish water estuary in North America, has one of the few comprehensive watershed management plans in operation anywhere in the world.

A number of other countries also have instituted river basin management schemes or are in the process of doing so. The Murray-Darling River Basin Commission in Australia, for instance, is an intergovernmental organization whose main aim is to coordinate the management of water resources across state borders within the Murray-Darling River Basin, the country's largest river system. The commission's technical abilities are comprehensive, covering river management and ecology, environmental impacts, finance and administration and communication. All development activities within the river basin fall under the jurisdiction of the commission and all government agencies connected to water management and its uses must collaborate.

In India, as a result of the 1987 National Water Policy Act, the states of Rajasthan and Gujarat set up a committee to regulate and control water use in the Sabarmati River Basin which encompasses parts of both states. The average amount of water available in the Sabarmati River Basin amounts to no more than 360 cubic metres per person per year, making it one of the most water-stressed regions in the country. Water is not only a very limited resource, but it is also increasingly polluted by irrigated agriculture.

To deal with these problems, the committee will regulate and manage water resources in the entire river basin, with a structure that gives a voice to representatives from each major water user group. The committee hopes to establish broad popular and institutional support and a structure capable of ensuring that polluters are fined and that major users pay a fair price for water. If the system works, it may be extended to other water-short areas of India with high population densities.

Freshwater supplies that originate in mountainous areas also can be better protected and managed at their source, observes Mountain Agenda, a nongovernmental organization interested in sustainable mountain development. According to the organization, in humid areas, the proportion of water generated in mountains can comprise as much as 60 per cent of the total freshwater available in the watershed areas, and as much as 95 per cent in arid areas.

2. *Building Institutional Capacity*

Managing watersheds and river basins sustainably means building institutional capacity, including the creation of cross-sectoral data collection and monitoring systems. Capacity building is a key theme of international organizations promoting change, including the World Bank, the United Nations Development Programme (UNDP) and the Global Water Partnership. To build capacity, the following measures are needed:

- Assessing national capacity-building requirements. It is vital for governments to know the capacities of their water-sector agencies as a first step towards improvements.
- Creating competent administrative and legal structures. The technical and administrative competence of national, regional and local agencies responsible for water management must be strengthened before progress can be made in water management.
- Making institutions more responsive and effective. Water-management agencies, both public and private, must also be able to respond to changing situations (political and social as well as environmental). Static organizations and outmoded procedures need to be overhauled, especially as countries enter the water-stressed or water-scarcity categories.
- Training senior water managers. Few hydrologists have been trained to consider water resources broadly. As well as an engineering approach to water management that considers supply needs and how to satisfy them, a demand-oriented approach is increasingly needed.
- Establishing closer ties to universities and research institutes. Since water issues embrace societal concerns and cultural values, water agencies should reach beyond the usual government channels and draw on a wide spectrum of opinion and expertise in order to assess freshwater issues and find solutions.

3. *Valuing Freshwater Resources*

Freshwater must be valued to reflect its status as a scarce resource, instead of being treated as a free or nearly free resource. As the Organization for Economic Cooperation and Development (OECD) points out, proper pricing policies can encourage environmentally responsible water-use behaviour as well as help to assure an adequate supply of water. To accomplish this, water should be valued appropriately in each of its various uses. The introduction of water markets and pricing mechanisms can have immediate and lasting impacts on water use.

There are several good examples of how water can be valued more appropriately than is the usual case. Chile established a water market in the mid-1980s that not only has saved water but also has enabled farmers to meet their needs by trading water rights among neighbouring farms. A World Bank study of the water market system concluded that it contributed greatly to better management and fairer pricing.

Similarly, in southern California, chronically one of the most water-short regions in a water-short state, the San Diego County Water Authority reached an agreement with farmers in the Imperial Valley area east of the city of San Diego.

The agreement encourages farmers to conserve up to 200,000 acre-feet of water a year and sell it to the county, which would finance the conservation measures and pay farmers cash incentives to participate. San Diego County would benefit from the guarantee of cheaper water, and the farmers would, in effect, be paid to conserve the resource. This approach to water management could change the dynamics of water use throughout California.

In São Paulo, Brazil's most populous state, where water resources already are stretched thin, increasing demands from municipalities, industries and agriculture threaten to cripple the state's capacity to manage scarce supplies.

In 1997, a draft Water Pricing Law was sent to the state legislature and formed the basis for an entirely new water management policy. Under the proposal, the price of water was determined by the source of supply, type of use (whether municipal, industrial, or agricultural), and the availability of water. The fees collected under the policy were to be re-invested in the water management infrastructure.

4. *Managing Water for Sectoral Needs*

A workable water management system requires the institutional capacity to balance sectoral needs for the good of society as a whole and also to consider ecosystem needs. Water allocation, rather than absolute scarcity of water, often lies at the heart of national water problems. Without policies that link the supply of freshwater to competing sectoral uses, local and regional water shortages often result and competition becomes increasingly bitter.

In developing countries, meeting sectoral demands is challenging because most lack efficient water management systems and equitable pricing policies that are based on how water resources are used. For example, although China passed a national water law in 1988, there is little coordination of sectoral water use between the Ministry of Water Resources, the river basin commissions and the various provincial and local authorities.

Local Responses

Locally led initiatives are showing that water can be used much more efficiently even in water-short areas, both urban and rural. Furthermore, when communities manage freshwater resources better, they also manage soils and forests better, increase crop production and reduce the incidence of illness and disease. Even where municipal governments have failed to finance a potable water supply or to provide proper sanitation, grassroots efforts have sometimes succeeded. Consider the following examples:

- **Managing the Mossi Plateau.** In Burkina Faso's main agricultural area, the Mossi Plateau, a group called the 'Six S's' (Se Servir de la Saison Seche en Savanne et au Sahel) has been promoting an integrated approach to water management since the late 1970s. The group encourages small-scale irrigation systems along with re-forestation and erosion control. It teaches village leaders new techniques for saving water and growing crops, provides basic hygiene education and helps with financing for water conservation.
- **Balinese rice farmers.** Balinese rice growers have used small-scale irrigation techniques for the past 500 years. Their system is not technically advanced but instead relies on loose stone dams and weirs to collect water, which is then distributed to terraced fields, using the hollowed-out trunks of coconut trees for piping. Accompanying this traditional system of water distribution is a social structure that regulates water among different communities, apportioning it according to the size of each rice paddy. The system works partly because women, the main source of paddy labour, have a hand in its management.
- **Urban sanitation in Karachi.** In Pakistan, the Orangi Pilot Project, carried out in one of the worst slums in Karachi, was able to provide 600,000 people with a sewer system and with covered latrines. The project, which was carried out with a small amount of external funding, worked because of progressive local leadership and strong community support. However, the benefits did not end with piped water. The project also increased access to better reproductive health and family planning services, which will help reduce future demand for water.

Potable piped water in Tegucigalpa. In Honduras, six poor communities in the country's capital city pooled limited resources to make a deal with the water utility to provide them with piped water. This scheme is notable because (1) the price that households paid for water actually dropped as a result of the piped water connections, since residents no longer had to buy water from street vendors, and (2) the average household connection rate in each of the six communities was 85 per cent, and the consumers themselves paid for the connections.

As this example demonstrates, even in poor urban areas clean piped water can be provided at a price that community members can afford to pay and that water utilities can accept. Recent studies in a number of countries make clear that poor people are prepared to pay for piped water and proper sanitation, if given the chance. In Onitsha, Nigeria, for instance, poor households were spending up to 18 per cent of their meagre monthly income on water purchased from street vendors, a percentage that dropped to under 5 per cent when piped water was provided.

Taking Action

Local communities should take an active part in planning and implementing water management schemes, if they are to be sustainable. Poor communities, in particular, have had notable success in introducing autonomous local distribution of water, either through special arrangements with the water authority or with private vendors. Communities have also set up community-managed vending kiosks or operated small, autonomous water supply systems.

Accessibility of clean water, as has been noted, promotes better household hygiene and improves health and well-being. Access to the water supply should be as close to homes as possible and should be reliable. Plans for piping water to poor households should consider the amount of water needed, choose the appropriate level of technology and price the water according to the ability to pay.

Water supply and public health programmes should both emphasize preventive health care education and encourage the use of clean water for personal and domestic hygiene.

Change in Direction

The world needs sustainable water management, but we are not headed in the right direction fast enough. A Chinese proverb holds that 'If we don't change course, we may end up where we are heading.' Without moving in a new direction, many more areas will face water shortages, many more people will suffer, more conflicts over water will occur, and more precious wetland ecosystems will be destroyed.

While a freshwater crisis appears inevitable in many water-short regions, in others the problem could be managed, if appropriate policies and strategies were formulated, agreed to and acted on soon. The international community is paying increasing attention to the world's water problems and a number of organizations are providing funding and assistance to help manage water supply and demand. Increasingly, mechanisms are being put in place that permit more equitable water management. Countries in water-stressed regions are introducing better pricing mechanisms, fostering community-based water management schemes, and moving towards watershed and river basin management regimes. Both the number and scale of these activities need to increase substantially.

Also, population growth has slowed, reflecting international and national attention to family planning programmes, together with rising popular demand for contraception. To meet people's needs, national governments and international donors need to increase their commitment to family planning, to improving sanitary conditions, to curbing pollution and to reducing the scourge of water-related diseases.

A vital part of a long-term solution is worldwide recognition of the links between rapidly growing populations and shrinking freshwater supplies. Recognition, knowledge and concern can help build the political will to avert a crisis and develop the commitment needed to assure that humanity's apparently unquenchable thirst for freshwater does not exhaust the world's finite water supply.

5

Challenge of the 21st Century

WATER scarcity affects all social and economic sectors and threatens the sustainability of the natural resources base. Addressing water scarcity requires an inter-sectoral and multidisciplinary approach to managing water resources in order to maximize economic and social welfare in an equitable manner without compromising the sustainability of vital ecosystems. Integration across sectors is needed. This integration needs to take into account development, supply, use and demand, and to place emphasis on people, their livelihood and the ecosystems that sustain them.

On the demand side, enhancing water productivity (the volume of production per unit of water) in all sectors is paramount to successful programmes of water scarcity alleviation. Furthermore, protecting and restoring the ecosystems that naturally capture, filter, store and release water, such as rivers, wetlands, forests and soils, is crucial to increasing the availability of water of good quality.

Experts are divided on whether the world is facing a water crisis today. Those who believe so can point with justification to the accumulation of reports throughout the world. For example, in just one week in mid-November 2006, national media sources reported local but high-profile shortages in parts of Australia, Botswana, Canada, China, Fiji, Kuwait, Liberia, Malawi, Pakistan, Philippines, South Africa, Uganda, United Arab Emirates and the United States of America.

Then there are the silent crises, the millions of people deprived of the water they need to live and to sustain their livelihood. It is indeed a powerful argument that a global crisis need not stem from a single cause with widespread impact alone, but rather that a crisis can be made up of many similar incidents across the globe, even if the incidents are isolated from one another.

The Multiple Dimensions of Water Scarcity

Water is essential for all socio-economic development and for maintaining healthy ecosystems. As population increases and development calls for increased allocations of groundwater and surface water for the domestic, agriculture and industrial sectors, the pressure on water resources intensifies, leading to tensions, conflicts among users and excessive pressure on the environment. The increasing stress on freshwater resources brought about by ever-rising demand and profligate use, as well as by growing pollution worldwide, is of serious concern.

There are several ways of defining water scarcity. In general, water scarcity is defined as the point at which the aggregate impact of all users impinges on the supply or quality of water under prevailing institutional arrangements to the extent that the demand by all sectors, including the environment, cannot be satisfied fully. Water scarcity is a relative concept and can occur at any level of supply or demand. Scarcity may be a social construct (a product of affluence, expectations and customary behaviour) or the consequence of altered supply patterns—stemming from climate change, for example. Scarcity has various causes, most of them capable of being remedied or alleviated. A society facing water scarcity usually has options. However, scarcity often has its roots in water shortage, and it is in the arid and semi-arid regions affected by droughts and wide climate variability, combined with high population growth and economic development, that the problems of water scarcity are most acute.

Symptoms of water scarcity include severe environmental degradation (including river desiccation and pollution), declining groundwater levels and increasing problems of water allocation where some groups win at the expense of others. A major study, the Comprehensive Assessment of Water Management in Agriculture, in 2007, revealed that one in three people faced water shortages. Around 1.2 billion people, or almost one-fifth of the world's population, live in areas of physical scarcity and 500 million people are approaching this situation. Another 1.6 billion people, or almost one quarter of the world's population, face economic water shortage (where countries lack the necessary infrastructure to take water from rivers and aquifers).

Imbalances between availability and demand, the degradation of groundwater and surface water quality, inter-sectoral competition, and interregional and international conflicts, all bring water issues to the fore.

Coping with Water Scarcity

Water Management

UN-Water is the mechanism coordinating the actions of the United Nations (UN) system aimed at implementing the agenda set by the Millennium Declaration and the World Summit on Sustainable Development (WSSD) in all aspects related to freshwater. UN-Water has grown out of many years of extensive collaboration and partnership among the UN agencies and the large number of UN agencies dealing with water reflects the multiple roles water plays in our society and the complex interactions it implies.

Advancing the implementation of sustainable water management for the benefit of all is a collective responsibility and challenge. It calls for coordinated action with other partners and stakeholders—including organizations from the public and private sectors, civil society and labour—as part of a global, comprehensive effort.

The main purpose of this is to complement and add value to existing programmes and projects by facilitating synergies and joint efforts in order to maximize the coherence and effectiveness of the support provided to countries pursuing the goals agreed upon by the international community. This is in line with the integrated water resources management (IWRM) approach, which calls for collaboration among all stakeholders in water management.

In most countries, the agriculture sector is the predominant consumer of water. Historically, large-scale water development projects have played a major role in poverty alleviation by providing food security, protection from flooding and drought and expanded opportunities for employment. In many cases, irrigated agriculture has played a major role in the development of rural economies, supporting economic growth and poverty reduction.

However, at the same time, poor communities have tended to suffer the greatest health burden from inadequate water supplies and, because of poor health, have been unable to escape from the cycle of poverty and disease. Thus, growing scarcity and competition for water stand as major threats to future advances in poverty alleviation, especially in rural areas.

In semi-arid regions, increasing numbers of the rural poor are coming to see entitlement and access to water for food production, livestock and domestic purposes as more critical than access to primary health care and education.

Most countries in the Near East and North Africa suffer from acute water scarcity, as do countries such as Mexico, Pakistan, South Africa, and large parts of China and India. Irrigated agriculture represents the bulk of the demand for water in these countries. It is also usually the first sector affected by water shortage and increased scarcity, resulting in a reduced capacity to maintain per-capita food production while meeting water needs for domestic, industrial and environmental purposes.

In order to sustain their needs, these countries need to focus on the efficient use of all water sources (groundwater, surface water and rainfall) and on water allocation strategies that maximize the economic and social returns to limited water resources, and at the same time enhance the water productivity of all sectors. In this endeavour, there needs to be a special focus on issues relating to equity in access to water and on the social impacts of water allocation policies.

Several factors drive the progression towards water scarcity and over-allocation of water, in many cases caused by a supply-driven approach to development that does not take sufficient account of the limits of the water systems. As water becomes scarce, logics based on increased supply or a lack of understanding of the interrelations between the different sectors depending on water resources lead to increased shortages and conflicts between users.

In most cases, the overriding political nature of water decisions takes precedence over the hydrological feasibility of projects, while their social consequences, in terms of deprivation of specific user groups are not well evaluated. In many places, the institutional and legal tools needed to adapt and manage water scarcity are not available, leaving the way open to abuse and inequitable access to the resource.

The appropriate scale for understanding water scarcity is at the local or regional level, notably within a river basin or sub-basin, rather than at the national or global level. In many countries, especially the larger ones, there are both water-scarce and water-abundant areas, such as in Brazil, China and Mexico. Such areas are often far away from each other with few opportunities for interbasin water transfers. Several other countries are naturally very arid within their own territory (for example, Egypt, Niger,

Mauritania, Turkmenistan) but their annual renewable freshwater resources are boosted by large perennial rivers flowing from much wetter areas upstream (the Nile, the Niger, the Senegal and the Amu Darya rivers, respectively).

In a context of rapid change, a number of questions arise:

- How are the many competing interests involved in water being balanced?
- On what basis are decisions to be made in favour of certain developments at the expense of others?
- What are the scope and conditions for increasing water productivity in different sectors?
- Which tools should be used to enable more efficient and equitable development and allocation of water?
- How can the best use be made of the water available?
- Which measures should be put in place to protect water resources and increase water supply?
- Which institutional and legal set-ups are most appropriate for ensuring adequate coordination?
- What kind of information is needed and how is wide public ownership of water-related problems to be ensured?

In conditions of water scarcity, the putting in place of effective and equitable management practices requires knowledge, expertise and investment at political, institutional and technical levels.

The Vicious Cycle of Water and Poverty

First and foremost, water scarcity is an issue of poverty. Unclean water and lack of sanitation are the destiny of poor people across the world. Lack of hygiene affects poor children and families first, while the rest of the world's population benefits from direct access to the water they need for domestic use. One in five persons in the developing world lacks access to sufficient clean water (a suggested minimum of 20 litres/day), while average water use in Europe and the United States of America ranges between 200 and 600 litres/day. In addition, the poor pay more. A recent report by the United Nations Development Programme shows that people in the slums of developing countries typically pay five to 10 times more per unit of water than do people with access to piped water.

For poor people, water scarcity is not only about droughts or rivers running dry. Above all, it is about guaranteeing the fair and safe access they need to sustain their lives and secure their livelihoods. For the poor, scarcity is about how institutions function and how transparency and equity are guaranteed in decisions affecting their lives. It is about choices on infrastructure development and the way they are managed. In many places throughout the world, organizations struggle to distribute resources equitably.

Water for Life, Water for Livelihood

While access to safe water and sanitation have been recognized as priority targets through the Millennium Development Goals (MDGs) and the Johannesburg plan of action of the World Summit on Sustainable Development (WSSD), there is increasing recognition that this is not enough. Millions of people rely in one way or another on water for their daily income or food production.

Farmers, small rural enterprises, herders and fishing people—all need water to secure their livelihood. However, as the resources become scarce, an increasing number of them see their sources of income disappear. Silently, progressively, the number of water losers increases—at the tail end of the irrigation canal, downstream of a new dam, or as a result of excessive groundwater drawdown.

It is probably in rural areas that water scarcity affects people most. In large parts of the developing world, irrigation remains the backbone of rural economies. However, small-holder farmers make up the majority of the world's rural poor, and they often occupy marginal land and depend mainly on rainfall for production.

They are highly sensitive to many changes—droughts, floods, and also shifts in market prices. However, rainwater is rarely integrated into water management strategies, which usually focus exclusively on surface water and groundwater. Countries need to integrate rainwater fully into their strategies to cope with water scarcity.

Growing Demand for a Finite Resource

If all the freshwater on the planet were divided equally among the global population, there would be 5000–6000 m^3 of water available for everyone, every year. As experts consider that people experience scarcity below a threshold of 1700 m^3/person, this global calculation gives an impression of abundance. However, the world's freshwater resources are distributed very unevenly, as is the world's population. The areas of most severe physical water scarcity are those where high population densities converge with low availability of freshwater. Many countries are already well below the threshold value. Jordan, like several other countries in the Near East, is an extreme case with less than 200 m^3/person per year.

Central to the debate on water scarcity are the ways in which we need and use water. Water for drinking and for general household use, comparatively small in terms of volume, needs to be available in the home or, at the very least, close by. The inexorable growth of cities, concentrating large numbers of people in small areas, exacerbates this challenge locally.

The water that supports ecosystems, fish, animals and invertebrates must, of course, be left to follow its natural pathways through the world's landscapes. The water that produces much of the world's energy, by hydropower generation or in cooling carbon-fired power stations, has to be available at the point of energy generation, with such decisions often dictated by factors other than water. The same is true of much of the water used in industry.

However, most significant is the water that produces our food. The basic metabolism of each of our bodies—heart-beats, respiration and maintaining body temperature—requires about 1,800–2,300 kcal every day. Every calorie of the food that releases the metabolic energy within us consumes about 1 litre of water in its production.

Crop production, the process of converting carbon and water into the biomass needed to sustain our daily energy requirements, is by far the largest water-consuming sector. To produce enough food to satisfy a person's daily diet requires about 2,000–3,000 litres of water. In contrast, about 2–3 litres are required for drinking purposes, and 200–300 litres for domestic needs. As the world population continues to increase, more people will require more water for the cultivation of food, fibre and industrial crops and for livestock and fish. It is estimated that food and feed crop demand will nearly double in the coming 50 years.

The two main factors driving how much more food we will need are population growth and dietary change. With rising incomes and continuing urbanization, food habits change towards richer and more varied diets—not only towards increasing consumption of staple cereals, but also leading to a shift in consumption patterns among cereal crops and away from cereals towards livestock and fish products and high-value crops that consume more water.

Agriculture accounts for more than 70 per cent of the world's total water use. Its share drops to about 40 per cent in countries that import food and have a developed and diverse economy, but rises to over 95 per cent in many of the countries where agriculture is the primary economic activity.

Securing our food supply is not negotiable. We all need safe and good-quality food in order to live a healthy life. However, the way food is produced and the type of diet people adopt can have significant impacts on the total volume of water used in agriculture.

Moreover, agricultural practices across the world have a substantial impact on the world's freshwater resources—the adoption of a clean and productive agriculture can have a positive impact on the quantity and quality of the water it uses.

Clearly, having 2 000 litres of water available to each of us in or near our homes every day is of little relevance to meeting our own metabolic needs. Many people are entirely isolated from food production, relying solely on purchasing food from shops or markets.

Where that food is produced is fundamental to the debate on water scarcity. Countries that are wealthy enough to import food and industrial goods can typically cope well with a low national endowment of water resources. They can mobilize their limited water resources towards domestic and environmental needs—water elsewhere is used to produce the food they need.

In the last century, the world population has tripled. It is expected to rise from the present 6.5 billion to 8.9 billion by 2050, before levelling off. Water use has been growing at more than twice the rate of population increase in the last century, and, although there is no global water scarcity as such, an increasing number of regions are chronically short of water.

By 2025, it is estimated that 1.8 billion people will be living in countries or regions with absolute water scarcity, and two-thirds of the world population could be under conditions of water stress. The situation will be exacerbated as rapidly growing urban areas place heavy pressure on local water resources.

There will be four main drivers of increasing water scarcity during the coming decades. First, as already mentioned, there is the inexorable growth in population. Second, the world is expected to become increasingly urbanized, focusing the demand for water among an ever more concentrated population. Asian cities alone are expected to grow by 1 billion people in the next 20 years. Third, per-capita consumption, the amount of domestic water that each person uses, is expected to rise as the world becomes more developed.

Fourth, while these factors will increase the demand for water, freshwater resources will change as a result of climate change. While the magnitude of this change is still subject to uncertainty and will vary from one region to another, semi-arid regions will probably see an increase in the variability of precipitations, leading to more frequent periods of drought.

As farmers in particular face the challenge of accessing an increasingly scarce resource, groundwater levels are falling further each year, causing more rivers to dry up. Water is a major determinant of the health and productivity of ecosystems, placed in jeopardy in many parts of the world by reductions in water flows and water quality standards. Increasing water extraction has threatened the integrity of natural ecosystems, leading to the loss of significant biological diversity and undermining the ecosystem productivity on which so many poor people depend. Half of the world's wetlands disappeared during the 20th century, many rivers no longer reach the sea and fish species are endangered.

The Strategic Role of Groundwater

In arid and semi-arid regions, where water scarcity is almost endemic, groundwater has played a major role in meeting domestic and irrigation demands. In many regions, massive use of groundwater has been practised for some time for irrigation. Groundwater mining and the lack of adequate planning, legal frameworks and governance have opened a new debate on the sustainability of the intensive use of groundwater resources.

Sharing Water—Conflict or Cooperation?

Water scarcity induces competition for water between users, between sectors of the economy and between countries and regions sharing a common resource, as is the case for international rivers. Many different interests are at stake and equitable solutions must be found between cities and rural areas; rich and poor; arid lands and wetlands; public and private; infrastructure and natural environments; mainstream and marginal groups; and local stakeholders and centralized authorities. Water conflicts can arise in water stressed areas among local communities and between countries because sharing a very limited and essential resource is extremely difficult. The lack of adequate legal instruments exacerbates already difficult conditions. In the absence of clear and well-established rules, chaos tends to dominate and power plays an excessive role, leading to inequitable allocation of water.

A greater focus is needed on the peaceful sharing and management of water at both international and local levels.

The fact that so many of the world's rivers and aquifers are shared by more than one country places a major emphasis on water allocation agreements. A mature debate is now emerging about sharing the benefits of water rather than focusing on setting up national quotas of bulk water. Analysts have shown that under the prevailing internationalist setting of the past decades, water has been a source of cooperation between nations rather than a source of conflict. There is an expectation that such cooperation will continue and indeed that there will be greater recognition of its importance to maximizing the benefits from water within development.

Water in Rural Areas—Vulnerability and Sustainability

As most of the world's poor live in rural areas, one of the most effective ways of reducing hunger and poverty is to raise their productive capacity through agricultural development. The ways forward are complex and vary from region to region, but the opportunities for increased productivity and diversification do exist and they are considerable.

Many households (about 80–90 per cent of all families in rural Africa) rely upon producing and eating their own food. Already compounded by longstanding problems of land degradation and desertification and suffering difficulties in securing inputs of fertilizer and seed they, more than others, face the very real world of water scarcity. Unpredictable seasonal rains and periods of just a few days without rain at critical stages in the cropping cycle can regularly decimate their production, leading to food shortages.

Irrigation is a direct source of livelihood for hundreds of millions of the rural poor in developing countries because of the food, income options and indirect benefits it generates. There are high political aspirations that agricultural development, in particular across sub-Saharan Africa, will lift many out of poverty, a few as producers of marketable products, others as wage labourers and others in small enterprises away from the farm. The anti-poverty effects of irrigation can be assessed at two levels: production, related to the national or regional economy; and livelihoods, related to the household and its well-being. The former has been the method traditionally used to assess irrigation impacts; conversely, a livelihood-based approach to irrigation places adequate and secure livelihood aims before increased production.

Rural farmers can be enabled to produce their own food through local soil and water conservation practices or through conservation agriculture. These are ways of farming that recognize that most poor farmers own nothing more than a hand-hoe, and make the most dependent on agriculture. For many African countries, bereft of alternative economic opportunities in rural areas, agriculture is viewed as the principal avenue for social development.

Expectations are high that agriculture can deliver national economic growth and at the same time lift millions of households out of poverty. Along with other factors such as markets, prices, inputs and security of land tenure, water is very important to meeting these aspirations.

Most importantly, farmers will be able to keep control over the small revenues earned within the households themselves. Critically, farmers are enabled to take that first step on the ladder towards the more commercial forms of agriculture that will create sustainable livelihoods.

Climate Change—Trouble Ahead

Now a major international issue, climate change is expected to account for about 20 per cent of the global increase in water scarcity. Countries that already suffer from water shortages will be hit hardest. Significantly, there will be major increases in water scarcity even if the water impacts of climate change prove to be neutral or even raise the world's hydrological budget. With neither being reasonably expected to happen, the impact of a changing climate will affect not only bulk water availability but also worsen the extremes of drought and floods. A study by the UK Meteorological Office concluded that with no mitigation of climate change, the severe droughts that now occur only once every 50 years will occur every other year by 2100.

The Way Forward

Addressing water scarcity requires actions at local, national and river basin levels. It also calls for actions at global and international levels, leading to increased collaboration between nations on shared management of water resources (rivers, lakes and aquifers) and of the benefits thereof. Being inter-sectoral in its nature, the response to water scarcity requires: collaboration; the sharing of joint vision and policy principles; and joint action in addressing the issue. A major challenge in addressing water scarcity successfully in countries is the institutional fragmentation of responsibilities in the water development sector.

Improving Investments in Water

Goals

Wise use of water will be needed if all the Millennium Development Goals, (MDG), most of them to be reached by 2015, are to be attained. In its own right, improved access to water and sanitation is an established MDG target.

In recent years, a very strong case has been made that improved access to water, sanitation and health will contribute across all of the MDGs, including targets in education and health. It would be advantageous to profile the wider contribution that must be made by water—beyond domestic water and sanitation alone—across all of the MDGs.

Judicious management of increasingly scarce resources is needed if benefits in economic growth, hunger reduction, lifting households out of extreme poverty and ensuring environmental sustainability, among others, are to be achieved. Failure to take action on water will be a detriment of MDG attainment.

With 2015 looming, now is not the time for weak governance. Worst of all, bad governance will bring with it real costs in terms of MDG attainment for millions.

Many countries are falling behind in their progress towards the specific MDG on water and, in particular, sanitation. While there are a few locations around the world where difficulties in access can be attributed to the physical scarcity of water, the overwhelming challenge is one of water governance.

Many actions are necessary to attain the MDGs that tackle poverty in ways that are entirely unconnected with water. However, water can play a key role as part of strategies for achieving most of the MDGs, including hunger reduction, universal education, empowerment of women, improved health and combating disease, environmental sustainability and advancing a global partnership for development. In particular, the eradication of poverty and hunger in rural areas is linked closely to fair and equitable access of the most vulnerable people to basic livelihood assets (including land and water) for domestic and productive uses. Because increased demand usually threatens the sustainability of the environment in situations of scarcity, water scarcity management is also crucial to achieving the goals of environmental sustainability.

This close relationship between MDGs and water is often not understood. Consequently, water management actions are poorly represented in the poverty reduction strategies of developing countries. Water can contribute both directly and indirectly by creating the conditions where the different goals and targets are more likely to be attained.

Studies by the World Health Organization have shown that the benefits of investing in water far outweigh the costs of making the improvements—by as much as 60 times (and never less than 3) in the major regions of the developing world.

Unlocking the Potential of Africa's Water

The doubling of Africa's irrigated area is currently very high on the political agenda. Achieving this goal means that the factors that have constrained investment will need to be addressed. With less than one-third of the continent's potential under irrigation, opportunities exist across much of the continent to invest further in water for agriculture.

Markets, commodity selection, ownership, land tenure, water storage for reliable supply and international agreements on water allocations within river basins are all key factors in unlocking this potential. Many see the importance of reducing the US$ 18-billion food-import bill borne by the continent. Many also see the potential for boosting household incomes by creating labour opportunities.

However, some recognize that, even in an optimistic scenario in which every hectare created two new jobs, the significant uplifting of 60 million households would be insufficient to make major inroads into the extreme poverty that pervades the continent.

Consequently, a dual approach is gaining ground, one in which improvements in rainfed food production for the very many vulnerable African farmers must take place alongside the seizing of viable irrigation opportunities.

Improved Health and Water

Globally, 1.1 billion people lack access to improved water supply, and 2.6 billion are without improved sanitation. Most of them live in rural areas, but the number of urban dwellers without adequate water and sanitation services is increasing rapidly. The majority of those without adequate sanitation services live in Asia, but sub-Saharan Africa has the highest proportion of people without water.

Water-related diseases, linked to inadequate access to safe water and basic sanitation, are endemic in many regions. There are 4 billion cases of diarrhoea each year, causing 2.2 million deaths (5,000 every day), mostly of children under the age of five. One million people a year, almost all under the age of five, are killed by malaria, and millions are affected by filariasis, schistosomiasis, intestinal worms and other water-related diseases.

Many women suffer permanent skeletal damage from carrying heavy loads of water over long distances day after day. Poor nutrition so weakens people that they die from illnesses and infections that are not usually fatal in developed countries. The numbers of deaths and illnesses from preventable diseases are dramatic in their own right. Their impact on the economies of countries and the livelihoods of poor households is even more insidious.

Water and health are intimately linked. Water conveys pathogens to people and provides the habitat for vectors and intermediate hosts of pathogens. Shortages of water and, above all, inadequate sanitation limit the ability of a family to cope with these threats. Worst of all, using poor quality water that is unsafe only exacerbates matters by causing further illness and infection. Diseases associated with water affect the poor in a disproportionate way, and this burden of ill health maintains the vicious cycle of poverty and sickness.

It is against this backdrop that the potential for access to improved water sources and best water management practices, basic sanitation and improved hygiene behaviour must be developed to the full. Major health gains can be achieved at household level through personal protection, whether through oral rehydration salts or the use of chlorination tablets for drinking water. Farmers can choose options that reduce health risks and their exposure to illness without detriment to their production. Communities can mobilize to work towards improved drinking water facilities. They can learn about drinking water contamination risks in their homes, and about the treatment and safe storage of drinking-water from the unreliable sources upon which so many depend.

Governments can take action to bring their health sectors and water managers together in successful partnerships.

Producing More with Less Water

Increasing water productivity holds the key to future water scarcity challenges. Without further improvements in water productivity or major shifts in production patterns, the amount of water used for agriculture, industrial and domestic activities will increase by 60–90 per cent by 2050, depending on population, incomes and assumptions about water requirements for the environment.

In agriculture alone, the total volume of water used in crop production would be 11,000–13,500 km^3, almost double the 7,130 km^3 of today. Cotton production, a high-demand agricultural practice, is projected to grow by 1.5 per cent annually, and a further burden is expected to come from increased demand for biofuel. By 2030, world energy demand will rise by 50 per cent, and two-thirds of this demand will come from developing countries.

However, there is scope for an accelerated increase in water productivity. Water productivity in agriculture has increased steadily in recent decades, largely owing to increasing crop yields, and the potential exists for further increase. However, the pace of such increase will vary according to the type of policies and investments put in place, with substantial variations in the impact on the environment and livelihoods of rural populations.

Targeted investments in all sectors, combined with a package of institutional measures that promote enhanced efficiency while guaranteeing equity in access to water, can do much to alleviate water scarcity and secure environmental sustainability.

Agriculture and Water Scarcity

Today, agriculture accounts for 70 per cent of all water use globally, up to 95 per cent in several developing countries. Adding to the pressures on agricultural use is the increased awareness of the instrumental value of water in maintaining environmental services and ecosystem resilience. Increasing the efficiency of water use and enhancing agricultural water productivity at all levels of the production chains are becoming priorities in a rapidly growing number of countries. A systematic approach to agricultural water productivity requires actions at all levels, from crops to irrigation schemes, and up to national and international economic systems, including the trade in agricultural products.

It calls for an informed discussion on the scope for improved water productivity in order to ameliorate inter-sectoral competition for water resources and optimize social and economic outcomes. To keep pace with the growing demand for food and taking into consideration an increase in water productivity, it is estimated that 14 per cent more freshwater will need to be withdrawn for agricultural purposes by 2030 in order to obtain the 55 per cent increase in food production that is needed.

As early as 2002, the international community acknowledged the importance of the water scarcity challenge by adopting the short-term target of developing 'integrated water resources management and water efficiency plans…with support to developing countries, through actions at all levels.' In particular, the Plan of Implementation called for:

- strategies and programmes for integrated river basin, watershed and groundwater management;
- measures to improve the efficiency of water use, to reduce losses and to increase recycling of water in a way that gives priority to the satisfaction of basic human needs while preserving or restoring ecosystems and their functions;
- programmes for mitigating the effects of extreme water-related events;
- diffusion of technologies and capacity building for non-conventional water resources and conservation technologies to developing countries and regions facing water scarcity conditions or subject to drought and desertification.

While there has been notable progress, still much remains to be done in order to develop and implement these plans.

Managing Uncertainty

The people facing the greatest problems of water scarcity on a day-to-day basis are the many rural poor. This is especially the case for those living in marginal areas where food production is at the mercy of the vagaries of climate and where they face the consequences of weak delivery of services in water and sanitation. This is a widespread and insidious problem that also affects urban dwellers, notably in Asian cities.

Many rural households produce their own food and in their particular case, it is essential that the 800–1,000 m of water per person they need to secure their annual food production is available locally on their fields. However, investments in household food security are rare and largely insufficient. Consequently, many millions of rural dwellers have to rely on rainfed agriculture, with all of the vagaries and vulnerabilities that accompany the unpredictability of that rain. It is this dependence on local rain for food production that makes the impacts of drought so widespread and so long-lasting. Few die of thirst during drought, but very many are affected by extreme hunger for a year or more.

Enhanced economic growth is essential for poverty reduction in most parts of the world, but the quality of growth and, in particular, the extent to which it creates new opportunities for the poor also matter. Improved water management can be a catalyst for such growth.

Water provides vital inputs into many productive activities and creates opportunities for local entrepreneurs in supplying technologies, constructing facilities and providing services. Local investments generate high returns and, importantly, they retain benefits in the local economy and generate significant multiplier effects. Improved water management can also be a catalyst for growth at the national and regional level, where major water infrastructure investments can transform development prospects. It is essential that such investments are accompanied by effective impact assessments and proper safeguards (taking into account all the costs and benefits generated). Where this is the case, and where major infrastructure investment is accompanied by incentives that trigger private enterprise and livelihood opportunities, then water investments can play a key role in poverty reduction.

There are massive opportunities to improve the ability of poor people to lift themselves out of poverty under conditions of greater water security and sustainability. Making sure that adequate and reliable supplies of water are available for agricultural activities (including producing the food that households grow to feed themselves and the extra they sell at markets to earn small amounts of cash, livestock, aquaculture and horticulture) is a key to rural poverty reduction throughout the developing world. Supporting domestic water schemes that make water available for home-based livelihood activities, such as vegetable production, pottery and laundering, is effective in targeting the poor and supporting diversified livelihoods. In many countries, broadbased agricultural growth represents the best opportunity for stimulating economic growth.

Investments to reduce vulnerability to water-related risks and to improve agricultural productivity are compelling for environmental and equity reasons. Realizing the potential of existing rainfed areas reduces the need for water withdrawals from rivers and groundwater for new large-scale irrigation development.

On the other hand, improving rainfed production also requires infrastructure, but often smaller and more distributed. Realizing this potential requires risk-mitigation measures. Water harvesting techniques are useful for bridging short dry spells, but longer dry spells may lead to crop failure. With the right incentives and measures to mitigate risks for individual farmers, improving rainfed agriculture holds considerable potential to increase food production and reduce poverty, while ensuring the maintaining of ecosystem services.

Pathways for Reducing Rural Poverty

- Ensure secure access to water for productive use for poor women and men through clarifying water rights is one example. At the same time, address the need for redistributive policies to solve the rural poor's lack of access to assets, markets and services.
- Target livelihood gains directly through small-scale, individually managed water management technologies that provide water at lower unit costs than large-scale hydraulic infrastructure and which can be easily implemented locally.
- Acknowledge indigenous knowledge, customary laws and informal institutions in water management.
- Promote multiple water-use systems—a single system for domestic use, crop production, aquaculture, agroforestry and livestock—that are effective for both reducing poverty and improving water productivity.
- Protect the natural resources on which the rural poor's livelihoods depend. Fisheries, in particular, represent an important source of livelihoods and nutrition in rural areas.

Social and Environmental Services

As water becomes scarce, a main question today is how to best support stakeholders in managing their water demands in a context of increasing competition and interdependence. This question is especially significant for agriculture as it is the largest water user globally and faces increasing difficulty in:

(i) securing a sufficient share of water resources to meet the needs of a growing world population; and

(ii) managing the impacts of its activities on the resource base.

Supporting stakeholders in managing their water resources means supporting them to make choices and to reach a common understanding on the necessary arrangements for sharing and allocating water-related goods and services.

Assessing and communicating the values associated with different water-related goods and services is the basis on which stakeholders have to seek a well-informed decision.

This explains the growing focus on water valuation as a means to support water resources management. Water valuation means expressing the value of water-related goods and services for sharing and allocation decisions. It covers use and non-use values, extractive and *in situ* use values and consumptive and non-consumptive use values. The notion of scarcity is central and this can refer to aspects of water quantity and quality, and have both temporal and spatial dimensions.

Valuation is an increasingly important tool in the process of allocating scarce water resources. However, the indiscriminate use of a purely economic approach risks over-emphasizing monetary expressions of value at the expense of environmental and social values.

Valuation frameworks are needed that recognize these three dimensions and in which stakeholders play a central role. Various methods have been developed that help to express the value of water-related goods and services in quantitative, monetary units.

Although potentially very useful, these methods are complicated and demanding in terms of the expertise, time and data required for their application. This hinders their widespread application, especially in developing countries.

As a result, their development in the field of water valuation has been mainly academic and much more effort is needed in order to apply valuation results and processes to support water resources management and decision-making effectively.

A multidisciplinary approach is needed in order to consider the social, economic, cultural, legal and institutional constraints relevant to local communities, urban centres, rural areas, user groups and administrative, public and private organizations. When reconsidering development schemes at local and national level, due consideration must also be given to societal and cultural changes that induce the transformation of related water management scenarios.

At national and local levels, many countries have developed scientific and technical knowledge, backed by policies and legislation, to prevent and remedy water scarcity impacts. There is a widespread need to share the results achieved with, and to raise awareness among, all decision-makers, managers and end users, including the general public.

6

Water: Conflicts and Opportunities

THE three water phenomena – dwindling freshwater supplies, inequitable access to water and the corporate control of water – pose the greatest threat of our time to the planet and to our survival. Together with impending climate change from fossil fuel emissions, the water crises impose some life-or-death decisions on us all. Unless we collectively change our behaviour, we are heading towards a world of deepening conflict and potential wars over the dwindling supplies of freshwater – between nations, between the rich and the poor, between the public and the private interests, between rural and urban populations and between the competing needs of the natural world and industrialized humans.

A Growing Source of Conflict

Around the world, more that 215 major rivers and 300 groundwater basins and aquifers are shared by two or more countries, creating tensions over ownership and use of the precious waters they contain. Growing shortages and unequal distribution of water are causing disagreements, sometimes violent, and becoming a security risk in many regions. Britain's former defence secretary, John Reid, warns of coming 'water wars.'

In a public statement in 2006, Reid predicted that violence and political conflict would become more likely as watersheds turn to deserts, glaciers melt and water supplies are poisoned. He went so far as to say that the global water crisis was becoming a global security issue and that Britain's armed forces should be prepared to tackle conflicts, including warfare, over dwindling water sources. 'Such changes make the emergence of violent conflict more, rather than less, likely,' former British prime minister Tony Blair told *The Independent*. "The blunt truth is that the lack of water and agricultural land is a significant contributory factor to the tragic conflict we see unfolding in Darfur. We should see this as a warning sign."

The London *Independent* gave several other examples of regions of potential conflict. These include Israel, Jordan and Palestine, who all rely on the Jordan River, which is controlled by Israel; Turkey and Syria, where Turkish plans to build dams on the Euphrates River brought the country to the brink of war with Syria in 1998, and where Syria now accuses Turkey of deliberately meddling with its water supply; China and India, where the Brahmaputra River has caused tension between the two countries in the past and where China's proposal to divert the river is re-igniting the divisions; Angola, Botswana and Namibia, where disputes over the Okavango water basin that have flared in the past are now threatening to re-ignite as Namibia is proposing to build a three-hundred-kilometre pipeline that will drain the delta; Ethiopia and Egypt, where population growth is threatening conflict along the Nile; and Bangladesh and India, where flooding in the Ganga caused by melting glaciers in the Himalayas is wreaking havoc in Bangladesh, leading to a rise in illegal and unpopular migration to India.

While not likely to lead to armed conflict, stresses are growing along the U.S.-Canadian border over shared boundary waters. In particular, concerns are growing over the future of the Great Lakes, whose waters are becoming increasingly polluted and whose water tables are being steadily drawn down by the huge build-up of population and industry around the basin. A joint commission set up to oversee these waters was recently bypassed by the governors of the American states bordering the Great Lakes, who passed an amendment to the treaty governing the lakes that allows for water diversions to new communities off the basin on the American side.

Canadian protests fell on deaf ears in Washington. In 2006, the U.S. government announced plans to have the U.S. coast guard patrol the Great Lakes using machine guns mounted on their vessels and revealed that it had created 34 permanent live-fire training zones along the Great Lakes from where it had already conducted a number of automatic weapons drills due to fierce opposition, firing three thousand lead bullets each time into the lakes. The Bush administration later temporarily called off these drills but is clearly asserting U.S. authority over what has in the past been considered joint waters.

Similar trouble is brewing on the U.S.-Mexican border, where a private group of U.S.-based water rights holders is using the North American Free Trade Agreement to challenge the long-term practice by Mexican farmers to divert water from the Rio Grande before it reaches the United States.

A Global Security Issue

Water has recently (and suddenly) become a key strategic security and foreign policy priority for the United States. In the wake of the terrorist attacks of 9/11, protection of U.S. waterways and drinking water supplies from terrorist attack became vitally important to the White House. When Congress created the Department of Homeland Security in 2002, it gave the department responsibility for securing the nation's water infrastructure and allocated US$ 548 million in appropriations for security of water infrastructure facilities, funding that was increased in subsequent years. The Environmental Protection Agency created a National Homeland Security Research Centre to develop the scientific foundations and tools to be used in the event of an attack on the nation's water systems, and a Water Security Division was established to train water utility personnel on security issues.

It also created a Water Information Sharing and Analysis Centre for dissemination of alerts about potential threats to drinking water and, with the American Water Works Association, a rapid e-mail notification system for professionals called the Water Security Channel. Ever true to market economy ideology, the Department of Homeland Security's mandate includes promoting public–private partnerships in protecting the nation's water security.

However, the interest in water did not stop there. Water is becoming as important a strategic issue as energy in Washington. In an August 2004 briefing note for the Institute for the Analysis of Global Security, a think tank that focuses on the link between energy and security, a senior analyst for the U.S. Department of Energy declared that the energy security of the United States actually depends on the state of its water resources and warned of a growing water-security crisis worldwide. "Just as energy security became a national priority in the period following the Arab oil embargo of 1973-74, water security is destined to become a national and global priority in the decades ahead," he said.

He noted that central to addressing water security issues is finding the energy to extract water from underground aquifers, transport water through pipelines and canals, manage and treat water for re-use and desalinate brackish and seawater—all technologies now being promoted by U.S. government partnerships with American companies.

He also pointed out that the U.S. energy interests in the Middle East could be threatened by water conflicts in the region: "Water conflicts add to the instability of a region on which the U.S. depends heavily for oil. Continuation or inflammation of these conflicts could subject U.S. energy supplies to blackmail again, as occurred in the 1970s." Water shortages and global warning pose a 'serious threat' to America's national security, top retired military leaders told the president in an April 2007 report published by the national security think tank, CNA Corporation. Six retired admirals and five retired generals warned of a future of rampant water wars into which the United States will be dragged.

The director of the Global Strategy Institute of the Centre for Strategic and International Studies, a research organization in Washington that calls itself a 'strategic planning partner for the government,' says that the United States must make water a top priority in foreign policy. "There is a very, very critical dimension to all these global water problems here at home," he said. 'The first is that it's in our national interest to see stability and security and economic development in key areas of the world, and water is a big factor with that whole set of challenges".

His centre has joined forces with ITT Industries, the giant water technology company; Proctor & Gamble, which has created a home water purifier called PUR and is working with the UN in a joint public-private venture in developing countries; Coca-Cola; and Sandia National Laboratories to launch a joint-research institute called Global Water Futures (GWF).

Sandia, whose motto is 'securing a peaceful and free world through technology' and that works to 'maintain U.S. military and nuclear superiority,' is contracted out to weapons manufacturer Lockheed Martin by the U.S. government, to operate, thus linking water security to military security in a direct way. The mandate of Global Water Futures is twofold: to affect U.S. strategy and policy regarding the global water crisis and to develop the technology necessary to advance the solution.

In a September 2005 report, Global Water Futures warned that the global water crisis is driving the world towards 'a tipping point in human history' and elaborated on the need for the United States to start taking water security more seriously: "In light of the global trends in water, it is clear that water quality and water management will affect almost every major U.S. strategic priority in every key region of the world. Addressing the world's water needs will go well beyond humanitarian and economic development interests....Policies focused on water in regions across the planet must be regarded as a critical element in U.S. national security strategy. Such policies should be part of a broader, comprehensive, and integrated U.S. strategy towards the global water challenges."

Innovations in policy and technology must be tightly linked, says the report, no doubt music to the ears of the corporations that sponsored it. GWF calls for closer innovation and cooperation between governments and the private sector and 'redoubled' efforts to mobilize public-private partnerships in the development of technological solutions.

And, in language that will be familiar to critics of the Bush administration who argued that the United States is not in Iraq to promote democracy, but rather to secure oil resources and make huge profits for American companies in the 'rebuilding' effort, the report links upholding American values of democracy with the profit to be gained in the process: "Water issues are critical to U.S. national security and integral to upholding American values of humanitarianism and democratic development." Moreover, engagement with international water issues guarantees business opportunities for the U.S. private sector, which is well positioned to contribute to development and reap economic rewards

Listed among the U.S. government agencies engaged in water issues in the report is the Department of Commerce, which 'facilitates U.S. water businesses and market research, and improves U.S. competitiveness in the international water market.'

The Alternative Water Future

Humanity still has a chance to head off these scenarios of conflict and war. We could start with a global covenant on water. The 'Blue Covenant', a concept promoted by Barlow, should have three components: a water conservation covenant from people and their governments that recognizes the right of the Earth and of other species to clean water and pledges to protect and conserve the world's water supplies; a water justice covenant between those in the global North who have water and resources and those in the global South who do not, to work in solidarity for water justice, water for all and local control of water; and a water democracy covenant among all governments acknowledging that water is a fundamental human right for all. Therefore, governments are required not only to provide clean water to their citizens as a public service, but they must also recognize that citizens of other countries have the right to water as well and to find peaceful solutions to water disputes between states.

A good example of this is the 'Good Water Makes Good Neighbours' project of Friends of the Earth Middle East, which seeks to use shared water and the notion of water justice to negotiate a wider peace accord in the region. Another example is the successful restoration of the beautiful Lake Constance by Germany, Austria, Lichtenstein and Switzerland, the four countries that share it.

The Blue Covenant should also form the heart of a new covenant on the right to water to be adopted both in nation-state constitutions and in international law at the United Nations. To create the conditions for this covenant will require concerted and collective international collaboration and will have to tackle all three water crises together with the alternatives: Water Conservation, Water Justice and Water Democracy.

7

Knowledge and Capacity Development

IN 1972, the Declaration of the United Nations Conference on the Human Environment emphasised the importance of education and the right institutions for the management of our environment. Since the Delft Declaration in 1991, capacity building has been recognized explicitly as a key tool for making development sustainable and for addressing the world's broad spectrum of water management challenges—from drinking water supply and sanitation to water resources management.

Across all sectors, funding for capacity development has grown tenfold since 1995. Donors are spending more than one quarter of their funds on education and capacity development today and this effort is indeed showing results.

Are these funds applied to optimum effect and are they helping our world to prepare well for future challenges? The world is in a state of accelerated change. Over the past two decades, the world's population has grown by two billion people, and most of them are poor. By 2030, nearly 60 per cent of the population in developing countries will live in urban centres—the engines of job creation and economic growth. These sprawling settlements are rapidly changing the land use in the watersheds around them, especially the river flood plains and thus exacerbating floods. People are demanding more clean tap water and sanitation that works.

Improving the often weak urban water systems in developing countries will become increasingly critical. All easily available water resources are now in use, so responding to increased demand for water now implies intense competition. With such large numbers of people and economies increasingly dependent on water, the new uncertainties and risks created by climatic variability pose a special challenge. By 2025, the number of people facing water scarcity is projected to double. The impacts on food production, health and livelihoods are still unclear, but it is sure that many communities will suffer from strong negative effects.

Our water systems and policies must be re-designed with the specific objective to enhance their resilience against climate change and other global changes. To achieve proper water resource management, coordination between institutions must be deepened and more structural capacity developed. It also follows that awareness raising and education for all stakeholder groups from local communities to politicians must be well-targeted and sustained.

Integrated water resources management (IWRM) must take into account the specific conditions of each situation. It is contextually shaped through dialogue and stakeholder involvement in order to encompass the different dimensions of sustainability (ecological, biophysical, economic, social and institutional). Thus, effective IWRM is knowledge-intensive. It cannot be imposed from outside and will require a slow incremental and patchy process.

Sustaining Global Development

UNDP states that 'Capacity is the ability of individuals, groups, institutions and organizations to identify and solve development problems over time.' The 1991 Delft Declaration suggested 'Capacity building involves developing institutions, their managerial systems, and their human resources, which in turn require favourable policy environments, to make the sector effective and sustainable.' Capacity implies the ability to understand, to act, and to learn. Proper knowledge may remain ineffectual if policies and regulations, or politically inspired preferences, preclude its application.

Learning is essential to continuously improve performance and prepare for upcoming changes. These transformations are global and affect all, rich and poor. They call for preparedness and innovation in industrialised and developing nations alike. Achieving effective solutions increasingly depends on getting a good fit between the technical solution (infrastructure) and what key stakeholders in society are willing to commit to. Stakeholder involvement is as critically important in industrialized countries to make large investments successful as it is in developing countries to make development efforts better targeted and more sustainable.

Developing countries remain especially vulnerable though: two billion people still lack access to clean water supply and to sanitation and the pace of economic growth is leading to rapid deterioration of land and water resources. Our efforts and coordination need to be better guided and scaled up in order to reach the Millennium Development Goals (MDGs). With finance now in good supply, communities and countries need to become able to absorb these funds.

Twenty years ago, capital was in short supply and water was predominantly a matter of government funding. This shortage determined the pace of international development. Nowadays, capital for investments is much more plentiful, also in developing countries. Private parties are becoming major actors and a growing slice of international investment. However, the knowledge and institutional capacity of many countries to readily 'absorb' all of these funds remain severely constrained—that is, key stakeholders are unable to rapidly bring to the table concepts and designs for projects and investments that are economically and socially robust and sustainable, and can be properly implemented, operated and maintained. The weakness in knowledge and capacity is becoming therefore the key constraint to sustainable development.

Yet, investing in Knowledge and Capacity Development (KCD) pays off. Recent evaluations have demonstrated that development projects in the water sector are now decidedly more effective and sustainable than previously. This can be attributed for a large part to stronger institutions, better governance and more technical and managerial competence in the developing countries whose capacity has been strengthened. Several studies on irrigation have shown that the best return on the investment in canal improvement is achieved when a substantial effort is also placed in capacity development—including empowerment—of irrigators and government officials.

Some of the recommendations presented below may sound all too familiar. Does that mean that the efforts for KCD have failed thus far? Not likely. The growth rate in the number and size of problems has outpaced the speed at which capacity could be put in place to deal with these problems; the population pressure has been increasing fast and water management has become much more complex. Also, our understanding of what needs to be done has improved; still, remarkably little is known about how KCD functions and how it can be made to work more effectively. There are major improvements to be achieved. Driven by these shifts, KCD is due to become an increasingly essential tool for sustainable development.

An irrigation canal designed and built without involving the users collapsed after two years (Indonesia). After capacity strengthening of irrigation staff and users, this irrigation canal was designed and rebuilt using users' knowledge and preferences—it is effective and well maintained. Local actors are at the front line as they are the first in addressing local problems. They hold valuable knowledge and experience and this still too often goes unrecognised.

Their knowledge and experience should be identified and reviewed—decision makers need to learn from these stakeholders and apply the lessons learned, such that they use local capacity and knowledge, work with local reformers, build capacity of local institutions and civil society, and apply the subsidiarity principle to empower local actors.

A balanced combination is called for to incorporate top-down (often larger-scale) and bottom-up (often smaller-scale) approaches and procedures. Importantly, just as there can be no solution if there is not first a problem, local actors are often the first to identify new issues and problems as well as offer simple solutions. These are critically important in preparing for the next generation of solutions. The local actors should therefore become more often partners in (national and international) knowledge networks, on equal footing with the 'solution providers'.

The role of water professionals is critical as they must become facilitators, able to engage with stakeholders at all levels; they should assist the local communities, user associations, businesses, local governments and other stakeholders in better articulating their issues, priorities, as well as existing insights and experiences. They should assist in articulating the demand. Local actors should receive access to information—in a format that is meaningful to them, as this empowers them to take part in decision-making and to hold service providers and government more accountable.

Information and communication systems (ICS) can be particularly useful to facilitate this process. Concrete steps to be taken include creating dialogue platforms involving local stakeholders and assisting local communities to play a meaningful role by training them. The focus should be on decision aiding rather than dispute resolution. A promising tool is the 'Negotiated Approach' in which all stakeholders, governmental and non-governmental, lay out the issues and seek consensus on key decisions.

Good governance aims to enhance equitable access and efficient use of water and must be contextually defined, which implicitly calls for a more democratic distribution of power and better accountability. Governance should start with tangible improvements that are meaningful for the community—fixing leaking pipes, improving maintenance, etc. Workable solutions are by definition 'local.' They reflect local and indigenous practices and knowledge, and aim to meet local priorities. At the same time, the larger-scale and exogenously developed technical solutions also remain valid options. Larger scale solutions bring synergies, economies of scale, mitigation of externalities and allow the negotiation of competitive upstream-downstream and cross-sectoral interests.

The balancing of the 'community focus' and the 'technical approach' calls for strong intellectual leadership and authority. KCD facilitates striking a balance between bottom-up and top-down approaches.

Conclusion and Recommendations

Actors outside the sector require more knowledge on water. Decisions on water are not only taken by water professionals but also in other sectors: power, land use, agriculture, fisheries, finance, etc. Therefore, water policies will be truly robust only when these policies are made mutually consistent. Politicians should be a priority focus group for capacity development.

Making decisions on water and on investments is pre-eminently political. The case should be made, and made again, that wise water use is in their interest. More effort must be put in making key technical information much more accessible—not only to the political decision-makers, but also to the water users to make them better informed and empowered.

There are important opportunities to promote local innovations by working with local businesses and other local organisations in developing and implementing new technologies, such as the necessary information and communication systems. The communication of research results and technical knowledge to politicians, local communities and decision-makers is essential to increase the relevance of research, as it helps to guide the selection of research topics and tests the resulting research and generated knowledge against 'field' practice. Useful tools which may be used to communicate scientific knowledge more effectively include a range of ICT tools, animations, and role-plays.

'Hot' water issues can be used to raise public awareness and understanding. This can be facilitated by encouraging 'research brokers' and 'science journalists.' However, scientists should avoid sensationalism and should make the hidden values and assumptions of their discipline explicit in order to promote dialogue, avoid misleading use of scientific information and facilitate interdisciplinary policy making.

Case Study: Uganda

Transforming organisations in the water sector is a necessary step to create the right vision, plans, environment and dedicated staff to improve service delivery. It requires vision from the politicians and leaders in the government and in the organisations. Through a 'stretch out' programme, the National Water and Sewerage Corporation (NSCW) in Uganda changed its organisation from one that was stagnant in its traditions to one that has been learning and improving performance steadily since 1998. To bring in much needed accountability, the change process introduced performance-based contracts between the local utilities and the NWSC, separating the functions of operations and maintenance from performance monitoring and regulation.

Through an incremental approach designed by multi-disciplinary teams, beginning with simpler performance contracts and then upgrading to a more complex arrangement, the capacity of utilities to work with this system was developed. Experience with this system is used to continually improve performance—NWSC has become a learning organisation. This process has created an environment where managers have to account for performance against goals and the attitude of staff has changed from passivity and tradition to one of purpose and innovation. 'Champions' were given the space to present business plans and make changes to their units. Significant salary and other performance-based incentives for managers and staff help sustain motivation.

As an integral part of the change strategy, NWSC actively supports utilities through targeted interaction and coordination, which has enhanced information flows and overall coordination. The abolishment of command and control structures is balanced with constructive interactions and monitoring of performance goals.

Promote Integrated Approaches

Workable and sustainable solutions in water management require further integration between land and water management, between the management of the different urban water systems, between the water and the energy and agricultural sectors, and between construction and operation and maintenance procedures. Integration can generally only be achieved incrementally in a step-wise process that can be long drawn out. In particular, dialogue between stakeholders facilitates integration, which is shaped by the context.

Multi-disciplinary Problem-Based Learning and demand-driven research agendas should be promoted. Educational and other knowledge institutions should play active roles in multistakeholder partnerships for water resources management. This will allow more effective problem solving and better sharing of traditional and formal knowledge.

Donor projects should recognise the complexity of the water sector and allow more flexibility in the budget, time schedules and objectives in order to create the space for the incremental progress that characterizes the development of integrated approaches.

Transform Organisations

The best organisations in public administration are 'learning' organisations, just as knowledge-driven corporations in the private sector tend to be the more successful businesses. They allow themselves to change in response to new challenges and to new knowledge. Structural, deep capacity cannot be enhanced without parallel institutional change in the organisation. Organisations that are static, which discourage change or are beholden to existing 'special interests,' under-perform.

They need to reform in order to anticipate and adapt better to future needs and demonstrate improved performance on key benchmarks. 'Champions,' or leaders, play a key role by being role models and shaping the attitudes for continuous learning and reform. KCD is an important tool to 'turn around' organisations, and help them develop their mission, vision, plans and learning capability.

Reform the Water Sector

The past decade has seen many countries across the globe going through deep administrative transformations: local governments are generally much more powerful now; market forces are exerting more economic discipline and people, goods, capital and ideas move more freely across borders. Yet experience shows that much investment is ineffectual because of poor operation and maintenance of the physical and institutional infrastructure. Lack of recurrent local budgets and political will; sectoral targets and technology based on inappropriate standards and practices, often from industrialised countries; lack of integration between planning, management and information systems; and poor governance and corruption in decision making, are critical issues to be tackled.

Too few resources are left to improve preparedness. The importance of national and regional land use planning is still poorly recognized. Water must receive a central role in this planning, particularly in flood- and drought-prone areas.

Migration is often driven by water insecurity. As such, special attention should be given to water management, to support the living conditions in urban slums, in unplanned settlements and in rural areas. An integrated urban water management plan should be a fundamental part of the urban plan; municipal budgets for operation and maintenance should be assured.

In order to increase efficiency in operations and accountability of providers to water users, the time may have come to introduce a new model of government-corporation-society (GCS) partnerships.

Responsible and capable civil society organizations should be brought in as project partners from the start, together with the government and private sectors. The transfer of standards, technology, policies and knowledge cannot occur without transformation.

The systems and technologies for developing countries should be based on standards and technologies that are appropriate, workable and financially feasible in developing countries—cutting-edge innovation may be necessary.

Policy instruments such as water pricing, markets and private sector participation are not straightforward solutions for all developing countries. Designing effective instruments calls for interdisciplinary contextual research that goes beyond prescription.

Whereas the EU Water Framework Directive is a very helpful tool, in a development context it often is applied too rigorously as it does not consider livelihood and does not facilitate the search for trade-offs between development and environmental objectives. Countries need to negotiate with each other and their respective stakeholders in order to come up with relevant frameworks.

Networks for KCD

Networks have proven their value in disseminating experiences and sharing knowledge. Networks are also becoming very helpful to disseminate and share informal knowledge, identify common problems, build attitudes and confidence and generate new knowledge. Learning networks are becoming much more important vehicles for KCD.

South-South and North-South networks provide platforms to share lessons and adapt them from one place to another. In addition to these horizontal networks of peers, the need is growing for 'vertical' connectivity of networks through which local stakeholders can access global networks and knowledge. South-North-South networks are desirable as the South-South flow stimulates sharing among countries with comparable development contexts and objectives, whereas the North can bring in other approaches that may be readily useful for Southern partners.

Appropriate solutions are best developed by the countries themselves, in close cooperation with the North and building on South-South learning. Vehicles like best-practice networks and change management forums should be strongly encouraged. Importantly, many future water challenges are of a global nature and impose the need for a global partnership.

Donors should facilitate the development of these networks, face-to-face meetings (in the real and virtual sense) and field trips because these can ensure that both formal and informal knowledge are shared. Importantly, to develop and manage effective networks, a critical mass of trainers needs to be developed who can disseminate and manage knowledge flows over networks from one node to the others.

Decision-makers and managers should give their knowledge workers the space to actively participate in networks. These networks should play a role in meeting the large and growing demand for training, innovation and research in the water sector at all levels, by facilitating collaboration and removing impediments for sharing experiences and knowledge. Educational institutions also have much to gain from collaboration as they do from competition. There is no lack of demand for education. Just some of the benefits of such networks of institutions are the development of 'dating services' for collaborative research projects, the sharing and development of new curricula, as well as the organisation of staff exchanges.

International networks connecting 'communities of practice' of professionals or institutions catalyze and facilitate the exchange and development of new knowledge and innovation, both through South-South and South-North-South exchanges. Current examples of working networks are:

- Nile Basin Capacity Building Network for River Engineers (NBCBN-RE): This comprises institutions and members from 10 countries across this large geographic region that, in general, is still poorly integrated. It has developed regional research clusters for collaborative research, training and academic exchanges, regular forums to meet face-to-face and an online collaborative platform which facilitates communication and the exchange of documentation.
- WaterNet is a Southern African network of 52 university departments and research and training institutes focusing on water. Now, WaterNet programmes together account for 15–20 per cent of all water-related peer reviewed publications from Africa. The network helps prepare and support regional symposia, and joint research, training and education.
- PoWER is a partnership of 18 educational institutes in the field of water across the globe. PoWER stimulated

    (i) development of new curricula to improve upon, and scale up the efforts of its partner institutions,

    (ii) joint specialized master programmes, and

    (iii) eleven online course modules.

    It is based on a synergetic approach to create economies of scale by pooling the strengths of all partners, to foster specialization and to enhance each institute's own capacity.
- Cap-Net is a global network supported by UNDP aiming to foster national and regional networks. It supports network development and the sharing of experiences. It offers training activities to rejuvenate local knowledge and strengthen the local networks, as well as online resources with a catalogue of training materials, network management tools, water management tools, and more.

Target and Encourage Leaders

A call was made for the training of 1,000 young water professionals, champions who can be tutored to lead critical developments. These champions should become catalysts who will transform and reform the sector and organisations. They should become the policy makers, engineers, scientists and researchers who explore new understanding and insights and develop innovative solutions; and they should become the advocates who seek to strengthen legitimacy.

One thousand professionals are definitely not enough, considering the huge challenges ahead, but it is a feasible figure to start with in the short term. They should be selected among young promising professionals, as they are less encumbered by tradition and open to new technologies and developments in the world. It is essential to encourage young professionals to engage in the sector and in government, as many feel increasingly disaffected by what they perceive as poorly performing and self-serving governments.

The tutoring should be done in those institutions where management and political leadership are willing to create the space for the new champions. Pre-conditions are providing quality education to these water sector professionals and equipping them with the skills and experiences necessary to become champions. Only by training many times the required numbers through a combination of international, regional and domestic programmes can a critical mass of champions and scientists be created in developing countries. Many of the trainees will inevitably leave the sector along the way.

Share Information and Knowledge

Free access to scientific literature for professionals and researchers in developing countries should become an increasingly important factor in reducing the knowledge gap that now exists between the North and the South. Information and communication systems (ICS) are potentially evolving into singularly important drivers in KCD and effective water management—facilitating transparent decision-making, speeding up and broadening communication and enabling social networks and knowledge transfer, empowering a growing circle of stakeholders by providing them with low cost real-time information and the capability to forecast the consequences of development scenarios.

E-learning offers major new opportunities, and needs to be embraced by education institutes. However, there are significant challenges to the adoption of ICS, which need to be overcome:

- Lack of information and communication skills training in the curricula of primary and secondary education. Open source software needs to become the subject of more extensive training.

- Lack of data, and restricted access in developing countries – sometimes for political reasons or because bureaucracies shy away from transparency. Data availability and free access need to be addressed jointly.
- Communication hurdles between information and communication technology (ICT) experts on the one hand and managers and policy makers on the other. ICT-driven cultural change is resisted, highlighting the generation gap that prevents the penetration of ICS in organisations. Decision-makers should adopt policies and set incentives for their organisations to overcome these hurdles and remove limits on the private sector to engage in ICS services. Donors should provide more fellowships dedicated to e-learning.

Open Access to Journals and Libraries

Providing unlimited access to the contents of research and innovation across the world will boost knowledge acquisition and development by professionals and researchers in the developing countries. It will help reduce the bias towards products from institutions in industrialised countries. The following initiatives help bridge this information gap:

- **OARE:** An initiative of UNEP, Yale University and the International Association of Scientific, Technical and Medical Publishers and leading science and technology publishing houses, the OARE collection includes on average, over 70 per cent of the world's most influential and widely cited scientific journals in diverse environmental disciplines for 106 countries. www.oaresciences.org
- **AGORA:** An FAO programme working with major publishers enables access to 958 journals to institutions in 107 countries. www.aginternetwork.org
- **DOAJ:** An online directory of open access journals. www.doaj.org
- **INSAH:** Institut du Sahel: Features an online electronic library focused on the Sahel. www.insah.org
- **HighWire Press:** The largest archive of free full text science articles. http://highwire.stanford.edu
- **CGIAR InfoFinder:** An online library in collaboration with Future Harvest Centres, CGIAR and FAO/WAICENT. http://infofinder.cgiar.org.

8

Water and Nature

More than one-half of the world's major rivers are being seriously depleted and polluted, degrading and poisoning the surrounding ecosystems, thus threatening the health and livelihood of people who depend upon them for irrigation, drinking and industrial water.

—World Commission on Water for the 21st Century

Water–Nature Interactions

Water is life and is necessary for all ecosystems. Sound ecosystems ensure balanced communities of species and rich livelihoods. Rich and diverse livelihoods are fundamental for our well-being and for the survival of the poorest. Currently, around 1.9 million species are described in the world and million of others are still to be discovered.

Our meals, our health and our livelihoods depend on biodiversity. Food resources from agriculture or fisheries, the diversity of medicinal herbs, water-consuming industries, or tourist activities developed next to lakes and rivers demonstrate that water resources are vital for both nature and man. In addition, nature plays a role of regulation and purification of water resources, thus contributing to better water supply and quality.

Regulating Water Flows

Some ecosystems such as wetlands or forests have strong water retention capacities. Water that penetrates into these ecosystems is stored, then restored. During wet periods, these ecosystems contribute to peak flow mitigation. During dry seasons, water is progressively released, which maintains a base-flow. Hence, the necessity of preserving these zones.

Improving Water Quality

When polluted water percolates into the soil, it is naturally filtered. This treats a certain amount of pollutants, which will not need human treatment afterwards. Wetlands and forests are particularly useful for this purpose.

Preserving ecosystems presents interests of an ethical, social and economical nature. Experts from the European Union estimate the financial value of goods and services provided by ecosystems at more than 26,000 billion euros per year, namely, almost twice the value of what human beings produce every year.

Current Threats: Water-Nature Equilibrium

Growth in human populations, increasing consumption, infrastructure development, land conversion, poor land use and massive use of pollutants in water, all threaten the ecosystem functions that produce our freshwater resources. Ecosystems evolve far too slowly to adapt to quick and brutal changes and cannot play their purifying and regulating role in such situations.

Pollution

With urbanization and industrialization, the quality of rivers, lakes, and aquifers may deteriorate seriously. This phenomenon has accelerated since the 1970s due to the increase of human and industrial waste. With current water treatment systems, eliminating some toxic particles is sometimes not possible any more. Surface water as well as groundwater run the risk of becoming dangerous for both human consumption and to ecosystems.

Biodiversity under Threat

Today, a growing number of species and habitats are disappearing. According to the IUCN Red List of Threatened Species, a total of 15,589 species of plants and animals are threatened, facing a high risk of extinction in the near future, in almost all cases as a result of human activities. Since the beginning of the century, 50 per cent of wetlands have disappeared. Since the 1990s, deforestation consumes 19.4 million hectares each year.

Water Scarcity

Water resources depletion generates tensions among water users and sometimes between states or countries. Every country wants to maintain sovereignty over its resources and to maximise its storage and withdrawals. Water scarcity already affects one-third of the total world population.

Mitigating Measures

First, simple everyday actions can reduce the phenomena threatening water resources. All actors from the water sector should be involved, namely, farmers, industrialists and also individuals. Responsible water-saving behaviour and a reduction in pollutants in agriculture can slow down the disappearance of water resources and the changes in ecosystems.

Collective measures should also be enforced. Space arrangements and water resources use should be taken in hand. Regulating natural river flows, carrying out soft changes and adapting water consumption to its availability may have much more sustainable and efficient effects than increasing the pressure on the resource, leading to short-term solutions. Effective cooperation should exist among actors, to ensure a consistent and environment-friendly water management.

9

The Concept of 'Virtual Water'

THE virtual water metaphor was created originally to gain the attention of public officials responsible for choosing policies that influence the use of water resources in arid regions. Over time, the metaphor has been used in both empirical and conceptual settings, primarily to describe the water used to produce crop and livestock products that are traded in international markets. Several authors have described how water-short countries can enhance their food security by importing water-intensive food crops.

Some authors have noted similarities between the virtual water metaphor and the economic theory of comparative advantage. The virtual water metaphor addresses resource endowments, but it does not address production technologies or opportunity costs. Hence, the metaphor is not analogous to the concept of comparative advantage. The metaphor can be helpful in motivating public officials to consider policies that will encourage improvements in the use of scarce resources, but comparative advantages must be evaluated to determine optimal production and trading strategies.

The theory of comparative advantage is explained and demonstrated in several scenarios that depict differences in resource endowments and production technologies. Optimal strategies are not always consistent with expectations based only on resource endowments. Policy discussions regarding water resources can be enhanced by considering comparative advantages when evaluating opportunities to import or export agricultural products.

Using the Concept of Virtual Water

Regional conflicts have mainly political causes and need to be addressed within political fora. Bad weather, though, unpredictable, is to be expected now and again, and tools exist which can be used for long-term forecasting. The concept of 'virtual water' is one such method. It refers to the amount of water required to produce a certain commodity or service. Maize, for example, requires a certain amount of water per tonne. A state can thus calculate roughly how much water it requires to produce the maize its citizens need.

The shortfall can be planned for and perhaps avoided. The question of whether a virtual water strategy can mitigate future food shortages is still under debate. Conflict aside, floods and drought were named as causes of a future food shortage. Of course, it was not only bad weather that has an impact. Political and market problems were also responsible.

Food Insecurity

The Food and Agricultural Organisation (FAO) of the UN defines food insecurity as a situation where people live in fear of hunger and starvation. A widely accepted definition of food security notes that all people should have access, at all times, to enough food for an active, healthy lifestyle. At present, many countries are experiencing massive food shortages. This is the direct consequence of the region's worst drought in 50 years. The precarious food security situation means that about 19 million people are in need of food aid. This does not include the four million people already facing starvation because many countries have already depleted their maize reserves.

Virtual Water

Given the food insecurity in the world, it becomes plain that some attempt should be made to look beyond the current crisis and reduce the risk that this will be repeated. Since water is an important variable in crop production, it is advisable to consider how much water is needed to produce the food the region requires. When a state imports a tonne of wheat or maize, it is in effect, also importing the water it requires to produce that crop. This is known as virtual water.

In international and regional economies, vast quantities of virtual water are present in the international cereal market. For instance, it takes about 1,000 tonnes of water to grow one tonne of grain. This is the virtual water value of grain. Similarly, to produce one tonne of rice, 2,000 tonnes of water are needed; one tonne of wheat requires 1,000 tonnes of water; and approximately 1,200 tonnes of water are needed to produce one tonne of maize. Because virtual water is embedded in the international political economy, every state in the international political system is subjected to trade in virtual water. This is evident in the cereal needs of many countries at present.

Almost all countries have to trade in foodstuffs because they cannot produce all their food locally. This is especially true of developing states. Virtual water can therefore be an important aspect of a country's food security. This infers that as countries trade in agricultural commodities, they are actually also importing and exporting water in a virtual sense. States with scarce water resources can also plant crops that require less water. In theory, when the region does not have enough water to supply its food, it can turn to the international market. The truth is that this is more complex and often quite difficult. The reasons for this are natural, political and economic in nature.

Natural Threats

One of the natural threats to regional food production is a region-wide drought. It is not only drought that can have an impact on the production of agricultural commodities. Other extreme weather events, like floods, can also wreak havoc. Floods can devastate farmland and wash away valuable topsoil needed for the production of foodstuffs. Under such circumstances, many countries can become reliant on the international food market for their food security needs.

Political Conditions

Unstable political conditions can make a bad situation even worse. The food crisis in Zimbabwe can be partly attributed to the actions of the ZANU-PF government and particularly the controversial land reform policies. Citizens in Angola and the DRC have had their food shortages made extreme because of conflict and political crises.

Economic Factors

Economic factors, such as the availability of foreign exchange and capital outlay on infrastructure also play a role. Where government finances are stretched to the limit by debt and mismanagement, countries can have difficulty implementing infrastructural projects to facilitate the distribution of food within the region. This also means that their agricultural sectors cannot develop to their full potential. For instance, irrigation schemes cannot be financed that could lead to a better food security situation. The implementation of irrigation schemes can make the production of agricultural commodities less dependent on rain.

The global trade in cotton and cotton products is a major element in the virtual water trade. A first objective of the research programme on virtual water trade is to assess virtual water flows between nations and to draw the virtual water trade balances of all nations of the world by analysing both imports and exports. Virtual water (also known as embedded water, embodied water, or hidden water) refers to the water used in the production of a good or service. Water is probably one of the most precious resources and vital for everyone's everyday life.

At the global level, virtual water trade has geo-political implications: it induces dependencies between countries. With the trade of food crops or any commodity, there is a virtual flow of water from producing and exporting countries to countries that consume and import those commodities. As water shortages emerge around the world – due to climate change and the sheer demand – the exporting countries are going to become increasingly unable, or unwilling, to export their virtual water.

Only this trade in virtual water – bound up in grains and vegetable oil, sugar and cotton, meat and dairy products from animals raised on fodder crops – has kept the world fed. The big exporters of virtual water are mostly countries with lots of water as well as the financial resources to harness the resource for productive use. Water footprints are used to give nations a better consumption-based indicator of water use. In spite of this obvious fact, people use large amounts of water: for drinking, cooking and washing, but even more for producing things such as food, paper, cotton clothes, etc.

The Stockholm International Water Institute (SIWI) stated that 'Virtual water has major impacts on global trade policy and research, especially in water-scarce regions, and has redefined discourse in water policy and management.' It both imports and exports on a large scale, but overall it is a net exporter. The per capita consumption of virtual water contained in our diets varies according to the type of diet, from 1m^3/day for a survival diet, to 2.6m^3/day for a vegetarian diet and over 5m^3 for a U.S.A. style meat-based diet. This is mainly relevant for agricultural products, where it refers to the total rainwater evaporation from the field during the growing period of the crop (including transpiration by the plants and other forms of evaporation).

Conclusion

While virtual water calculations are an essential planning tool, and can be useful in determining how seasonal water can be used most efficiently to provide more food at the right times, they are dependent on all other factors (political, economic and natural) being equal—seldom the case in sub-Saharan Africa. Nevertheless, the awareness of how water is an invisible part of the food economy is already a positive step. Once states, farmers, citizens and aid agencies have more accurate information about the virtual water that is involved in their numerous transactions, they will be better able to decide on their own course of action.

10

How Much Water is Enough Water?

IT is difficult to estimate the amount of water needed to maintain acceptable or minimum living standards. Moreover, different sources use different figures for total water consumption and for water used by various sectors of the economy. A range of 20 to 40 litres of freshwater per person per day is generally considered to be a necessary minimum to meet needs for drinking and sanitation alone, according to Peter Gleick, president of the Pacific Institute for Studies in Development, Environment and Security. If water for bathing and cooking is included as well, this figure varies between 27 and 200 litres per capita per day.

Several different amounts have been proposed as minimum standards. Gleick proposes that international organizations and water providers adopt 'an overall basic water requirement of 50 litres per person per day' as a minimum standard to meet four basic needs – drinking, sanitation, bathing, and cooking. In 1990, Gleick estimated, 55 countries with a population of nearly 1 billion people did not meet this standard as a national average. Falkenmark uses the figure of 100 litres of freshwater per capita per day for personal use as a rough estimate of the amount needed for a minimally acceptable standard of living in developing countries, not including uses for agriculture and industry.

Population Growth and Water Shortage

The amount of water that people in a country actually use depends not only on minimum needs and how much water is available for use but also on the level of economic development and the extent of urbanization. Globally, of the three standard categories of freshwater use—for agriculture, industry and domestic (personal, household and municipal)—agriculture dominates. On a worldwide basis, agriculture accounts for about 69 per cent of all annual water withdrawals; industry, about 23 per cent; and domestic use, about 8 per cent.

There are wide differences by region. In Africa, an estimated 88 per cent of all freshwater use is for agriculture, 7 per cent for domestic purposes and 5 per cent for industry. In Asia, water is also used mostly for agriculture, estimated at 86 per cent of total use, while industry accounts for 8 per cent and domestic use 6 per cent. In Europe, however, most water use is for industry, at 54 per cent, while agriculture accounts for 33 per cent and domestic use 13 per cent.

Freshwater and Economic Development

A country's level of freshwater use reflects—and, in fact, is one of the key measures of—its level of economic development. In the developing regions of the world, people use far less water per capita than in developed regions.

In Africa the annual per capita water withdrawals for personal use average only 17 cubic metres (equal to 47 litres of water per day), and in Asia, 31 cubic metres (equal to 85 litres per day). In contrast, comparable water use in the U.K. is estimated at 122 cubic metres per year (334 litres per day), and in the U.S.A., 211 cubic metres per year (578 litres per day).

Developing countries devote most of their water supplies to agriculture. India, for instance, uses 90 per cent of all water for agricultural purposes, with just 7 per cent for industry and 3 per cent for domestic use. The higher the level of development, the more water is used for domestic and industrial purposes and the less for agriculture. There are some important exceptions to this rule, however.

For example, Japan still uses the largest share of its freshwater for irrigating rice. Also, in some arid areas of Europe, such as Spain and Portugal, most of the available water is used for irrigated agriculture.

Around the world, freshwater demand per capita is rising substantially as countries develop economically. Withdrawals of water have grown in all three major categories of use—to meet rising industrial demand, rising domestic demand, including for municipal use and increasing reliance on irrigation to produce food.

Urbanization

The level of water use also reflects the level of urbanization in a country. Low household water use in many developing countries today often reflects difficulty in obtaining freshwater. Piped water systems are rare in rural areas. Two-thirds of the world's population, the majority in developing countries, get their water from public hand pumps, community wells, rivers and lakes, or rainfall collected off roofs. Often rural people—usually women and girls —must walk many kilometres and spend many hours fetching water for their households. In Africa, for instance, women and girls spend 40 billion person-hours a year hauling water.

Urbanization increases water use dramatically. For example, in 1900 the average American household used as little as 10 cubic metres of water per year compared with more than 200 cubic metres today. Why? A century ago, most Americans obtained their freshwater from wells or public standpipes. Running water was largely unavailable to households except in big cities and most people lived in the rural areas. In contrast, virtually every American household today has running water available, and this water costs its users very little.

As the world becomes predominately urban, while agriculture depends more and more on irrigation, it will be difficult for cities to meet the rising demand for freshwater. In developing countries, rapid urban growth often puts tremendous pressure on antiquated, inadequate water supply systems. For instance, between 1950 and 1980, the populations of many cities in Latin America, such as Bogota, Mexico City, São Paulo and Managua, tripled or even quadrupled.

Such African cities such as Nairobi, Dar-es-Salaam, Lagos, and Kinshasa grew sevenfold, primarily because of a rural exodus. In the 1990s, cities of developing countries have had to cope with about 60 million new arrivals every year. Yet many agencies are not equipped to manage the urban water supply, while some countries have ineffective water allocation systems that allow cities to run short of water at the same time that water resources are being used for subsidized agriculture.

The Coming Water Crisis

Freshwater is emerging as one of the most critical natural resource issues facing humanity. The world's population is expanding rapidly. Yet there is no more freshwater on earth now than there was 2,000 years ago, when the population was less than 3 per cent of its current size.

Water is, literally, the source of life on earth. The human body is 70 per cent water. People begin to feel thirst after a loss of only 1 per cent of bodily fluids and risk death if fluid loss nears 10 per cent. Human beings can survive for only a few days without freshwater. Yet, in a growing number of places people are withdrawing water from rivers, lakes and underground sources faster than they can be recharged—'unsustainably mining what was once a renewable resource,' as one researcher puts it. Currently, 31 countries—mostly in Africa and the Near East face water stress or water scarcity.

Population growth alone will push an estimated 17 more countries, with a projected population of 2.1 billion, into these water-short categories within the next 30 years. By the year 2025, 48 countries, with more than 2.8 billion people—35 per cent of the projected global population in 2025—will be affected by water stress or scarcity. Another nine countries, including China and Pakistan, will be approaching water stress.

Beyond the impact of population growth itself, the demand for freshwater has been rising in response to industrial development, increased reliance on irrigated agriculture, massive urbanization, and rising living standards. In the last century, while world population tripled, water withdrawals increased by over six times.

Since 1940, annual global water withdrawals have increased by an average of 2.5 per cent to 3 per cent a year compared with annual population growth of 1.5 per cent to 2 per cent. In developing countries, over the past decade, water withdrawals have been increasing by 4 per cent to 8 per cent a year.

Moreover, the supply of freshwater available to humanity is shrinking, in effect, because many freshwater resources have become increasingly polluted. In some countries, lakes and rivers have become receptacles for a vile assortment of wastes, including untreated or partially treated municipal sewage, toxic industrial effluents and harmful chemicals leached into surface and groundwater from agricultural activities.

Caught between finite and increasingly polluted water supplies on the one hand and rapidly rising demand from population growth and development on the other, many developing countries face uneasy choices. The lack of freshwater is likely to be one of the major factors limiting economic development in the decades to come, warns the World Bank.

11

Women: The Worst Sufferers

HAVING an ample supply of safe water is something most of us do not think much about. Turning on the kitchen or bathroom tap is usually an effortless decision. Yet, when we flush the toilet, we use as much water as most people in Kenya use in an entire day. Imagine that day in Kenya. You spend six hours fetching and hauling heavy loads of water across a dangerous expanse. Once you get the water home, you conserve and manage every drop to have enough for drinking, cooking, cleaning, bathing the children and watering the vegetable garden that keeps your family from going hungry. Since the water is untreated, you never know what kind of microbes or pollution you and your family are drinking.

For many rural women, that imaginary day is every day. For others who live in cities, water is just as scarce and unsafe because of economic policies that reward pollution and price clean water out of reach. In total, 17 per cent of the world's people lack access to safe water. This is a human rights abuse of staggering proportion—threatening more than a billion people and undermining a range of other human rights, including rights to health, environmental sustainability, economic justice and peace. Around the world, it is women and girls who are responsible for providing water to households. That division of labour makes water a critical women's human rights concern.

Water and Health

Every year, nearly 1.8 million people (90 per cent of them children under five) die from diarrhoea caused by dirty water. Typhoid, cholera and other deadly diseases are also spread by contaminated water, bringing the death toll from water-related diseases to a staggering 3.5 million people a year. In fact, unsafe drinking water is the source of 80 per cent of disease worldwide and kills more children every year than wars, malaria and HIV/AIDS combined.

Without clean water, it is nearly impossible for people to maintain good hygiene for themselves and their children. Lack of personal hygiene contributes to the spread of infectious diseases and compromises people's dignity and confidence. Whether or not a community chronically lacks water, no mother wants to send her child to school with a dirty face.

The daily task of carrying water over distances is back-breaking work for women. In rural Africa, women commonly walk 10 kilometres a day to a water source and back—and twice that distance in the dry season. Often, women carry loads of up to 50 pounds on the head, hip, or back. Over time, the strain can deform the spine and pelvis, causing extreme pain and disability. An immediate worry for many women and girls is the threat of sexual attack as they venture far from home in search of water.

Tremendous health benefits are achieved when people gain access to even small quantities of clean water. Simple measures, like washing hands with soap and water, reduce the spread of deadly diarrhoeal diseases by more than 35 per cent. Ensuring clean water for washing can also prevent trachoma, a leading cause of blindness.

The UN Millennium Development Goals call for reducing by half the number of people without sustainable access to safe drinking water and basic sanitation. Achieving this target would mean more than 200,000 fewer child deaths in 2015 and more than one million children's lives saved over the following decade.

Across the world, children would gain another 272 million days of school, thanks to fewer episodes of diarrhoea. In addition, economic benefits of about $ 38 billion would accrue to some of the poorest countries. Financing these gains would cost about $ 10 billion—less than half of what rich countries spend each year on mineral water.

Water and Environmental Sustainability

Today, many women find that they must walk farther to fetch water as it becomes increasingly scarce. Only about 2.5 per cent of the Earth's water is fresh and suitable for drinking. Climate change, pollution and the unsustainable use of water for industry and factory farming are depleting this limited supply. In Peru, nearly all drinking water comes from glaciers that are melting fast and may be completely gone by 2015. Across Africa, all 667 major lakes are drying up. Lake Chad, once the third-largest lake in Africa, has shrunk by 90 per cent, mainly because its waters have been diverted into canals. In Indonesia and Brazil, timber and biofuel plantations are monopolizing and depleting water sources. Around the world, industrial agriculture is contaminating groundwater with toxic pesticides.

These are serious problems, but they have clear solutions, including reclamation of polluted water, water conservation, renewable energy, sustainable agriculture and government investment in water infrastructure. Where these measures have been implemented, they have worked well. The U.S. Clean Water Act, for example, detoxified more than half of the country's polluted rivers and lakes (before the law was gutted by the Bush Administration). Organic farming is proving to be a reliable way to feed people and protect the planet. The problem is not that we lack solutions, but that we have not yet achieved the political momentum to guarantee that our solutions are implemented.

Water and Peace

Increasingly, competition over scarce fresh water is sparking violent clashes between parched communities. The bloodshed in Darfur, for instance, is as much a 'resource war' for water as an ethnic conflict. In the Middle East, the drive to control water is one of the less recognized objectives of Israel's occupation of the West Bank. On average, each Israeli settler there uses nine times as much water as each Palestinian.

Since water flows across scores of national boundaries, symptoms of our growing global water crisis—including rivers that no longer reach the sea, sinking groundwater tables, and shrinking lakes—threaten to cause new conflicts between countries. As former World Bank President Ismail Serageldin had said: "If the wars of the last century were fought over oil, the wars of the next century will be fought over water."

This is a chilling prediction, but not inevitable. Humanity has a strong record of accomplishment of peacefully sharing water. In fact, the world's first known peace treaty, signed over 4,000 years ago in Mesopotamia (today's Iraq), was a water-use agreement. Now that fresh water supplies are more endangered than ever, the challenge is to build on that heritage of cooperative resource use and support policies that can promote an equitable distribution of this common global resource.

Water and Economic Justice

Though water scarcity is threatening ecosystems on every continent, the biggest problem is not that the world's water supply is literally running out, but that water is used unsustainably and unequally. Water needs vary from place to place, but a minimum threshold for daily use is about 20 litres a person. The average North American uses 600 litres of water a day. The average person in Africa uses six. Scarcity, then, is mainly the result of poverty and unequal access to resources.

For communities in places like Kenya, Guatemala and Nicaragua, lack of water services is a direct result of government discrimination against poor communities and indigenous peoples. However, cash-strapped governments themselves are pressured by international financial institutions such as the World Bank to privatize their water sources (meaning sell them to corporations) as a way to make money to pay back loans. Once corporations 'own' a country's water, they sell it back to communities, often at unaffordable prices.

In the cities of the Global South, poor people pay the highest prices for water—sometimes 10 times more than wealthier people living in the same city. Millions of families living in slums have no access to water at all. Until women in the Barcenas neighbourhood of Guatemala City organized to install public water taps, they had to choose between spending 30 per cent of their sweatshop earnings on bottled water or relying on water they knew to be contaminated by industrial pollution and sewage.

Clearly, those suffering the most from lack of water also lack the political voice needed to assert their right to water. This includes poor communities in general and women in particular. Therefore, resolving the world's water crisis requires a political mobilization by and for those most threatened by the crisis. This mobilization is already underway and important victories have been won, many in Latin America. In Bolivia, Argentina, and Chile, activists have compelled private water corporations to relinquish control over municipal water systems. Uruguay now recognizes the public's right to water in its constitution. Porto Alegre, Brazil, has created a model public water utility that provides affordable and safe water to all residents.

Water as a Human Right

Access to water is a human right. Not only does it underpin the most basic of human rights—people's right to life—access to safe water is also essential to the enjoyment of all other human rights. However, international standards do not reflect that reality. Because water is defined as a need instead of a right, control over this critical resource has largely been ceded to corporations. That means that human rights standards need to be changed.

The United Nations must pass a water covenant that would commit governments to treat water as an entitlement, guaranteeing that every person has a secure, accessible and affordable supply of healthy water. Policies that are inadequate or unjust must be changed. We have done it before, and we can do it again and create a world with clean water for all.

12

Water: The Real Food Crisis

AFTER decades in the doldrums, food prices soared in 2008, causing more misery for the world's poor than any credit crunch. The geopolitical shockwaves spread round the world, with food riots in Haiti, strikes over rice shortages in Bangladesh, tortilla wars in Mexico and protests over bread prices in Egypt.

The immediate cause is declining grain stocks, which has encouraged speculators, hoarders and panic-buyers. However, what are the underlying trends that have sown the seeds for this perfect food storm? Biofuels are part of it, clearly. A quarter of U.S. corn is now converted to ethanol, powering vehicles rather than filling stomachs or fattening livestock. And the rising oil prices (till July 2008) that encouraged the biofuels boom also raised food prices by making fertilizer, pesticides and transport more expensive.

However, there is something else going on that has hardly been mentioned, and that some believe is the greatest slow-burning, and hopelessly underreported, resource crisis of the 21st century: water. In the first half of 2008, it is being called 'scarcity,' not 'crisis.' The perspective scenario is grim and it is expected to take under two decades for the scarcity to become a real crisis if palliative steps are not taken now.

Climate change, over-consumption and the alarmingly inefficient use of this most basic raw material are all to blame. Three years ago, a book was written, *When The Rivers Run Dry* which probed why the Yellow River in China, the Rio Grande and the Colorado in the United States, the Nile in

Egypt, the Indus in Pakistan, the Amu Darya in Central Asia and many others are all running on empty. The confident blue lines in a million atlases simply do not tell the truth about rivers sucked dry, for the most part, to irrigate food crops.

We are using these rivers to death. And we are also pumping out underground water reserves almost everywhere in the world. With two-thirds of the water abstracted from nature going to irrigate crops – a figure that rises above 90 per cent in many arid countries – water shortages equal food shortages.

Consider the two underlying causes of the current crisis over world food prices: falling supplies from some of the major agricultural regions that supply world markets and rising demand in booming economies like China and India. Why falling supplies? Farm yields per hectare have been stagnating in many countries for a while now. The green revolution that caused yields to soar 20 years ago may be faltering.

However, the immediate trigger, according to most analysts, has been droughts, particularly in Australia, one of the world's largest grain exporters, and also in some other major supplier countries, like Ukraine. Australia's wheat exports were 60 per cent down last year; its rice exports were 90 per cent down.

Why rising demand? China has received most of the blame here – its growing wealth is certainly raising demand, especially as richer citizens eat more meat. But China traditionally has always fed itself – what is different now is that the world's most populous country is no longer able to produce all its own food.

A few years ago, the American agronomist and environmentalist Lester Brown wrote a book called *Who Will Feed China?: Wake Up Call for a Small Planet*. It predicted just this. China can no longer feed itself largely because demand is rising sharply at a time when every last drop of water in the north of the country, its major breadbasket, is already taken. The Yellow River, which drains most of the region, now rarely reaches the sea, except for the short monsoon season.

Some press reports have recently suggested that China was sucked dry to provide water for the Beijing Olympics. Would that it were so simple. The Olympics would have required only trivial amounts of water. China's water shortages are deep-seated, escalating and tied to agriculture. Even hugely expensive plans to bring water from the wetter south to the arid north will only provide marginal relief.

The same is true of India, the world's second most populous country. Forty years ago, India was a basket case. Millions died in famines. The green revolution then turned India into a food exporter. Its neighbour, Bangladesh, came to rely on India for rice. However, Indian food production has stagnated recently, even as demand from richer residents has soared. And the main reason is water.

With river water fully used, Indian farmers have been trying to increase supplies by tapping underground reserves. In the last 15 years, they have bought a staggering 20 million Yamaha pumps to suck water from beneath their fields. The director of the International Water Management Institute's groundwater research station in Gujarat, estimated those farmers were pumping annually to the surface 100 cubic kilometres more water than the monsoon rains replace. Water tables are plunging, and in many places water supplies are giving out.

"We are living hand-to-mouth," says the president of the All India Grain Exporters Association, who blames water shortages for faltering grain production. In 2007, India began to import rice, notably from Australia. In 2008, it stopped supplying its densely populated neighbour Bangladesh, triggering a crisis there too.

More and more countries are up against the limits of food production because they are up against the limits of water supply. Most of the Middle East reached this point years ago. In Egypt, where bread riots occurred this spring, the Nile River no longer reaches the sea because all its water is taken for irrigation.

A map of world food trade increasingly looks like a map of the water haves and have-nots, because in recent years the global food trade has become almost a proxy trade in water – or rather, the water needed to grow food. 'Virtual water,' some economists call it. The trade has kept the hungry in dry lands fed. Now that system is breaking down, because there are too many buyers and not enough sellers.

According to estimates by UNESCO's hydrology institute, the world's largest net supplier of virtual water until recently was Australia. It exported a staggering 70 cubic kilometres of water a year in the form of crops, mainly food. With the Murray-Darling Basin, Australia's main farming zone, virtually dry for the past two years, that figure has been cut in half. The largest gross exporter of virtual water is the United States, but its exports have also slumped as corn is diverted to domestic biofuels and because of continuing drought in the American West.

The current water shortages will not mark an absolute limit to food production around the world. However, it could do three things. It could encourage a rethinking of biofuels, which are themselves major water guzzlers. It could prompt an expanding trade in food exported from countries that remain in water surplus, such as Brazil. And it should trigger much greater efforts everywhere to use water more efficiently.

In Australia. in the midst of the 2006 drought, farmers even in the most arid areas still irrigated their fields mostly by flooding them. Until the water runs out, that is. Few have adopted much more efficient drip irrigation systems, where water is delivered down pipes and discharged close to the roots. And while many farmers are expert at collecting any rain that falls on their land, they sometimes allow half of that water to evaporate from the surfaces of their farm reservoirs.

For too long, we have seen water as a cheap and unlimited resource. Those days are coming to an end—not just in dry places, but everywhere. For if the current world food crisis shows anything, it is that in an era of global trade in 'virtual water,' local water shortages can reverberate throughout the world—creating higher food prices and food shortages everywhere.

13

Using Water Like There's No Tomorrow

As populations grow and water use per person rises, demand for freshwater is soaring. Yet the supply of freshwater is finite and threatened by pollution. To avoid a crisis, many countries must conserve water, pollute less, manage supply and demand and slow population growth.

Caught between the growing demand for freshwater on the one hand and limited and increasingly polluted water supplies on the other, many developing countries face difficult choices. Populations continue to grow rapidly. Yet there is no more water on earth now than there was 2,000 years ago, when the population was less than 3 per cent of its current size. Rising demands for water for irrigated agriculture, domestic (municipal) consumption, and industry are forcing stiff competition over the allocation of scarce water resources among both areas and types of use.

Today 31 countries, accounting for under 8 per cent of the world population, face chronic freshwater shortages. By the year 2025, however, 48 countries are expected to face shortages, affecting more than 2.8 billion people—35 per cent of the world's projected population. Among countries likely to run short of water in the next 25 years are Ethiopia, India, Kenya, Nigeria and Peru. Parts of other large countries, such as China, already face chronic water problems.

In much of the world, polluted water, improper waste disposal, and poor water management cause serious public health problems. Such water-related diseases as malaria, cholera, typhoid, and schistosomiasis harm or kill millions of people every year. Overuse and pollution of water supplies also are taking a heavy toll on the natural environment and pose increasing risks for many species of life.

What Can Be Done?

It may already be too late for some water-short countries with rapid population growth to avoid a crisis. Many other countries can avoid the coming crisis if appropriate policies and strategies are formulated and acted on soon. Whether water is used for agriculture, industry, or municipalities, there is much room for conservation and better management. Effective strategies must consider not only managing the water supply better but also managing demand better.

To avoid catastrophe over the long term, it is also important to act now to slow the growth in demand for freshwater by slowing population growth. Currently, in many developing countries millions of people want to plan their families and use contraception. Family planning programmes have played an important role in assuring individual reproductive health and in reducing national fertility levels. Continuing and expanding these programmes also can help assure that population growth eventually slows to sustainable levels in relation to the supply of freshwater.

Towards a Blue Revolution

The world needs a Blue Revolution to conserve and manage freshwater supplies in the face of growing demand from population growth, irrigated agriculture, industries and cities—just as the Green Revolution transformed agriculture in the 1960s. A Blue Revolution will require coordinated responses to problems at local, national, and international levels.

Locally led initiatives show that water can be used much more efficiently. When communities manage freshwater resources efficiently, they also manage other natural resources better, improve sanitation, and reduce disease. At the national level, especially in water-short regions with dense populations, adopting a watershed or river-basin management perspective is a needed alternative to uncoordinated water-management policies by separate jurisdictions. At the international level, countries that share river basins can fashion workable policies to manage water resources more equitably. Development agencies need to focus more on assuring the supply and management of freshwater resources and on providing sanitation as part of development and public health programmes.

A water-short world is an inherently unstable world. In the 21st century, water crises in more and more countries will present obstacles to better living standards and better health and even bring risks of outright conflict over access to scarce freshwater supplies. Finding solutions should become a high priority now.

The Coming Water Crisis

Water is, literally, the source of life on earth. The human body is 70 per cent water. People begin to feel thirst after a loss of only 1 per cent of bodily fluids and risk death if fluid loss nears 10 per cent. Human beings can survive for only a few days without freshwater. Yet, in a growing number of places people are withdrawing water from rivers, lakes and underground sources faster than they can be recharged—'unsustainably mining what was once a renewable resource,' as one researcher puts it. Currently, 31 countries—mostly in Africa and the Near East—face water stress or water scarcity.

Population growth alone will push an estimated 17 more countries, with a projected population of 2.1 billion, into these water-short categories within the next 30 years. By the year 2025, forty-eight countries, with more than 2.8 billion people—35 per cent of the projected global population in 2025—will be affected by water stress or scarcity. Another nine countries, including China and Pakistan, will be approaching water stress.

Beyond the impact of population growth itself, the demand for freshwater has been rising in response to industrial development, increased reliance on irrigated agriculture, massive urbanization and rising living standards. In the 20th century, while world population tripled, water withdrawals increased by over six times.

Since 1940, annual global water withdrawals have increased by an average of 2.5 per cent to 3 per cent a year compared with an annual population growth of 1.5 per cent to 2 per cent. In developing countries, over the past decade, water withdrawals have been increasing by 4 per cent to 8 per cent a year.

Moreover, the supply of freshwater available to humanity is shrinking, in effect, because many freshwater resources have become increasingly polluted. In some countries, lakes and rivers have become receptacles for a vile assortment of wastes, including untreated or partially treated municipal sewage, toxic industrial effluents and harmful chemicals leached into surface and groundwater from agricultural activities.

Caught between finite and increasingly polluted water supplies on the one hand and rapidly rising demand from population growth and development on the other, many developing countries face uneasy choices. The lack of freshwater is likely to be one of the major factors limiting economic development in the decades to come, warns the World Bank.

Slowing Demand

To avoid a water crisis, particularly in water-short countries with rapid population growth, it is vital to slow the growth in demand for water by managing the resource better, while at the same time slowing population growth as soon as possible. Family planning programmes play an important role not only for individual reproductive health but also for sustainability of the use of freshwater and other natural resources in relation to population size.

As population grows, so does demand for freshwater for food production, household (municipal) consumption, and industrial uses. The availability of freshwater limits the number of people that an area can support and affects standards of living. In turn, population growth and density typically affect the availability and quality of water resources in an area, as people attempt to assure their water supply by digging wells, constructing reservoirs and dams and diverting the flow of rivers. If needs consistently outpace available supplies, at some point, overuse of water leads to the depletion of surface and groundwater resources, triggering chronic water shortages.

Scarce and unclean water supplies are critical public health problems in much of the world. Polluted water, water shortages and unsanitary living conditions kill over 12 million people a year.

Competition for freshwater supplies breeds social and political tensions. River basins and other water bodies do not respect national borders. For example, one country's use of upstream water often subtracts from the supply available for use by downstream countries. In this first decade of the 21st century there is a growing risk that wars will be fought over access to freshwater supplies.

If a crisis is to be averted, the world's overuse and misuse of freshwater must end as soon as possible. We cannot afford to keep wasting and fouling our precious supplies of freshwater. Increasingly, human activities are altering the flow of water and drawing down freshwater supplies faster than they can be replenished. Throughout the world enormous amounts of water are wasted due to inappropriate agricultural subsidies, inefficient irrigation systems, leaky municipal pipes, improper pricing of municipal water, poor watershed management and other imprudent practices. It is time for widespread conservation measures, effective water management policies and growing attention to assuring freshwater supplies and decent sanitation as part of development and public health projects.

Water Availability and Use

Some 70 per cent of the earth's surface is water, but most of that is ocean. By volume, only 3 per cent of all water on earth is freshwater and most of this is largely unavailable. About three-quarters of all freshwater is locked away in the form of ice caps and glaciers located in polar areas far removed from most human habitation; only about 1 per cent is easily accessible surface freshwater.

This is primarily the water found in lakes, rivers and the soil at underground levels shallow enough to be tapped at an affordable cost. Only this amount is regularly renewed by rain and snowfall and thus available on a sustainable basis. In all, only one-hundredth of one per cent of the world's total supply of water is considered easily accessible for human use.

Globally, between 12.5 and 14 billion cubic metres of water (12,500 to 14,000 cubic kilometres) are considered available for human use on an annual basis. This amounts to about 9,000 cubic metres per person per year (1 cubic metre equals 1,000 litres). By the year 2025, global per capita availability of freshwater is projected to drop to 5,100 cubic metres per person as another 2 billion people join the world's population. Even then, this amount would be enough to meet human needs if it were distributed equally among the world's population.

Global per capita figures on water availability give a false picture, however. The world's available freshwater supply is not distributed evenly around the globe, throughout the seasons, or from year to year. In some cases, water is not where we want it, nor in sufficient quantities. In other cases we have too much water, in the wrong place, at the wrong time. We 'live under the tyranny of the water cycle,' observes hydrologist Malin Falkenmark, referring to the earth's hydrological cycle.

The earth's hydrological cycle acts like a giant water pump that continually transfers freshwater from the oceans to the land and back again.

In this solar-driven cycle, water evaporates from the earth's surface into the atmosphere and is returned as rain or snow. Part of this precipitation evaporates back into the atmosphere. Another part flows into streams, rivers and lakes, commencing a journey back to the sea. Still another part sinks into the soil and becomes soil moisture or groundwater. Plants incorporate soil moisture into their tissues and release it into the atmosphere in the process of evapotranspiration. Much of the groundwater eventually works its way back into the flow of surface waters.

Freshwater Distribution

The hydrological cycle comes with no guarantees for humankind. About three-quarters of annual rainfall comes down in areas containing less than one-third of the world's population. Put the other way around, two-thirds of the world's population lives in areas receiving only one-quarter of the world's annual rainfall. For instance, about 20 per cent of the global average runoff each year is accounted for by the Amazon Basin, a vast region with fewer than 10 million people, a tiny fraction of the world's population. Similarly, the Congo River and its tributaries account for about 30 per cent of the entire African continent's annual runoff, but the watershed contains only 10 per cent of Africa's population.

More than half the global runoff occurs in Asia and South America (31 per cent and 25 per cent, respectively). On a per capita basis, however, North America has the most freshwater available, at over 19,000 cubic metres per year, estimated in 1990. In contrast, the per capita amount is just over 4,700 cubic metres in Asia (including the Near East).

By country, the amount of renewable freshwater available per capita on an annual basis ranges from over 600,000 cubic metres in Iceland to only 75 cubic metres per person in Kuwait.

There are also striking differences in water availability within countries. In Mexico, less than 10 per cent of the land area provides more than half of the national rainwater runoff each year. Despite the fact that 90 per cent of Mexico is arid and chronically water-short, its total per capita water availability in 1990 was over 4,000 cubic metres. Such a figure is grossly misleading as a measure of actual water availability for most Mexicans.

"The disparities between the rich and poor are never more stark than when it comes to access to water", according to the UN publication *Earth Times*. "Ask a person in New York what he thinks about the water problem and he will probably say, 'what problem?' Ask a person in New Delhi and you will be lucky if you escape with a 15-minute lecture on how the water flows once a day, it has to be stored, it smells and, if you drink it without boiling, chances are you will get sick".

Throughout much of the developing world freshwater supply comes in the form of seasonal rains. Such rains run off too quickly for efficient use, as during the monsoons in Asia. India, for instance, gets 90 per cent of its rainfall during the summer monsoon season, which lasts from June to September. For the other eight months, the country gets barely a drop of rain. As a result of the seasonal nature of the water supply, India and some other developing countries can make use of no more than 20 per cent of their potentially available freshwater resources.

Altering Natural Supply Systems

As water-short societies have done for centuries, many countries attempt to move water from where it occurs in nature to where people want it and also to store water for future use. The Egyptians built thousands of canals and irrigation ditches to capture the Nile's waters in order to grow crops. In the first century AD, Roman engineers brought water into Rome via huge aqueducts from as far away as 100 kilometres.

Worldwide, there are some 40,000 dams higher than 15 metres, most of them built in the last 50 years. Although dams help ensure a steady water supply, they often imperil aquatic ecosystems by disrupting flood cycles, blocking river channels, altering water flows in rivers, floodplains, deltas and other natural wetlands, and imperilling plant and animal life.

How Water is Used

It is difficult to estimate the amount of water needed to maintain acceptable or minimum living standards. Moreover, different sources use different figures for total water consumption and for water use by the various sectors of the economy.

A range of 20 to 40 litres of freshwater per person per day is generally considered to be a necessary minimum to meet the needs for drinking and sanitation alone, according to Peter Gleick, president of the Pacific Institute for Studies in Development, Environment and Security. If water for bathing and cooking is included as well, this figure varies between 27 and 200 litres per capita per day.

Several different amounts have been proposed as minimum standards. Gleick proposes that international organizations and water providers adopt 'an overall basic water requirement of 50 litres per person per day' as a minimum standard to meet four basic needs—for drinking, sanitation, bathing and cooking.

In 1990, Gleick estimates, 55 countries with a population of nearly 1 billion people did not meet this standard as a national average. Falkenmark uses the figure of 100 litres of freshwater per capita per day for personal use as a rough estimate of the amount needed for a minimally acceptable standard of living in developing countries, not including uses for agriculture and industry.

The amount of water that people in a country actually use depends not only on minimum needs and how much water is available for use but also on the level of economic development and the extent of urbanization. Globally, of the three standard categories of freshwater use—for agriculture, industry and domestic (personal, household, and municipal)—agriculture dominates. On a worldwide basis, agriculture accounts for about 69 per cent of all annual water withdrawals; industry, about 23 per cent; and domestic use, about 8 per cent.

There are wide differences by region. In Africa, an estimated 88 per cent of all freshwater use is for agriculture, 7 per cent for domestic purposes and 5 per cent for industry. In Asia, water is also used mostly for agriculture, estimated at 86 per cent of total use, while industry accounts for 8 per cent and domestic use, 6 per cent. In Europe, however, most water use is for industry, at 54 per cent, while agriculture accounts for 33 per cent and domestic use, 13 per cent.

Freshwater and Economic Development

A country's level of freshwater use reflects—and, in fact, is one of the key measures of—its level of economic development. In the developing regions of the world, people use far less water per capita than in developed regions. In Africa, the annual per capita water withdrawals for personal use averages only 17 cubic metres (equal to 47 litres of water per day), and in Asia, 31 cubic metres (equal to 85 litres per day). In contrast, comparable water use in the U.K. is estimated at 122 cubic metres per year (334 litres per day), and in the U.S.A., 211 cubic metres per year (578 litres per day).

Developing countries devote most of their water supplies to agriculture. India, for instance, uses 90 per cent of all water for agricultural purposes, with just 7 per cent for industry and 3 per cent for domestic use. The higher the level of development, the more water is used for domestic and industrial purposes and the less for agriculture. There are some important exceptions to this rule, however. For example, Japan still uses the largest share of its freshwater for irrigating rice. Also, in some arid areas of Europe, such as Spain and Portugal, most of the available water is used for irrigated agriculture.

Around the world, freshwater demand per capita is rising substantially as countries develop economically. Withdrawals of water have grown in all three major categories of use—to meet rising industrial demand, rising domestic demand, including for municipal use, and increasing reliance on irrigation to produce food.

Urbanization

The level of water use also reflects the level of urbanization in a country. Low household water use in many developing countries today often reflects difficulty in obtaining freshwater. Piped water systems are rare in rural areas. Two-thirds of the world's population, the majority in developing countries, get their water from public standpipes, community wells, rivers and lakes, or rainfall collected off roofs.

Often rural people—usually women and girls—must walk many kilometres and spend many hours fetching water for their households. In Africa, for instance, women and girls spend 40 billion person-hours a year hauling water.

Urbanization increases water use dramatically. For example, in 1900, the average American household used as little as 10 cubic metres of water per year compared with more than 200 cubic metres today. Why? A century ago, most Americans obtained their freshwater from wells or public standpipes. Running water was largely unavailable to households except in big cities, and most people lived in the rural areas. In contrast, virtually every American household today has running water available, and this water costs its users very little.

As the world becomes predominately urban, while agriculture depends more and more on irrigation, it will be difficult for cities to meet the rising demand for freshwater. In developing countries, rapid urban growth often puts tremendous pressure on antiquated, inadequate water supply systems. For instance, between 1950 and 1980, the populations of many cities in Latin America, such as Bogota, Mexico City, São Paulo and

Managua, tripled or even quadrupled. Such African cities as Nairobi, Dar-es-Salaam, Lagos and Kinshasa grew sevenfold, primarily because of a rural exodus. In the 1990s, cities of developing countries have had to cope with about 60 million new arrivals every year. Yet many agencies are not equipped to manage the urban water supply, while some countries have ineffective water allocation systems that allow cities to run short of water at the same time that water resources are being used for subsidized agriculture.

Years of rapid population growth and increasing water consumption for agriculture, industry and municipalities have strained the world's freshwater resources. In some areas, the demand for water already exceeds nature's supply, and a growing number of countries are expected to face water shortages in the near future.

Population Growth, Water Shortages

The world's population, at nearly 6 billion, is growing by about 80 million people each year. This number implies an increased demand for freshwater of about 64 billion cubic metres a year—an amount equivalent to the entire annual flow rate of the Rhine River. While population growth rates have slowed somewhat, the absolute number of people added to the population each year—the relevant figure when considering the availability of and need for freshwater—remains near historic highs. For example, because nearly 2 billion people have been added to the planet since 1970, per capita availability of water is one-third lower now than it was then.

China and India, the world's first and second most populous countries, provide examples of how even modest population growth rates translate into large absolute numbers when the population base is large. In China, the population growth rate is about 1 per cent per year. Nevertheless, because China's population is over 1.2 billion people, even a low population growth rate means 12 million additional people each year. India's population growth rate, which is substantially higher than China's, at about 1.9 per cent per year, means about 18 million people are added each year to India's current population of over 1 billion.

In the two regions of the world that already face the most serious absolute or seasonal shortages of water—Africa and the Near East—population growth rates remain among the highest in the world. In sub-Saharan Africa, population is growing by an average 2.6 per cent a year; in the Near East and North Africa, by 2.2 per cent. These population growth rates have ominous implications for per capita water supply in the countries of these regions.

Water Stress and Scarcity

As their populations grow, more and more countries are facing water shortages. A country is said to experience 'water stress' when annual water supplies drop below 1,700 cubic metres per person. At levels between 1,700 and 1,000 cubic metres per person, periodic or limited water shortages can be expected. When annual water supplies drop below 1,000 cubic metres per person, the country faces water scarcity.

Once a country experiences 'water scarcity', it can expect chronic shortages of freshwater that threaten food production, hinder economic development and damage ecosystems.

Malin Falkenmark developed the concepts of water stress and water scarcity based on an index of per capita freshwater needs. She estimated a minimum need of 100 litres per day per person for household use and from 5 to 20 times as much for agricultural and industrial uses. These concepts have been widely accepted and used by hydrologists, the World Bank and other organizations. For example, Population Action International (PAI) has relied on them to make projections of per capita water availability and to forecast water shortages in 2025 and 2050.

Calculations of water stress and water scarcity are based on estimates of a country's renewable freshwater supplies and do not include water withdrawn from fossil groundwater. Fossil groundwater is essentially a non-renewable resource: It takes tens of thousands of years for these deep aquifers to replenish themselves.

A country may temporarily avoid the effects of water stress by mining its non-renewable water supplies, but this practice is not sustainable, particularly if the population continues to grow rapidly and per capita demand for freshwater increases.

As at the end of the last century, 31 countries, with a combined population of over 458 million, faced either water stress or water scarcity. This represents an addition of only 3 countries since 1990, when 28 countries, with a combined population of 335 million faced chronic water stress or water scarcity. The number of people estimated to live in water-scarce and water-stressed countries rose by nearly 125 million during these 10 years, however, largely reflecting population growth in water-short countries.

The Coming Era of Water Stress and Scarcity

Already evidence of a serious problem, these numbers are about to explode. By 2025, more than 2.8 billion people will live in 48 countries facing water stress or water scarcity, PAI projects, based on the recently revised United Nations medium population projections.

Of these 48 countries, 40 are either in the Near East and North Africa or in sub-Saharan Africa. Over the next two decades, population increase alone—not to mention growing demand per capita—is projected to push all of the Near East into water scarcity. By 2050, the number of countries facing water stress or scarcity will rise to 54 and their combined population to 4 billion people—40 per cent of the projected global population of 9.4 billion.

The Near East and North Africa

The 20 countries of the Near East and North Africa face the worst prospects. The Near East is the most water-short region in the world. In fact, the entire Near East 'ran out of water' in 1972, when the region's total population was 122 million, according to Tony Allan, a University of London expert on water resources.

Since then, the region has withdrawn more water from its rivers and aquifers every year than is being replenished. Currently, for example, Jordan and Yemen withdraw 30 per cent more water from groundwater aquifers every year than is replenished. Also, Israel's annual water use already exceeds its renewable supply by 15 per cent.

Saudi Arabia presents one of the worst cases of unsustainable water use in the world. This extremely arid country now must mine fossil groundwater for three-quarters of its water needs. Fossil groundwater depletion in Saudi Arabia has been averaging around 5.2 billion cubic metres a year.

Of 14 countries in the Near East, 11 are already facing water scarcity. In five of these countries the populations are projected to double within the next two decades.

Water is one of the major political issues confronting the region's leaders. Since virtually all rivers in the Near East are shared by several nations, current tensions over water rights could escalate into outright conflicts, driven by population growth and rising demand for an increasingly scarce resource.

Four Gulf states—Bahrain, Kuwait, Saudi Arabia, and the United Arab Emirates—have so little freshwater available that they resort to desalinization, the costly conversion of sea water into freshwater. Without desalinization, the Gulf states would be unable to support anywhere close to their current populations. Bahrain's population depends completely on desalinization of seawater from the Gulf. It has virtually no freshwater at all. Desalinization, however, is far too expensive and impractical for most water-short countries, not to mention land-locked countries, either today or in the foreseeable future.

Sub-Saharan Africa

Much of sub-Saharan Africa is facing serious water constraints. Nearly 200 million people live in Africa's water-stressed countries. While only 6 million live in countries facing water scarcity, rapid population growth will make this problem worse. By 2025, as many as 230 million people will be living in African countries facing water scarcity. Another 460 million will be in water-stressed countries of Africa.

Water Problems within Countries

Parts of many large countries, such as India, China and the United States, would be considered to face water stress or water scarcity if calculations were made regionally rather than nationally. Already, 19 major Indian cities face chronic water shortages. India as a whole is expected to enter the water-stress category by 2025.

China, which has 22 per cent of the world's population but only 7 per cent of all freshwater runoff, will narrowly miss the water stress category's cut-off point of 1,700 cubic metres per capita in 2025. China's freshwater supplies have been estimated to be capable of sustainably supporting 650 million people—only half of the country's current population of over 1.2 billion.

Despite periodic flooding in the south, along the Yangtze River, China faces chronic freshwater shortages in the northern part of the country affecting 92 million people in the Hai river basin alone. Many of China's cities, including Beijing, face critical water shortages. The water table under Beijing has been dropping by roughly two metres per year, and one-third of the wells have dried up.

Even in the U.S.A., which has plenty of water on a national basis, groundwater reserves are being depleted in many areas. Overall, groundwater is being used at a rate 25 per cent greater than its replenishment rate. In the western part of the country, groundwater aquifers are being depleted at even faster rates in some areas. In particular, the huge Ogallala aquifer, which underlies parts of six states and irrigates 6 million hectares, has been overexploited. In some regions half of its available water has been withdrawn.

Competition for Scarce Water Supplies

In developed and developing countries alike, competition among water users is increasing. As might be expected, tensions are particularly high in water-short areas where population pressures, urbanization and development needs combine to create intense demand for limited freshwater resources.

A number of developed water-short countries currently face tensions over water, including Belgium, the United Kingdom, Poland, Singapore and the U.S.A. In southern Britain, for instance, urban demand for water is growing so fast that it is outpacing the capacity of rivers and aquifers to supply it during the drier summer months.

In the western U.S.A., farmers who want more irrigation water for their crops face off against fast-growing urban areas that demand more water for households and other municipal uses.

India's states have become embroiled in disputes over water rights and over dams that might provide more water for one state but at the expense of another. "Water disputes, if not attended to, will become a major headache for the stability of Indian society," says Mohan Katarki, a lawyer representing Karnataka state in a water dispute with Andhra Pradesh. These two states are arguing in court over the height of a dam on the Krishna River, which could affect the amount of water available for use by both states.

China already is practising what some water experts call the 'zero sum game of water management.' The zero sum game—when authorities increase water supply to one user by taking it away from another—is played both between competing areas of the country and between competing types of use, as when cities compete with farmers.

China's Yellow River is a classic case of the zero sum game. The river is so oversubscribed that, for an average of 70 days a year for the past decade, its waters have dried up before reaching the Bohai Sea. In 1995, the dry period lasted for 122 days. In 1996, one of the few years when there was enough water for farming villages near the river's mouth to feed their crops, the government authorities ordered them not to touch a drop. All of the water flowing by their parched fields was destined for use by a state-run oil field farther downstream.

Also, to meet urban needs, the government of China is planning a huge aqueduct that will carry water from the Danjiangkou Reservoir in Henan Province to Beijing, across 1,300 kilometres of heavily farmed land – land that also needs the water for food production.

If China diverts too much water from agricultural uses, grain production is likely to suffer, probably forcing China to import more grain. Other grain-producing countries, however, have little potential to boost exports, warns the Worldwatch Institute. In the U.S.A. and Europe, for example, increases in agricultural productivity are just keeping up with population increases.

Australia and Canada depend on dryland farming and are constrained by limited rainfall. Thus 'China's water scarcity could soon become the world's grain scarcity,' the Worldwatch Institute predicts. Increasing demand for grain in China could raise prices on the world market beyond the reach of some poor countries.

Regional Conflicts

In nearly all water-short areas the threat of regional conflicts over limited water supplies is emerging as a serious issue. In Africa, for example, about 50 rivers are each shared by two or more countries. In particular, access to water from the Nile, Zambezi, Niger and Volta river basins has the potential to ignite conflicts.

In Central Asia, the Aral Sea Basin is beset by international conflicts over water. Turkmenistan, Uzbekistan, Kazakhstan, Kyrgyzstan and Tajikistan all depend for their survival on the waters of the Amu Darya and Syr Darya rivers. The flows of both rivers are almost wholly diverted to feed water-intensive crops such as cotton and rice. In most years, only a trickle reaches the Aral Sea.

As demand for this water grows, the countries are increasingly at odds over its division, with all five Central Asian republics demanding a greater share. Disputes are growing between Kyrgyz and Uzbeks over water and land in the fertile Fergana Valley; between Kyrgyz and Tajiks over the allocation of irrigation water from the Syr Darya; and between Turkmens and Uzbeks over the distribution of irrigation water from the Amu Darya.

In the U.S.A., the Colorado River, which flows through the south-western part of the country, has fed irrigated agriculture and enabled the explosive growth of desert cities. Now, however, demands on the river's water supply for irrigation and urban use have become so great that the river no longer reaches its mouth in Mexico's Gulf of California. Instead, its waters trickle out somewhere in the desert south of the U.S.-Mexican border. The river's premature disappearance has been a source of bickering between the U.S.A. and Mexico.

14

The Role of Governance in Water Control

MANY governments recognize the need to localize water management but fail to delegate adequate powers and resources to make it work. Local groups and individuals are often without access to information, are excluded from water decision-making, and thus lack a capacity to act. Good water governance is a complex process, influenced by a given country's overall standard of governance, its customs, mores and politics and conditions, events within and around it (for example, conflict) and by developments in the global economy. There is no blueprint for good water governance.

Reforms of water governance are being driven by internal pressures on water resources and environmental threats, growing population and the focus of the international community on poverty alleviation and socio-economic development (for example, Millennium Development Goals). However, the rate of reform is patchy and slow. There are significant and serious gaps in developing countries between land- and water-use policies and governance *and* between policymaking and its implementation, often due to institutional resistance to change, corruption, etc.

In many countries, water governance is in a state of confusion: in some countries, there is a total lack of water institutions and others display fragmented institutional structures or conflicting decision-making structures. In many places, conflicting upstream and downstream interests regarding riparian rights and access to water resources are pressing issues that need immediate attention; in many other cases there are strong tendencies to divert public resources for personal gain, or unpredictability in the use of laws and regulations and licensing practices impede markets and voluntary action and encourage corruption.

Citizens and organized interests are demanding much more transparency and influence in water decision-making. Very complex and dynamic events and processes external to the water sector define how we relate to water. Changes in water-use patterns are continuously redefined through such things as culture, macroeconomic and development trends, processes of democratization and social and political stability or unrest.

Examples given below point at complex urban and rural water-use dynamics, the increasing need for integrated approaches to water, the range of international targets for local action and the multitude of stakeholder interests. Finally, some overarching challenges are identified, which relate to specific water governance issues, challenges and potential solutions with respect to their fields.

The Water-Poverty Link

How societies choose to govern their water resources has profound impacts on people's lives and their ability to prosper, as well as on environmental sustainability. On the ground, this means that some groups or individuals will benefit while others will lose out when water allocation changes are made. Having a fair water provision can be, for many people, a matter of daily survival. How and for whom water is being governed has impacts on river flows, groundwater tables and pollution levels, affecting both upstream and tail-end water users.

The capacity of countries to pursue poverty reduction strategies and Integrated Water Resources Management (IWRM) plans, meet new demands and manage conflicts and risks depends largely on their ability to promote and put into place sound and effective governance systems. Improved governance is essentially about improving people's livelihood opportunities, while providing the backbone for governments worldwide to alleviate poverty and increase the chances of sustainable development.

One of the most striking features of the link between water and poverty is that each year, thousands of African and Asian children die from water- and sanitation-related diseases. In the poorest countries, one out of every five children fails to reach his or her fifth birthday, mainly due to infectious and environmental diseases that arise from poor water quality. Over the last two decades, the number and scale of water-related disasters –

either too much water (floods) or too little (droughts)—have increased greatly because of changing climate patterns. Many countries in sub-Saharan Africa and the Indian and Pacific oceans, along with low-lying small island states, are the most vulnerable to climate change, because widespread poverty limits their capabilities to adapt to climate variability.

Water Governance Today

A basic insight—which has not yet garnered enough attention—is that the insufficiency of water (particularly for drinking water supply and sanitation), is primarily driven by an inefficient supply of services rather than by water shortages. Lack of basic services is often due to mismanagement, corruption, lack of appropriate institutions, bureaucratic inertia and a shortage of new investments in building human capacity, as well as physical infrastructure.

Water supply and sanitation have recently received more international attention than water for food production, despite the fact that in most developing countries agriculture accounts for 80 per cent of total water use. It is increasingly agreed in development circles that water shortages and increasing pollution are to a large extent socially and politically induced challenges, which means that there are issues that can be addressed by changes in water demand and use and through increased awareness, education and water policy reforms.

The water crisis is thus increasingly about how we, as individuals, and as part of a collective society, govern the access to and control over water resources and their benefits. In many places of the world, a staggering 30 to 40 per cent of water or more goes unaccounted for due to water leakages in pipes and canals and illegal tapping.

Better governance exerts a powerful effect on per capita incomes. As recently as 200 years ago, per capita incomes were not very different across countries. Today's wide income gaps across countries reflect the fact that countries that are currently rich have grown rapidly over the past two centuries, while those that are poor have not.

It has been suggested that a substantial fraction of these vast income gaps is due to 'deep historical differences in institutional quality'. Water-use efficiency in developing countries is very low in both urban and rural areas, and there is great room for improving the water situation through improved water distribution and management.

The political empowerment dimension points at granting water stakeholders and citizens at large equal democratic opportunities to influence and monitor political processes and outcomes. At both national and international levels, marginalized citizens, such as indigenous people, women, slum dwellers, etc., are rarely recognized as legitimate stakeholders in water-related decision-makers, and typically lack voices, institutions and capacities for promoting their water interests to the outside world. Empowering women, as well as other socially, economically and politically weak groups, is critical to achieving more focused and effective water management and actions to ensure greater equity.

The environmental sustainability dimension shows that improved governance allows for enhanced sustainable use of water resources and ecosystem integrity (so often, those affected by such disasters are the poor, who do not have the means to escape poverty traps).

The Dimensions of Water Governance

The conceptual development of water management has paved the way for an IWRM approach, which is considered by many as an appropriate vehicle to resolve the world's water challenges. As defined by the Global Water Partnership (GWP), IWRM is 'a process which promotes the co-ordinated development and management of water, land and related resources in order to maximize the resultant economic and social welfare in an equitable manner without compromising the sustainability of vital ecosystems.' IWRM should be seen as a comprehensive approach to the development and management of water, addressing its management both as a resource and the framework for provision of water services.

The social dimension points to the equitable use of water resources. Apart from being unevenly distributed in time and space, water is also unevenly distributed among various socio-economic strata of society in both rural and urban settlements. How water quality and quantity and related services are allocated and distributed have direct impacts on people's health as well as on their livelihood opportunities.

It is estimated that daily water use per inhabitant totals 600 litres in residential areas of North America and Japan and between 250 and 350 litres in Europe, while daily water use per inhabitant in sub-Saharan Africa averages just 10 to 20 litres. Currently, 1.1 billion people lack sufficient access to safe drinking water and 2.6 billion people lack access to basic sanitation. People in slums have very limited access to safe water for household uses. A slum dweller may only have 5 litres to 10 litres per day at his or her disposal. A middle- or high-income household in the same city, however, may use some 50 to 150 litres per day, if not more. Similarly, water for food production often benefits large-scale farmers to the detriment of small-scale and landless farmers.

The economic dimension draws attention to the efficient use of water resources and the role of water in overall economic growth. Prospects for aggressive poverty reduction and economic growth remain highly dependent on water and other natural resources.

Studies have illustrated that per capita incomes and the quality of governance in particular can be said to be made up of the range of political, social, economic and administrative systems that are in place, which directly or indirectly affect the use, development and management of water resources and the delivery of water services at different levels of society.

Governance systems determine who gets what water, when and how and decide who has the right to water and related services and their benefits. The representation of various interests in water decision-making and the role of politics are important components in addressing governance dynamics.

Water is power, and those who control the flow of water in time and space can exercise this power in various ways. It is often claimed that clean water tends to gravitate towards the rich and wastewater towards the poor. Sandra Postel has aptly noted that "water grabs and power plays are legendary in the western United States."

The water tensions of the American west have been captured in popular movies such as *Chinatown*, where farmers were being 'sucked dry' by Los Angeles.

As water demands and uses increase at exponential rates due to population growth, stakes rise in many parts of the world. As opportunities to expand water supplies decrease, competition over current supplies escalate, creating the need for improved governance.

The way in which societies govern their water resources has profound impacts on settlements, livelihoods and environmental sustainability, yet governance has traditionally not received the same attention as technical issues. Sufficient flow of quality water is critical to maintaining ecosystem functions and services and sustaining groundwater aquifers, wetlands and other wildlife habitats.

A worrisome sign is that water quality appears to have declined worldwide in most regions with intensive agriculture and large urban and industrial areas. With the reduction and pollution of natural habitats, the diversity of freshwater flora and fauna is becoming increasingly threatened. Poor people's livelihood opportunities, in particular, depend directly upon sustained access to natural resources, including water—especially since they tend to live in marginalized areas that are prone to pollution, droughts and floods.

The essential role of water for maintaining a healthy environment is being increasingly emphasized in the change of attitudes towards wetlands, which is an encouraging sign.

Decisions about water are being made by the minute around the world within urban and rural households, neighbourhoods, small businesses, and corporate boardrooms and in the offices of local, state and national governments, as well as on the international scale.

The particular settings vary, as do the people and groups involved. Water decisions are anchored in governance systems across three levels: government, civil society and the private sector. Facilitating dynamic interactions among them is critical for developed and developing countries alike. The water sector is a part of a broader society and its politics and is thus affected by decisions that lie outside of the water sector.

The United Nations Development Programme (UNDP) defines governance as 'the exercise of economic, political and administrative authority to manage a country's affairs at all levels. It comprises the mechanisms, processes and institutions, through which citizens and groups articulate their interests, exercise their legal rights, meet their obligations and mediate their differences.' The way we perceive and govern our water resources is also rooted in culture.

Although water is considered by most cultures to be something critical for all life, with a prominent place in cultural and religious beliefs, it is something of a paradox that water is often taken for granted and is increasingly polluted, with many people having limited access to clean drinking water and water for productive activities.

The development of governance and management systems within the water sector is closely related to overall development trends in which the role of the state has shifted from the provider to the enabler of development and welfare (the 'rolling back of the state').

Privatization, Conflicts and Democratization

The past decades have witnessed tremendous social, political and economic changes. The end of the cold war and the process of decolonization continue to shape current societal events. Globalization and the increasing speed of information exchange have had tremendous impacts on societies. Terrorism has also had a major impact on how countries interact with each other and on how governments interact with their citizens. Some commentators worry that we are heading towards a more closed 'barbed-wire' society in an effort to keep out direct and indirect impacts on how water is being used and governed.

Increasing water demands will lead to a decline of per capita supply in the future. Currently, an estimated 26 countries with a combined population of more than 350 million people are located in regions with severe water scarcity where the available water resources seem to be sufficient to meet reasonable water needs for development activities, but only if these countries take appropriate water demand and supply management measures. In many countries, there will also be additional, sometimes severe, local water scarcities, even within countries that have sufficient aggregate water resources, such as within the U.S.A. and India.

A comparison of water shortages and governance challenges shows that many countries, particularly in the Middle East and North Africa, are facing a double challenge. It is also evident that countries that have bountiful water resources are facing governance challenges to provide water and sanitation services and for fundamental changes in society that can lead to improved policy-making, which in turn can benefit a nation's water prospects. Democratization, macroeconomic changes, population growth and other demographic changes and social and political instability, often have much greater impacts on water use and demands than any water policy itself.

Global market conditions and trade regimes are factors that affect crop choices and thus, also, have serious implications for water use and demands in agriculture. Market liberalization can contribute to improving the water situation for many people but can also increase pressures to overexploit water and the environment.

The cases of India (low levels of water services) and southern Spain (dwindling groundwater) indicate that democracy itself is not sufficient. It also depends on how political rights and civil liberties are exercised, as well as on other factors, such as demographic development, economic growth, institutional effectiveness and how welfare is generated and distributed within and between societies. This does not mean that water managers should refrain from trying to make a difference, but rather underlines an urgent need to collaborate with new actors outside the water realm and establish more inclusive water development networks.

Political change has to begin somewhere, and in some cases, the promotion of improved water governance may even serve as a preliminary for inducing broad-based reform. It has been pointed out that cooperative water development in the Netherlands in the earlier part of the 20th century was an important part of nation-building for the modern Dutch welfare state. Improved governance and impacts on water resources management and related services are both complex and dynamic.

If a country lacks essential freedoms, like the freedom of speech and the right to organize, promoting participatory approaches in water development programmes is compromised. If citizens cannot access basic information on water quantity and quality, it seriously curtails their chances of halting environmentally unsound water projects or to hold relevant government agencies accountable.

International Responses to Improve Water Governance

The concept of water governance has gained a lot of ground and evolved over the past decade. Within the international political arena, the concept has evolved from a political taboo in North–South development cooperation dialogue to gain wider acceptance as a critical issue at international, national and local levels.

The framing of water challenges in terms of governance has allowed a broadening of the water agenda to include the scrutiny of democratization processes, corruption, power imbalances between rich and poor countries and between rich and poor people. Governance and politics are necessary to protect water resources. For example, countries in Central Africa, which have ample water resources, have not been able to provide their citizens with a sufficient supply of water; hence the point that water provision is often less a question of available water resources than of properly functioning institutions and proper infrastructure management.

Despite limited democratic provisions in some countries, water can still be managed in more democratic ways at the local level, such as through water-user associations or other types of local organizations. It has been suggested that partial democratization, without the appropriate checks and balances, can, at least in the short run, lead to an increase in the exploitation of water, land and forests through patronage politics. It has also been suggested that within well-established democratic polities, politicians can make environmental 'pay-offs' to groups that financially support the campaigns of a particular party or candidate. These 'pay-offs' can include, for example, circumventing certain environmental regulations and allowing the lax enforcement of pollution control.

Despite the fact that democracy has flourished in Western Europe, more than half of European cities are currently exploiting groundwater at unsustainable rates. Chronic water shortages already affect 4.5 million people in Catalonia, where authorities are pressing for the construction of a pipeline to divert water from the Rhone in France to Barcelona. It is thus apparent that many water development 'principles' – IWRM, participation, transparency, community involvement and decentralization – require improved governance in order to be successfully implemented.

It is unlikely that effective participation and transparency within the water sector will take place unless there are overall changes in how societies and political systems function. Water policy reform, IWRM implementation and meeting the Millennium Development Goals (MDGs) all require that we address issues in the water and development interface, as well as issues that have traditionally been considered outside the scope of water. If we wish to increase stakeholder participation, make decentralization more effective and hold water agencies and utilities accountable; enhanced democratization is required.

Yet fairly little is known about the local and practical links between water shortages and democratization. The general notion is that democratization is beneficial to improved water governance and would open up far more transparency, decentralization and participation. But partial democratization, without the appropriate checks and balances can, potentially lead to an increase in the exploitation of water, land and forests through patronage politics.

During recent years, the international water community has centre-staged governance as the most important challenge to improve water management and services provision. A serious weakness is that very few, if any, robust indicators exist to monitor and assess trends for water governance. A key challenge for all development actors is to publish disaggregated data on water governance issues to assess if countries are on the right track in their reform efforts. Water governance indicators should be useful to national stakeholders as a tool for priority setting and strengthening the responsiveness of institutions and processes to the water needs of water users. There has been great progress in quantifying and standardizing governance indicators. The progress in research, measurement and indicator development has helped identify the many components of governance.

Improved governance can result in higher economic growth, more productive investments, lower transaction costs and more effective implementation of policies and legislation. Thus, if a country's governance is improved through increased transparency, strengthening of local democracy, improvements in the judiciary system, etc., such changes will also spill over to the water sector.

However, due to limited research and indicator development there is currently little evidence that can help us understand to what extent and how this is occurring. It is thus critical that the water governance knowledge base be enhanced on, among other things:

1. What type of governance is favourable to improved water resources management and water services provisions?
2. Are some governance components more critical to address than others to improve water supply and sanitation coverage as well as the sustainable use of water resources?

The development and application of appropriate water governance indicators will make a major contribution to the type of water policy interventions that are required by governments and the whole development community.

Within the water sector, there is a widespread belief that we now have most of the needed principles in place in order to make a lasting improvement to the world's water resources situation, which will also make a major contribution to the overall work of alleviating poverty. What is lacking today are the concerted actions and the means for effective implementation of various water policies and development programmes. The implementation of existing water policies of countries would go a long way in meeting the MDGs and the water targets set in Johannesburg, increasingly viewed as an integral part of water crises and thus as a part of resolving them.

An important part of the work of bilateral and multilateral organizations has been to support the enhancement of capacities to strengthen national and local water agendas and policies and investment priorities, while providing useful examples for scaling up activities. Despite these efforts, water is not considered a main priority in most countries. Investment in the water sector is still at a very low level in developing countries, and despite promises of action-oriented outcomes by the world's governments at the WSSD, much remains to be done about water governance issues in donor budgets.

Trends in Reform and Rights Governance

Why and how are certain decisions made? What stakeholders are involved? What principles, rules and regulations (formal and informal institutions) apply? Governance is process-oriented and thus intrinsically linked to politics and preoccupied with how various actors relate to each other. Because of the varying characteristics of water resources and the myriad socio-economic and political frameworks, governing mechanisms vary considerably across countries, including differences such as reform items, the pace at which countries are moving towards implementing water reforms, the level of the reform and the degree of targeting environmental and social objectives.

National Water Policies in the Making

Reform of the water sector is now taking place in many countries around the world. The reasons for reforms can vary according to the particular situation. In most cases, water reforms in a particular sector appear to be associated with a larger reform agenda. For example, pricing reforms are often complicated by financial constraints and cost recovery affects the fiscal budget.

In Pakistan, the central government has to subsidize the budgets of the irrigation departments and in Morocco the public budget used to be the sole source of funding of water services provided mainly by irrigation districts. The Republic of Yemen, where macroeconomic measures accompanied water reforms, provides a good example of the importance of having a wide-ranging agenda for reform.

In the case of South Africa, water reform was made part and parcel of the overall political changes in the early 1990s. Water policies have too often been driven by assumptions about the need to increase supplies through investing in physical infrastructure. Current water sector reform, particularly in developing countries, has increasingly tried to balance issues of infrastructure and technology with governance and management issues, such as multi-stakeholder participation, as well as measures for enhancing demand management, decentralization and various elements of integrated and basin management approaches.

Another example includes water reform in Nicaragua, where current water legislation covers a wide range of issues from water rights, participation and economic incentive instruments to technology. In recent water sector reform—in South Africa, Zimbabwe, Kazakhstan and the European Union (EU)—water framework directive management, for example, the basin level constitutes an important component of improved integrated management of water.

Kazakhstan, for example, has established eight river basin organizations that are responsible for water resources governance and use, water plan preparation, water allocation and permit provision. The ongoing water reform in Kazakhstan also includes provisions for public involvement and decentralization that can take the form of local self-governance

In many cases, water management at the basin level also extends to the management of river basins and groundwater aquifers shared between sovereign states. The increased water cooperation between nations will require building mutual trust as well as long-term commitments from the parties involved. Normally, this necessitates a whole sequence of cooperative actions that can start off with agreeing on methodologies and standards for collecting hydrological data and joint monitoring plans.

Other actions can include the harmonization of water policies and joint water management plans. It is important that trans-boundary water management not stop with cooperation at a technical level, but that such cooperation 'spill over' to joint development plans for a river basin or even to broader issues of sharing the benefits of river basins and groundwater aquifers.

There is currently a wide range of various sub-regional river basin commissions on all continents; however, their mandates and impacts on water resources use efficiency and sustainability vary to a great extent. Despite the growing call for integrated approaches, there is, in reality, limited practical experience of how it can be implemented.

Water Policies, Politics and Resistance

No reform is stronger than its weakest link, which is to say, implementation. Recent years have seen the development of sophisticated water policies and plans in many parts of the world, such as in South Africa, in Europe with the EU Water Framework Directive and in Chile with water privatization. Some of the reforms in developing countries have been assisted by the international community and have frequently been motivated, at least in part, by active international debate on these issues. These achievements also need to be balanced, however, by a recognition that policy changes at the national level have often only been imperfectly followed through to effective implementation.

A recent example is Zimbabwe, where the actual content of water reform is considered progressive, but where reform has stalled due to recent political instability and weak implementation capacity.

There is a tendency to separate policy-making processes from implementation. The notion is that policy-making is ascribed to decision-makers, while implementation is linked to administrative capacity. This kind of thinking is too rigid and fails to acknowledge that policies are often modified as they move through public administrations.

Water Policy Reform: Where to Begin?

While there has been progress in water policy development during the past decade, this progress is uneven and considerable challenges remain. Many government reforms fail because once enacted, they yield unsatisfactory outcomes as they never get past implementation. How can the prospects for success be improved? It has been noted that 'a reform programme will be successful if there is economic rationality in its design, political sensitivity in its implementation and close and constant attention to political-economic interactions and socio-institutional factors, so as to determine in each case the dynamics to follow.'

In particular, there needs to be a more complete understanding of the forces that lead to policy development in the first place and, critically, a concerted drive to make sure that policies are followed through to implementation. There also needs to be effective feedback and assessment mechanisms, so that the consequences of policy implementation can inform future policy development.

There are many components that are critical for successful policy reform. For example, some studies in policy implementation suggest that in order to maximize the likelihood of success, or minimize national bureaucracies to local levels for ultimate enforcement. Policy implementers can respond to policy change in different ways: they can implement reforms fully or partly, or if internal reform resistance is high in combination with lax monitoring from policy-making levels, they can ignore new policies altogether. It is clear, then, that policy-makers should not escape the responsibility of implementation and making sure that adequate capacities and financing is available for effective implementation.

Because reforms change the status quo, one can expect both support for and opposition to reform agendas by affected groups. Institutional reforms generate the active involvement of interest groups that may be affected directly or indirectly.

In some cases, the implementing agency may not have a reform agenda that coincides with that of the government initiating the reform.

For example, a stakeholder analysis of the parties involved in a proposed pricing reform for the capital of Honduras, Tegucigalpa, shows that the public agency in charge of supplying water to the city was a major opponent to the reform. A main aim of the agency was to seek continued power over water allocation and administration.

Interestingly, the case of Tegucigalpa also showed that the main support for reform was provided and driven by external international development agencies, but, in this case, this was not sufficient for reform to take effect. It was noted that for the reform to go forward, it would require the support from critical national power centres, such as the president and key government ministries.

A similar situation of opposing reform is described by Wambia (2000) in the case of Pakistan, where certain government agencies along with ministries opposed reform because it was felt that it would affect them negatively. Part of the reform was to transfer power and financial resources from the irrigation ministry and its regional offices to what were called Area Boards.

In governance systems that foster a non-implementation policy climate, decision-making tends to be discretionary, unpredictable and largely non-conducive to influence by citizens.

The implementation and allocation of resources tend to benefit the ruling elite or certain groups or individuals tightly connected to the ruling elite. Many civil society actors in developing countries are well aware of limited government commitment and capacities to follow through on policy development and external pressures.

National Ownership of Policy

The limited funding opportunities in low-income countries expose domestic decision-makers and policy development to pressure from international lending institutes and donors. If a country does not develop a certain 'internationally' required policy, it may face difficulties attracting international loans and development project funds. It is not uncommon in many low-income countries that due to external pressure they are required to put into place policies, plans and development programmes that lack 'national ownership' and have little chance of actually being implemented.

Allow for Incremental Change

Reforms should be well prepared, because once they are in place, they are often difficult to modify. If possible, keep the reform as simple as possible and avoid addressing many reform objectives at the same time. Reform is an incremental process, which sometimes can be painstakingly slow and managing policy processes is laborious and time-consuming and should not be underestimated. Although policy reform is an ongoing process and modification occurs over time, it is important that the main thrust of the policy can be sustained over time.

Compensate Policy Reform Losers

Adequate compensation mechanisms, negotiated with stakeholders, are an important part of a reform. Those who are losing out considerably in a reform should be adequately compensated: paying a fair amount of compensation is important for building support and avoiding social and political clashes that can jeopardize or slow down the reform. In the case of water pricing reforms, several groups or issues, such as the poor, or the environment, may need to be specifically addressed. For example, addressing the needs of poor people may mean including a differentiated tariff structure.

Water Rights

Ownership or the right to use a resource means power and control. While it may seem simple, water rights and ownership often have a complex relationship with water governance. How property rights are defined, who benefits from these rights and how they are enforced are all central issues that need further clarification in current water policies and legislation.

Insecurity of water rights, mismatches between formal legislation and informal customary water rights and an unequal distribution of water rights are frequent sources of conflict that can lead to poor decisions on efficient water resource use and equitable allocation.

Also, the problem of managing dwindling groundwater supplies or fish stocks—which many a time lack clear user rights—is a problematic water governance challenge. Water rights can be defined as 'authorized demands to use (part of) a flow of surface water and groundwater. Including certain privileges, restrictions, obligations and sanctions accompanying this authorization, among which a key element is the power to take part in collective decision-making about system management and direction.'

Water rights are inextricably linked to property. Well-defined and coherent water rights are fundamental to dealing with situations of increased competition between water users. Water management is a complex activity; it is a mobile resource that is attached to many different and sometimes competing, economic, social and environmental values. While water users compete for the same resource and struggle for increasing control, they also need to cooperate if they want to make effective use of water and sustain the quantity and quality of water in the long run.

This often occurs in 'pluralistic' legal contexts, where formal and informal normative systems sometimes clash. For example, in South Africa, water management moved from a pre-colonial collective activity to a publicly regulated resource under Roman-Dutch law. It was then transformed under Anglo-Saxon jurisprudence when it was captured as a private resource to the benefit of a small minority.

Conclusion

The challenge remains to develop governance frameworks and institutions that are flexible and adaptive. More attention needs to be given to resilient institutions and approaches that can govern or guide the complex, often surprise-laden, process of water governance central to long-term management at a regional, basin, aquifer or even local level.

This suggests that specific solutions—the ideal solution—may be less relevant and emphasizes the importance of enabling processes and frameworks that can be applied to resolve certain issues in situations of economic or other constraints and in contexts of change, that is, 'second or third best' solutions.

Many countries are currently at a crossroads about whether to provide the required political and financial capital to enhance efforts to improve water governance. 'Business as usual' is no longer a viable option. If investment levels and reform speed are not stepped up, the abilities of countries to provide water and sanitation for all, increase food production, while maintaining the environment, will be seriously compromised. This will, in the long- and short-run, curtail the prospect of societies for development.

There is no blueprint for improved governance. With social, political and economic preconditions as a base, any society must find its own way of improving governance. Despite the variety in design and implementation of improved governance across the world, there are also certain characteristics of the water sector that must be taken into account:

- Water is a renewable resource, as it reproduces itself through the hydrological cycle. While there is plenty of freshwater at the global scale, there is a challenge of having sufficient water, of the right quality, at the right place and at the right time.
- The nature of water resources is multi-purpose and hydrologically interconnected.
- Water is mainly considered a public good, but due to its multi-purpose nature, it is also at times an economic good. Importantly, water has economic, social and environmental value, which, among other things, calls for dialogue between water users and enhancement of participation and multi-stakeholder processes.
- The provision of water-related services is often characterized as being close to monopoly situations, particularly for water supply and sanitation. This can limit the effectiveness of water markets and can also require regulated price ceilings to protect consumers from monopolistic power abuses.
- The capital-intensive nature of water-related infrastructure is often combined with low-cost recovery and heavy subsidization. Water infrastructure investment is also considered a 'sunk cost', meaning that investments made to provide water services cannot be transferred or redeployed for other purposes, hence increasing capital investment risks. It is important to develop institutions and governance systems that can effectively respond to situations characterized by variability, risk, uncertainties and change.

15

Coping With Water Scarcity

Q&A with the Director-General, FAO

How serious is the problem of water scarcity?

Global water use has been growing at more than twice the rate of population growth in the last century.

Water scarcity already affects every continent and more than 40 per cent of the people on our planet. By 2025, 1.8 billion people will be living in countries or regions with absolute water scarcity, and two-thirds of the world's population could be living under water stressed conditions. In order to really understand how serious the problem is we first must take stock of the immense impact water has on our daily lives and our ability to provide for a better future.

Lack of access to adequate, safe water limits our ability to produce enough food to eat or earn enough income. It limits our ability to operate industries and provide energy. Without access to water for drinking and proper hygiene it is more difficult to reduce the spread and impact of life-threatening diseases like HIV/AIDS. Every day, 3 800 children die from diseases associated with lack of safe drinking water and proper sanitation.

Is water scarcity being caused by climate change?

The water scarcity situation is being exacerbated by climate change, especially in the driest areas of the world, which are home to more than 2 billion people and to half of all poor people.

The human impact on the earth's environment and climate must be addressed in order to protect the world's water resources.

But there are other factors involved, such as increases in the amount of water needed to grow the food for a growing population. Agriculture is the number-one user of freshwater worldwide.

Also, the trend towards urbanization and increases in domestic and industrial water use by people who live in more developed areas are factors that lead to growing water use.

Ultimately, though, the problem is one of the way in which we manage existing water resources and whether we as a global community truly have the political will to support policies and invest in programmes that protect our natural environment, conserve water and use less water to do more.

Political will and investment aren't going to make the Sahara desert disappear?

Certainly not. But political will, international cooperation and investment can help to stem the loss of water from huge river basins like those of the Nile and Lake Chad. That is something that FAO and other United Nations agencies are involved in doing as we speak.

Political will and investment can help to bring available water to the millions of small farmers around the world who are struggling to grow enough food to eat, by supporting locally-based programmes that directly involve those farmers and their neighbours in conserving rainfall, using water more efficiently and protecting water resources.

Political, and moral, will can help us to bring water to the 1.1 billion people who do not have access to the minimum of 20-50 litres of freshwater required to meet their most basic needs and the 2.6 billion people who don't have enough water to provide proper sanitation.

You say that agriculture is the world's number-one user of freshwater. Shouldn't the solution to water scarcity lie in agriculture?

First of all, there is no magic wand, no flip of the switch that is going to suddenly eliminate water scarcity. But there are concrete ways to turn the tide against water shortages. We at FAO recognize that the agriculture sector must take the lead in coping with water scarcity by finding more effective ways to conserve rain-fed moisture and irrigate farmlands.

There is no question that growing enough food is fundamental to fighting hunger and improving lives on every continent. But agriculture consumes about 70 per cent of all freshwater withdrawn and up to 95 per cent in several developing countries. To tackle water scarcity even as the demand for food increases, we must support initiatives to produce more food with proportionally less water. Again, this means protecting our waterways, keeping our forests healthy and improving the way in which we irrigate crops and manage livestock.

Can you give an example of how you would do that?

By thinking both big and small. First FAO advocates short-term, small-scale irrigation projects at the village level, including the development of low-cost and relatively simple, cost-effective methods which can be used by small farmers to irrigate crops. We have organized and supported pilot programmes in places like South Africa, Turkey and Mexico that focus on small scale irrigation or community-based systems for harvesting rainfall.

Often, one must help people to recover from severe water and food shortages by providing new crops and livestock while setting up irrigation projects, as we are doing right now with the support of the government and international donors in Niger. But the secret to long-term success is to break out of the cycle of responding to one water emergency after another and to put into place workable, sustainable long-term programmes.

This requires policy changes and cooperation on a larger scale. It means upgrading and improving the management of the facilities and then working across national borders to develop and protect water basins.

You had stated that the world was off-target for meeting the Millennium Development Goal of halving hunger by the year 2015. How can we be sure that it will be any different with the goal of improving access to water?

The two go hand-in-hand. Access to water is intricately linked to the achievement of most of the Millennium Development Goals, which include halving extreme poverty and hunger by 2015, halting the spread of HIV/AIDS and ensuring primary education for all children in the same time period. This is why we cannot make real progress in worldwide development without addressing the water scarcity issue.

Coping with water scarcity requires addressing a range of issues, not all of them directly linked to agriculture. They range from protection of the environment and global warming to fair pricing of water services and equitable distribution of water for irrigation, industry and household use. This is why not only the agriculture sector, but everyone—international organizations, governments, local communities—must share the responsibility.

As a global community, we have the capacity to greatly improve the management of our water resources and provide access to water for more people. But again, we cannot do it without placing greater political priority on ensuring that everyone has access to water and without investing in programmes which improve water conservation and delivery systems, protect the earth's ecosystems, conserve rain-fed moisture and use water for food production more efficiently.

16

Good Management can Prevent Crisis

WATER policies in most nations are failing to protect life's most vital resource. This fact is reflected in growing water scarcity and alarming declines in the health of aquatic ecosystems worldwide. More precious than oil, yet routinely wasted, water is arguably the world's most pressing resource issue.

Ensuring Water Supply

Human development depends on adequate water—a fact that has driven the location of communities, the extent of agriculture, and the shape of industry and transportation for centuries. Because of its central place in our activities, water is also the focus of much engineering activity and investment in the form of dams, canals, pipelines, and irrigation systems. Today, there are more than 45,000 large dams (dams more than 15 metres high) in the world—most of them built in the last 35 years. This storage capacity represents a 700 per cent increase in the standing stock of water in river systems since 1950.

The increase in storage capacity has permitted the expansion of agriculture through the use of irrigation, as well as the capability to distribute water more evenly throughout the year in many areas of the world where seasonal water shortages are a problem. But water demand is growing quickly, jeopardizing the availability of the supplies we would like to collect, store and use. Global water consumption rose six-fold between 1900 and 1995—more than double the rate of population growth—

and continues to grow rapidly as agricultural, industrial, and domestic demand increases.

Not surprisingly, the environmental impacts of our water consumption are growing rapidly as well. For example, the enormous increase in the number of dams has fragmented and seriously altered the flow of roughly 60 per cent of the world's major river basins. These fragmented rivers carry nearly 90 per cent of the water flowing through these major basins. As population increases and freshwater systems are modified to a point where many of their basic functions are affected, it becomes increasingly difficult to ensure that there is enough water for both people and nature.

How Scarce is Water?

Humans now withdraw about 4,000 km^3 of water a year—about 20 per cent of the base flow (the average dry-weather flow) of the world's rivers. Understanding what this means in terms of the global water cycle requires some context: scientists estimate that the average amount of global runoff (the amount of water that is available for human use after evaporation or absorption into groundwater aquifers) is between 39,500 km^3 and 42,700 km^3 a year.

However, not all of this water is available to humans. Much of the runoff occurs in flood events or is inaccessible to people because of its remote location. In addition, part of the runoff needs to remain in waterways so that aquatic ecosystems continue to function. In fact, only around 9,000 km^3 is readily accessible to humans every year as runoff. An additional 3,500 km^3 is stored in reservoirs.

In any case, such global averages fail to portray the details of the world's water situation. Water supplies are unevenly distributed around the globe, with some areas containing abundant water and others a much more limited supply. For example, arid and semiarid regions receive only 2 per cent of the world's runoff, even though they occupy roughly 40 per cent of the terrestrial area. In river basins with high water demand relative to the available runoff, water scarcity is a growing problem.

New estimates of water scarcity calculated by the World Resources Institute in collaboration with the University of New Hampshire show that some 41 per cent of the world's population, or 2.3 billion people, live in river basins under 'water stress,' meaning that per capita water supply is less than 1,700 m^3/year. An area in 'water stress' is subject to frequent water shortages.

In many of these areas, water supply is actually less than 1,000 m^3 per capita. In these 'highly stressed' river basins, the consequences of water scarcity can be much more severe, leading to problems with local food production and economic development unless the region is wealthy enough to apply new technologies for water use, conservation, or reuse. Some 1.7 billion people (out of the 2.3 billion noted above) live in such high water-stress basins.

Assuming that current water consumption patterns continue unabated, projections show that at least 3.5 billion people—or 48 per cent of the world's projected population—will live in water-stressed river basins in 2025. Even regions where per capita water availability appears sufficient when averaged over the year may actually face water shortages in the dry season.

The results of this analysis make it clear that many of the most populous river basins will gradually slip into water stress (with water per capita falling below 1,700 m^3 per year) over the next quarter century as water consumption rises.

Wasting Water: Inefficiency, Overuse, and Pollution

Global food production must increase in the years ahead to accommodate population growth. United Nations projections put global population at nearly 8 billion in 2025—up 1.7 billion from today. This means the world's farmers will need more water for irrigation.

Growth in food production in the last 50 years has been roughly matched by a proportional increase in water use, with grain yields rising 2.4-fold between 1950 and 1995 and irrigation water use rising 2.2-fold.

At present, irrigated agriculture accounts for 40 per cent of global food production, even though it represents just 17 per cent of global cropland. As a consequence, agriculture is society's major user of water, withdrawing some 70 per cent of all water.

Unfortunately, most irrigation systems are relatively inefficient and result in massive water waste. Global estimates of irrigation efficiency show that around 60 per cent of irrigation water never reaches the crop and is lost to evaporation and runoff.

Adding to the problem of inefficient irrigation techniques is the fact that farmers usually pay low prices for irrigation water, giving them little incentive to conserve. Government water subsidies that artificially lower water prices are the primary culprit.

In the western United States, for example, water subsidies total some $ 2-2.5 billion per year. Throughout the world, government support typically allows water utilities to sell irrigation water for far less than the cost of supplying it.

In arid Tunisia, farmers pay no more than one-seventh the cost of their water. Such low prices and subsidies encourage inefficient use and discourage the adoption of water-saving technology like drip irrigation.

Water pollution adds enormously to existing problems of local and regional water scarcity by removing large volumes of water from the available supply. In many parts of the world, rivers and lakes have become so polluted that their water is unfit even for industrial uses.

Groundwater is Also Scarce

Global concerns about water scarcity include not only surface water sources but groundwater sources. More than 1 billion people in Asian cities and 150 million in Latin American cities rely on groundwater from wells or springs. In addition, although there are no complete figures on groundwater use by the rural population, many countries are increasingly dependent on this resource for both domestic and agricultural uses.

Currently humans withdraw approximately 600-700 km^3 of groundwater per year—about 20 per cent of global water withdrawals. Some of this water is fossil water (ancient water that isn't routinely replenished) that comes from deep sources isolated from the normal runoff cycle, but much groundwater comes from shallower aquifers that draw from the same global runoff that feeds freshwater ecosystems.

Indeed, overdrafting of groundwater sources can rob streams and rivers of a significant fraction of their flow. In the same way, pollution of aquifers by nitrates, pesticides and industrial chemicals often affects water quality in adjacent freshwater ecosystems.

Although overdrafting and contamination of groundwater aquifers are known to be widespread and growing problems, comprehensive data on groundwater resources and pollution trends are not available at the global level.

Management for More Water

Better management of water resources is the key to mitigating water scarcities in the future and avoiding further damage to aquatic ecosystems. In the short term, more efficient use of water could dramatically expand available resources. This is particularly true in the agricultural sector, where experience shows that drip irrigation systems routinely cut water use 30-70 per cent, while simultaneously increasing crop yields 20-90 per cent. Although the use of drip irrigation has grown more than 50-fold over the last 20 years, it is still used in only 1 per cent of the world's irrigated areas.

More efficient water technology alone will not be sufficient to fully address the looming water crisis. It will also require difficult policy choices that reallocate water to the most economically and socially beneficial use. This may mean diverting water from agriculture to commercial or household uses. In China, for example, planners estimate that a given amount of water used in industry generates more than 70 times more economic value than the same water used in agriculture.

To a certain extent, the transfer of water from low-value uses to higher-value uses is already well under way, especially where individuals hold legal water rights that they can sell to others. Farmers outside the city of Tirupur in southern India, for example, have begun to abandon farming so that they can sell their groundwater at a premium to water-hungry industries and urban users. Such 'water markets' are becoming more common in arid regions of the western United States and Australia.

An important key to using and allocating water more efficiently is phasing out subsidies and allowing water prices to reflect the true cost of supply. Price reforms in Chile reduced irrigation water use 22-26 per cent and saved $ 400 million in costs for developing new water supplies. In Bogor, Indonesia, price increases cut domestic consumption by 30 per cent. However, effective water pricing, particularly of irrigation water, remains a highly sensitive issue in low-income countries, where agriculture still dominates the economy and most farmers have limited incomes.

17

'Think Local' to Conserve Freshwater

WATER, covering 71 per cent of the Earth's surface, gives our planet its distinctive blue hue when seen from space. Yet for all that water, an astonishing small amount is available for human use. If we were to imagine all the Earth's water in a 1000-litre bucket filled to the brim, the fraction that is freshwater and not locked in ice is a mere 25 ml. Rough estimates place South America's share of that total at about half. Asia gets almost 6.25 ml, leaving the remainder—another 6.25 ml—for everyone living in North and Central America, Europe, Australia, Africa, and the Middle East.

The lion's share of the water we use goes to growing our food: irrigation siphons off roughly two-thirds of all the water we consume. Industrial and other economic activities draw somewhat less than a third. The trickle that is left—or about 5 per cent of the total—accounts for all common household uses, most of which are low quality uses, such as watering lawns and flushing toilets.

Over the past 70 years, human numbers have tripled but our thirst for water has surged six-fold. To keep pace, we have diverted rivers, tapped lakes, and pumped aquifers. Everywhere, the best and cheapest sources of water are now being used. In some regions, we are approaching the limits: in the Middle East, 58 per cent of all reasonably available fresh water is already being withdrawn. In Eastern Europe, the figure stands at 41 per cent. While strategies to increase water supply by desalinating seawater or by shipping large volumes by pipeline or sea are technically feasible, they will be neither cheap nor easy, and they will likely incur severe ecological and political costs.

Supply is only one part of the growing water crisis. For an increasing number of people, water quality is every bit as threatening. Population growth, industrialization, and urbanization are not only depleting lakes, rivers, and aquifers, they are polluting them as well.

Already more than 1 billion people lack access to safe drinking water; 3 billion lack access to basic sewerage systems. For millions, life-sustaining water is now a deadly menace. Water- and sanitation-related diseases will rob many more of their health and a productive future.

So what are the options? The answer is deceptively simple: we must manage our current supplies better. Past approaches, enthusiastically endorsed by development banks and agencies, favoured large-scale, capital-intensive projects. While they did deliver water to many households and many farms, most fell short of their original promise.

Thirty years of applied research supported by the International Development Research Centre (IDRC) offers a new focus for global efforts to curb water demand and alleviate poverty: community-based or local water management. It is at this level that the effects of water scarcity are most keenly felt and it is here that solutions must be implemented.

As the examples that follow demonstrate, some of the most powerful responses to water scarcity are already being mounted in households, farmers' fields, villages and city neighbourhoods across the developing world. If these efforts are to continue and to expand, local people will need ongoing support from their governments. In some cases, this will include delegating power to make decisions about which options to pursue and which techniques to employ.

Underscored in this chapter are some of the key lessons gleaned from IDRC's three decades of support for water-related research. They can serve as starting points or notions to consider in developing new community-based initiatives or in improving those currently under way.

Harvesting Rain

The history of rain harvesting is rich in technique and innovation. The Greeks, the Mayans, and island peoples around the world all developed ways of harvesting or holding back rain as it cascaded from their roofs or flowed across their fields. IDRC-supported researchers tapped into this broad base of traditional knowledge and used the tools of modern science to improve water-harvesting techniques and safeguard water quality.

In the crowded settlements of the Gaza Strip and the dusty villages of the Jordan Valley, for example, 'textbook' rooftop rainwater-collection systems were adapted to local circumstances.

The main technical hurdles were in keeping the water clean and engineering cost-effective storage. The principal obstacles to deploying the rooftop systems were partly organizational: inhabitants not only had to be shown how to build and maintain the systems, they also had to be convinced that the technology was effective and durable.

There was an economic hurdle as well: the ferro-cement holding tank—priced at US$ 200—was beyond the means of most households in the Gaza Strip. Two policy options presented themselves: a subsidy or alternative pricing scheme; or scaling-up to serve several families or a city block, thereby producing economies of scale and cutting unit costs. This second option also required some system of fair distribution and ongoing maintenance.

A benefit-cost analysis found rainwater harvesting to be economical where rainfall averages between 100 to 500 millimetres per year. More rain than that and costs exceed benefits; less, and benefits fail to cover costs.

Lesson

Scaling-up from households to villages or neighbourhoods is a common solution for improving the cost efficiency of traditional techniques. However, scaling-up requires capital or large tracts of land. These factors favour the well-to-do. Research and policies that fail to account for these unequal effects can make a difficult situation worse for the poor or disadvantaged.

Aquifer Protection and Recharge

In Mexico City, overpumping of the underlying aquifer has dropped the water table 20 metres in only 50 years. This situation is not unusual. Research in Latin America has shown that overuse and pollution are common threats to urban water supplies.

The same body of research also offers solutions: vigorous programmes of aquifer protection and recharge. Recharge techniques can be as simple as digging pits or trenches to gather rainy-season water, or as technically challenging as injecting clean water under pressure into fissures or fractures in the surrounding bedrock.

To protect aquifers, regulations are required to keep pumping rates below inflow rates. These should include measures to control competitive drilling, investment in ever-deeper wells, and careless dumping of wastes that all too often pollute groundwater stocks.

Putting proposed solutions into practice has proven difficult. The reasons, not fully understood, undoubtedly include the common practice of pricing water far below the cost of extraction and delivery. In most cases, far from benefiting ordinary people, such subsidies enrich the better-off. In developing countries as in industrialized ones, power politics and vested interests pay close attention to policies and regulations controlling access and use of water.

Lesson

Three decades of experience warn us to expect the worst when managing groundwater and aquifer supplies. But even when the outcomes of research are disappointing, it can still pay rich dividends. The discovery of fresh and basic information can open new opportunities to solve old problems.

Community-based Water Quality Monitoring

Developed-world approaches to ensuring the safety of drinking water rely on sophisticated tests carried out in expensive laboratories. Where these are duplicated in the South, they usually benefit citizens in the urban core and wealthier suburbs. In the mid-1980s, IDRC brought together a network of Southern and Northern researchers to develop low-cost, sensitive methods to test water for microbiological contaminants, such as faecal bacteria. The network proposed four methods suited to conditions in rural communities across the South: the hydrogen sulphide test, the presence-absence test, the A1 broth, and the coliphage test.

Field trials in Canada's north and in Chile proved the tests' effectiveness and ease of use by locally trained staff. Further efforts to broaden the scope of community-based water management activities to include remedial actions also pointed to the need for closer linkages between the communities, local institutions providing test supplies and technical advice, and state and national bodies charged with water supply and quality. Significantly, the Government of Chile is in the process of adapting its regulations and policies to include the hydrogen sulphide test as a standard procedure for monitoring drinking water quality in rural areas.

Lesson

Decision-makers frequently overlook small groups and simple solutions. Yet, seemingly humble innovations, such as check dams to slow the runoff from farmers' fields, can produce surprisingly powerful benefits that spread quickly through community networks.

Wastewater Recycling

Reusing wastewater is an obvious response to local water shortages. But recycled wastewater can pose a threat to public health, soil, and water if wastewater is not reused carefully. Because of the technical difficulty in safely treating 'black water' from toilets, much of the IDRC-supported research at the household and village level dealt with recycling 'grey water' from showers, kitchens and laundry facilities.

In the poorer communities surrounding the Senegalese capital of Dakar, researchers tested the technical and socioeconomic feasibility of exploiting aquatic plants, like water lettuce, to convert household wastewater into water fit for irrigating small market gardens. Results here, and from a similar project in Peru, found no significant health problems. Risks in consuming crops raised on recycled waste grey water, where measured, also appeared negligible.

In Cambodia's second largest city, Battambang, IDRC also supported an evaluation of an engineered wetland to treat all of the city's wastewater. Comparative economic analysis of small-scale grey water recycling systems and large-scale systems show many of the benefits in keeping things small.

From a cost viewpoint, large-scale systems, as with Battambang, will not pay for themselves. Selling the water (and fish) may cover the operational costs, but not capital costs. Smaller household and village grey water systems, on the other hand, can generate enough income to cover building and maintenance costs. The revenue gained from selling additional produce is often enough to encourage local participation. And where these systems replace septic tanks, households further save on the cost of pumping them out.

To operate effectively in the long-term, large-scale operations also require that governments develop means of allocating costs and revenues, encourage or oblige those used to disposing of wastewater for free to use the new system, and reform building codes or land-use regulations to permit and encourage wastewater recycling.

In small-scale systems, skills gained through training and in running the system stay in the community and with local authorities and nongovernmental organizations that frequently act as executing agencies. This capacity-building feature of small-scale systems frequently favours women, as they play leadership roles in financing, operating and managing both water treatment systems and market gardens.

Lesson

Social and economic factors are always important in local water management. Gender issues are particularly pertinent, as women bear the burden of providing water for domestic use. Changing water-management practices, even for the better, is rarely gender-neutral. Researchers and policymakers looking to improve water management ignore this aspect of programme or project implementation at their peril.

Watershed Management and Irrigation

Irrigation is vital to our survival. Some 40 per cent of all the food we eat is grown on irrigated land. But irrigated agriculture has not kept pace with population growth. Moreover, irrigated farmland is steadily removed from production because of soil salinity and contamination and because of urban encroachment. In the developing world, huge gains in water supply can be achieved simply by reducing the waste in irrigated agriculture. As much as 75 per-cent of water diverted or pumped on to fields is lost to evaporation, leakage, seepage, or just bad management. However, changes to irrigation practices must take into account two other factors. First, water in irrigation canals is used for more than growing crops. It is also used to raise fish, wash clothes, water animals, flush away wastes and, sadly, as drinking water. Conserving water for these uses would contribute to productivity and public health. Second, some of the water apparently lost to leakage and seepage goes back to groundwater and appears in the next field lower in the watercourse.

For these and other reasons, improving the management of watersheds and irrigation raises difficult issues of equity and efficiency. Large-scale irrigation is capital intensive and so favours those with money and influence. For poor farmers, remote communities, and indigenous communities, securing a say in such arrangements is often difficult. In arid and semi-arid regions, these communities rely upon surface water sources, often seasonal; groundwater, often from hand-dug wells; or a combination of both. The local environment has shaped water-management practices for centuries, so that many of these communities are experts in dealing with water scarcity. On India's Deccan Plateau, for example, researchers relied on local expertise to help the tribal people of the Akole Taluka region improve their crop yields and their year-round access to water. The strategies put in place to improve the water supply were simple. Gullies were plugged and water was diverted, thus slowing down runoff and reducing erosion. Water pooled and seeped into the soil. This increased crop yields and served to replenish groundwater supplies.

Later, rooftop harvesting and storage tanks were built, filled first by rains each year and later, in the dry season, by bullock-cart deliveries. The outcome: healthier people; higher food production; rising incomes; stocks of water that last virtually all year. And villagers are embracing the new strategies.

Lesson

Scarcity forces trade-offs. To determine fairly who gets what, when and for how much requires institutional capacity. That is the ability to gather and assess information, to deliberate, to execute policies and to answer responsibly to community members. Building this capacity is necessary for local water management and for other sustainable resource-management decisions.

A Path Forward

The merits of local water management speak for themselves in the examples shown here and in research conducted across the developing world. Approaches that engage local users in water management are simply more efficient, more effective, more equitable, and more environmentally sustainable than the usual top-down practices. They are not panaceas, but must complement wider reaching water-management approaches. Local water management, however, does offer an immediate path forward in divining solutions to growing water scarcity.

Building the Foundation for Success

Community-based water management strategies can play a critical role in solving water scarcity problems. The following elements should be considered in developing any new local water-management initiatives or in improving current programmes.

Up, down, and sideways, get the big picture with a three-part economic analysis.

Benefit-cost analysis is a top-down approach for determining whether using a particular technique or technology makes economic sense. While this can be revealing, it fails to identify why local communities choose not to adopt promising research. A bottom-up analysis, looking at the community level, will often reveal the value individuals or communities place on a particular solution. It should also reveal how women and men will be affected differently. A sideways perspective examines how economic and non-economic values interact. Non-economic values, such as maternal-health benefits from having more clean water or the gains from a healthy ecosystem, are difficult to measure, but should be included nevertheless. Together, these three elements provide a complete economic analysis of local water management.

Accept social custom and cultural norms as a given, but not sacrosanct.

Traditional practices and local knowledge are not static collections of beliefs and practices. But they will change only when people see the value in change. The role of research is to convince people of the need for change, then design and test remedies that are socially and culturally acceptable, and that fit well with local tradition. It is as wrong to romanticize tradition as it is to exalt science.

Conduct evaluation that is transparent, participatory, and continuous.

The key to deciding how well a particular solution works is to monitor it over time. Yet taking time to conduct a thorough evaluation is frequently neglected. This is dangerous, wasteful, and undemocratic. Dangerous because it can allow problems to accumulate or go undetected. Wasteful because costs and benefits go untallied. Undemocratic because evaluation is a central element to transparency and accountability.

Include water rights in any analysis.

In rural areas and in developing countries tradition often rules access to water. Having a 'right to water,' however, does necessarily determine who gets what, when, and for what purpose. When water is scarce, for example, women will typically demand a greater share for household uses whereas men will want to use as much as possible for cash crops. Whatever the local situation, the management of water rights is a crucial element of policy-making.

Appendix I

UN-Water: Coping with Water Scarcity

UN-Water is the mechanism coordinating the actions of the United Nations (UN) system aimed at implementing the agenda set by the Millennium Declaration and the World Summit on Sustainable Development (WSSD) in all aspects related to freshwater. UN-Water has grown out of many years of extensive collaboration and partnership among the UN agencies.

These efforts have helped to achieve significant progress and to bring water and water-related issues to the top of the political agenda. Advancing the implementation of this complex and ambitious international agenda is a collective responsibility and challenge. It calls for coordinated action within the UN system and with other partners and stakeholders – including organizations from the public and private sectors, civil society and labour – as part of a global, comprehensive effort.

The main purpose of UN-Water is to complement and add value to existing programmes and projects by facilitating synergies and joint efforts in order to maximize coordinated action, coherence and the effectiveness of the support provided to countries pursuing the goals agreed upon by the international community. This is in line with the integrated water resources management (IWRM) approach, which calls for collaboration among all stakeholders in water management.

UN-Water has identified coping with water scarcity as part of the strategic issues and priorities requiring joint action. This note presents the UN-Water joint plan of action (PoA) for this thematic initiative and describes its elements.

A strategic issue and priority for system-wide action is essential for all socio-economic development and for maintaining healthy ecosystems. As the population increases and development calls for increased allocations of groundwater and surface water for the domestic, agriculture and industrial sectors, the pressure on water resources intensifies, leading to tensions, conflicts among users, and excessive pressure on the environment. The increasing stress on freshwater resources brought about by ever rising demand and profligate use, as well as by growing pollution worldwide, is of serious concern.

There are several ways of defining water scarcity. The definition used in framing this programme refers to water scarcity as 'the point at which the aggregate impact of all users impinges on the supply or quality of water under prevailing institutional arrangements to the extent that the demand by all sectors, including the environment, cannot be satisfied fully'.

Water scarcity is a relative concept and can occur at any level of supply or demand. Scarcity may be a social construct (a product of affluence, expectations and customary behaviour) or the consequence of altered supply patterns stemming from climate change. Scarcity has various causes, most of which are capable of being remedied or alleviated. A society facing water scarcity usually has options.

However, scarcity often has its roots in water shortage and it is in the arid and semi-arid regions affected by droughts and wide climate variability, combined with population growth and economic development, that the problems of water scarcity are most acute. Water use has been growing at more than twice the rate of population increase in the last century, and, although there is no global water scarcity as such, an increasing number of regions are chronically short of water.

By 2025, 1,800 million people will be living in countries or regions with absolute water scarcity, and two-thirds of the world population could be under stress conditions. The situation will be exacerbated as rapidly growing urban areas place heavy pressure on neighbouring water resources. Most countries in the Near East and North Africa suffer from acute water scarcity, as do countries such as Mexico, Pakistan, South Africa, and large parts of China and India. Irrigated agriculture, which represents the bulk of the demand for water in these countries, is also usually the first sector affected by water shortage and increased scarcity, resulting in a decreased capacity to maintain per capita food production while meeting water needs for domestic, industrial and environmental purposes.

In order to sustain their needs, these countries need to focus on the efficient use of all water sources (groundwater, surface water and rainfall) and on water allocation strategies that maximize the economic and social returns to limited water resources and at the same time enhance the water productivity of all sectors.

In this endeavour, there needs to be a special focus on issues relating to equity in access to water and on the social impacts of water allocation policies. Imbalances between availability and demand, the degradation of groundwater and surface water quality, inter-sectoral competition, inter-regional and international conflicts, all bring water issues to the fore.

Freshwater bodies have a limited capacity to process the pollutant charges of the effluents from expanding urban, industrial and agricultural uses. Water quality degradation can be a major cause of water scarcity.

In most countries, the agriculture sector is the predominant consumer of water. Historically, large-scale water development projects have played a major role in poverty alleviation by providing food security, protection from flooding and drought, and expanded opportunities for employment. In many cases, irrigated agriculture has been a major engine for economic growth and poverty reduction.

However, at the same time, poor communities have tended to suffer the greatest health burden from inadequate water supplies and, as a result of poor health, have been unable to escape from the cycle of poverty and disease. Thus, growing scarcity and competition for water stand as a major threat to future advances in poverty alleviation, especially in rural areas.

In semi-arid regions, increasing numbers of the rural poor are coming to see entitlement and access to water for food production, livestock and domestic purposes as more critical than access to primary health care and education.

Rainwater is the primary source of water in agriculture. It has also been used successfully to augment water for industrial and domestic purposes, while being an essential element in the functioning of natural ecosystems.

However, rainwater is rarely integrated into water management strategies, which usually focus exclusively on surface water and groundwater. Countries need to integrate rainwater harvesting more fully into their IWRM strategies and to promote its use to alleviate water scarcity.

In this context of rapid change, a number of questions arise:

- How are the many competing interests involved in water being balanced? On what basis are decisions to be made in favour of certain developments at the expense of others?
- What are the scope and conditions for increasing water productivity in different sectors?
- Which tools should be used to enable the more efficient and equitable development and allocation of water?
- How can the best use be made of the water available?
- Which measures should be put in place to protect water resources and increase water supply?
- Which institutional and legal set-ups are the most appropriate for ensuring adequate coordination?
- What kind of information is needed and how is wide public ownership of water-related problems to be ensured?

In conditions of water scarcity, putting in place effective and equitable management practices requires knowledge, expertise and investment at political, institutional and technical levels. Water development is linked closely to poverty reduction, especially in low-income countries that are highly dependent on a rural economy.

In arid and semi-arid regions, where water scarcity is almost endemic, groundwater has played a major role in meeting domestic and irrigation demands. In many regions, massive use of groundwater has been practised for some time for irrigation. Groundwater mining and the lack of adequate planning, legal frameworks and governance have opened a new debate on the sustainability of the intensive use of groundwater resources.

Water conflicts can arise in water stressed areas among local communities and between countries because sharing a very limited and essential resource is extremely difficult. The lack of adequate legal instruments exacerbates already difficult conditions. There should be a greater focus on the peaceful sharing and management of water at both international and local levels. In short, water scarcity is also about equity and rights, and cultural and ethical issues warrant due consideration.

Water scarcity affects all social and economic sectors and threatens the sustainability of the natural resources base. Addressing water scarcity calls for an inter-sectoral and multidisciplinary approach to water resources management, one that ensures the coordinated development and management of water and related resources in order to maximize economic and social welfare in an equitable manner without compromising the sustainability of vital ecosystems.

Integration across sectors is needed. This integration needs to take into account development, supply, use and demand and to place the emphasis on people and the ecosystems that sustain them. On the demand side, enhancing the productivity of water use in all sectors is paramount to successful programmes of water scarcity alleviation.

Furthermore, protecting and restoring the ecosystems that naturally capture, filter, store and release water, such as rivers, wetlands, forests and soils, is crucial to increasing the availability of water of good quality. Addressing water scarcity requires actions at local, national and river basin levels.

It also calls for actions at global and international levels, leading to increased collaboration between nations on shared management of water resources (rivers, lakes and aquifers) and of the benefits thereof. Being inter-sectoral in its nature, the UN-system response to water scarcity requires collaboration; the sharing of joint visions and policy principles; and joint action in assisting countries to address the issue.

A major challenge in addressing water scarcity in countries successfully is the institutional fragmentation of responsibilities in the water development sector.

Water scarcity issues and the way they are addressed will affect the successful achievement of most of the Millennium Development Goals. The eradication of poverty and hunger in rural areas is related closely to fair and equitable access for the most vulnerable people to basic livelihood assets (including land and water) for domestic and productive uses. Because increased demand usually threatens the sustainability of the environment in situations of scarcity, water scarcity management is also crucial to achieving the goals of environmental sustainability.

Water scarcity is also linked closely to the five key areas for action identified by the UN Secretary General on the occasion of the WSSD: water, energy, health, agriculture and biodiversity.

Last, it also has an impact on all the issues identified in the WSSD Johannesburg Plan of Implementation and, in particular, on poverty eradication; changing unsustainable consumption and production patterns; and protecting and managing the natural resources base of economic and social development.

Coping with water scarcity can achieve:

- Eradication of extreme poverty and hunger.
- Achievement of universal primary education.
- Promotion of gender equality and empowering women.
- Reduction of child mortality and improvement of maternal health.
- Promotion of global partnerships.
- Ensuring environmental sustainability.
- Combating HIV/AIDS, malaria and other diseases.

Water scarcity increasingly calls for reinforced international cooperation in the fields of technologies for enhanced water productivity, financing opportunities, and an improved environment to share the benefits of scarce water management.

—Extracted from the document *UN-Water*

Appendix II

4th World Water Forum

MINISTERIAL DECLARATION

We, the Ministers assembled in Mexico City on the occasion of the Fourth World Water Forum, 'Local Actions for a Global Challenge' on March 21st and 22nd, 2006,

1. Reaffirm the critical importance of water, in particular freshwater, for all aspects on sustainable development, including poverty and hunger eradication, water-related disaster reduction, health, agricultural and rural development, hydropower, food security, gender equality as well as the achievement of environmental sustainability and protection. We underline the need to include water and sanitation as priorities in national processes, in particular national sustainable development and poverty reduction strategies.

2 Reaffirm our commitment to achieve the internationally agreed goals on integrated water resources management (IWRM), access to safe drinking water and basic sanitation, agreed upon in Agenda 21, the Millennium Declaration and the Johannesburg Plan of Implementation (JPOI). We reiterate the continued and urgent need to achieve these goals and to keep track of progress towards their implementation, including the goal to reduce by half, by the year 2015, the proportion of people unable to reach or afford safe drinking water.

3. Reaffirm, in particular, our commitment to the decisions adopted by the 13th session of the United Nations Commission on Sustainable Development (CSD-13), in April 2005, on policy options and practical measures to expedite implementation in water, sanitation and human

settlements. We note with interest the importance of enhancing the sustainability of ecosystems and acknowledge the implementation and importance in some regions of innovative practices such as rain water management and the development of hydropower projects.

Further reaffirm the importance of the involvement of relevant stakeholders, particularly women and youth, in the planning and management of water services and, as appropriate, decision-making processes.

4. Take note of the Ministerial Declaration of the Third World Water Forum and recognize the work done within the UN System in support of member States, in order to reach the aforementioned goals. In this regard, we support the coordinating role of UN–Water and highlight the need to strengthen its work within its mandate among the relevant UN organizations, funds and programmes.

   We appreciate the inputs from the UN Secretary General's Advisory Board on Water and Sanitation to reinforce ongoing implementation efforts towards reaching water and sanitation targets.

   We express our continued support to initiatives like the Water for Life Decade and our interest in the United Nations Secretary General's WEHAB Initiative.

5. Recognize the contributions of the 4th WWF and its preparatory regional process to building capacity at international, regional and national levels and promoting the exchange of best practices and lessons learned on international water and sanitation issues.

6. Acknowledge the input of the Forum for the follow up segment on water and sanitation of the 16th Session of the CSD, to be held in 2008 which will play an important role to monitor and follow-up decisions on water and sanitation and their inter-linkages taken at CSD-13, and as an example of coordinated participation and involvement of governments at all levels, civil society, intergovernmental organizations, non-governmental organizations, private sector, scientific institutions, partnerships, and international financial institutions regarding water issues and other relevant stakeholders.

7. Reaffirm also the decision of the 13th Session of the Commission of Sustainable Development regarding, inter alia:

   (a) that a substantial increase of resources from all sources, including domestic resources, official development assistance and other resources will be required if developing countries are to achieve the internationally agreed development goals and targets, including those contained in the Millennium Declaration and the JPOI, and

(b) that Governments have the primary role in promoting improved access to safe drinking water, basic sanitation, sustainable and secure tenure, and adequate shelter, through improved governance at all levels and appropriate enabling environments and regulatory frameworks, adopting a pro-poor approach and with the active involvement of all stakeholders.

8. Recognize the importance of domestic and international policies that foster and assist building capacities and cooperation at all levels to mitigate water-related disasters including prevention, preparedness, risk assessment, community awareness, resilience and response.

9. Recognize the important role that parliamentarians and local authorities are playing in various countries to increase sustainable access to water and sanitation services as well as to support integrated water resource management.

   An efficient collaboration with and between these actors is a key factor to meet our water-related challenges and goals.

10. Note with appreciation the work of stakeholders at the regional preparatory process towards the 4th WWF as well as during the Forum itself, and take note of the documental output of the said regional preparatory stakeholder process.

    As appropriate, this output can be used as a source of information for our tasks.

    We also thank participating parliamentarians and local authorities for their valuable views and opinions expressed during our joint working session at the Fourth World Water Forum, and take note of their statements.

11. Welcome the launch at the 4th WWF of the CSD Water Action and Networking Database (CSD WAND), as a means of implementing the decision from CSD-13 to develop 'web-based tools to disseminate information on implementation and best practices' on water and sanitation. The CSD-WAND will serve as a platform for exchanging information and best practices, lessons learned and relevant international agreements and policy recommendations. We note that the CSD WAND has been built upon information collected during the 2003–05 CSD Cycle, in the Portfolio of Water Actions—as an output of the Ministerial Conference of the Third World Water Forum, and in the database of local actions of the 4th WWF.

12. Encourage all stakeholders, including national and international agencies, and other international and regional fora, such as World Water Week in Stockholm and the water weeks of the regional development banks, to contribute to and exchange information through the WAND.

13. Thank the Government of Mexico and the World Water Council for the organization of the 4th WWF and for their determination to promote better water management through dynamic local actions for a global change.

Mexico City, March 22, 2006.

Appendix III

Water Briefs

1. The Coastal Connection

WORLDWIDE, population is concentrated along or near coasts and river valleys occupying just 10 per cent of the earth's land area. Human activities in coastal areas are in the process of annihilating coastal and ocean ecosystems and the wealth of biodiversity that they harbour.

Around the world, people cluster near coasts. Over half of the world's population—about 3.2 billion—occupy a coastal zone 200 kilometres wide. With the exception of India, most of Asia's population is coastal.

In China, for example, close to 60 per cent of the population of 1.2 billion live in 12 coastal provinces, along the Yangtze River valley, and in two coastal municipalities—Shanghai and Tianjin.

Along China's 18,000 kilometres of continental coastline, population densities average between 110 and 1,600 people per square kilometre.

The population of Latin America and the Caribbean is even more coastal. Among the region's coastal countries, with a total population of around 610 million, a full three-quarters of the population lives within 200 kilometres of the seacoast.

Only in Africa do more people live in the interior of the continent than along or near coastlines. Over the past two decades, however, Africa's coastal cities—centres of trade and commerce—have been growing by 4 per cent a year or more, as millions of people migrate from the interior.

Accra, Abidjan, Dakar, Dar-es-Salaam, Lagos and other coastal cities have seen their populations soar from inward migration.

In recognition of rapid population growth and increasing water pollution, representatives of Africa's 38 maritime countries met in July 1998 in Maputo, Mozambique, to consider ways to 'protect, manage, and value' the continent's coastal environment in the face of limited resources, poor sanitation, and development needs.

Environmental Consequences

Population growth, urbanization and industrialization with little regard for the environment are polluting and depleting coastal and ocean resources. Consider the following trends:

- The world has lost half its coastal wetlands, including mangrove swamps and salt marshes. Over the past century, mangrove forests have been decimated. An estimated 25 million hectares have been destroyed or grossly degraded.
- In virtually all inhabited coastal areas, sea-grass beds, vital as fish nurseries and feeding areas, are diminishing.
- Coral reefs, the rainforests of the sea, are being pillaged in the name of development. Of the world's 600,000 square kilometres of reefs found in tropical and sub-tropical seas, 70 per cent could be lost within 40 years.
- Coastal and ocean fisheries are in serious decline. According to the UN Food and Agriculture Organization (FAO), in 1995 nearly 70 per cent of the world's marine fish stocks were either fully-to-heavily exploited, overexploited, depleted, or slowly recovering.
- As coastal waters become clogged with raw sewage and agricultural and industrial pollutants, ecosystems begin to unravel.

Links to Freshwater

When human activities damage freshwater ecosystems, they ultimately damage the salt water environment as well. Oceans are connected to the land through a complex network of rivers, streams and lakes that comprise watersheds. Managing freshwater resources better will help protect the world's coastal waters. Protecting the coastal environment, rather than treating oceans and seas as garbage dumps, would help avoid a possible ecological disaster in the future.

2. Wars over Water?

Conflicts over water—both political and violent—could erupt in coming decades as more countries, with larger and larger populations, face water stress and outright water scarcity, according to Peter Gleick of the Pacific Institute for Studies in Development, Environment and Security. To Gleick, the potential for conflict is 'symptomatic of our inability in general to manage limited supplies of freshwater on a sustainable basis'.

In particular, problems could erupt in a number of areas where freshwater use has already reached or even exceeded natural limits. In these areas, mostly in North Africa and the Near East, countries not only face mounting internal competition for limited supplies of freshwater as a result of rapid population growth and escalating demand, but also find themselves squabbling with their neighbours over water rights. For example:

- Water has been at the centre of a continuing controversy between Israel and Jordan. In May 1997, a ceremony to create a joint 'peace park' on the site where seven Israeli schoolgirls were killed by a Jordanian border guard was cancelled after Jordan charged Israel with delaying implementation of a water agreement in the Jordan-Israeli Peace Treaty of 1994. Under the treaty, Jordan was to receive an additional 50 million cubic metres of water a year from Israel, mostly from the Yarmuk River, one of the River Jordan's main tributaries. The treaty did not state who would pay for the water and its transportation, however. Since the May 1997 'peace park' crisis, Israel has offered to foot half the bill, and the Israeli cabinet has approved a plan to supply Jordan with 50 million cubic metres of water, constituting the second transfer under the treaty.
- Israel already has used its military power to maintain access to the Jordan River. In the early 1960s, Israeli soldiers halted a Syrian-Jordanian scheme to divert the river for irrigation. Later, Israel occupied vital sections of the Jordan River's headwaters, thus making sure that most of its flow would be available for Israeli towns and farms.
- Egypt has threatened Ethiopia with war if it carries out plans to divert more water from the Blue Nile for agricultural use. The Egyptian government sees this issue as one of life or death. Without the Nile's nourishing waters, Egypt could not exist as a nation, since it depends on the Nile for 98 per cent of its freshwater needs.
- The Southeast Anatolia Project in Turkey is one of the largest irrigation and power generation schemes in the Near East. This vast complex of dams, canals and irrigation systems began operating in July 1992. By the early decades of the 21st century it was expected to divert at

least half of the flow of the Euphrates River—some 4 trillion gallons of water a year—into Turkish dams and irrigation canals. This diversion would leave the downstream countries, Syria and Iraq, with less than half of the stable flow they had access to. Syria is also planning to take some 3.5 trillion gallons out of the Euphrates before it enters Iraq, thus depriving Iraqi farmers of badly needed irrigation water—water that people in the area have had access to for the past 6,000 years. The entire region is set for a potentially ruinous conflict over limited water resources.

3. Successful Watershed Management

Watershed management is complicated and can be contentious because watershed boundaries do not coincide with those of political or administrative jurisdictions. Thus, management involves many levels of government and many different communities, each with its own constituencies and concerns. Balancing the multitude of interests involved is so time consuming and troublesome that watershed management rarely succeeds.

It can be done, however, as shown by the example of the Chesapeake Bay, North America's largest brackish water estuary. Managing the Chesapeake watershed presents unique and seemingly insurmountable obstacles. Although the Bay itself covers only 2,200 square miles (5,500 square kilometres) and averages just 21 feet deep (6.5 metres), its watershed is vast, sprawling over 64,000 square miles (160,000 square kilometres) through six U.S. states. Moreover, 15 million people live in the watershed, which is one of the most heavily populated areas on the East Coast.

By the early 1980s, planners were confronted with the consequences of decades of accumulated abuse of water resources in the Chesapeake watershed. Signs of decay were everywhere:

- By 1987, the Bay was receiving about 184,000 metric tons of nitrogen and 74,000 metric tons of phosphorus a year from human and animal wastes and commercial fertilizers.
- The Bay had lost more than half of its natural tidal and non-tidal wetlands and 40 per cent of its watershed forests.
- Sea-grass beds, which once covered over half the Bay's bottom, amounting to several hundred thousand acres, had been reduced to no more than 34,000 acres (14,000 hectares) by 1984—10 to 20 per cent of their original area.

- Chronic over-harvesting, along with mounting pollution and habitat degradation, contributed to the dramatic decline in the Bay's fish and shellfish populations. Commercial catches of rockfish (striped bass) dropped from 2,608 metric tons in 1970 to just 272 metric tons in 1983. The Bay's oyster fishery had plunged catastrophically. From an all-time peak of 20 million bushels in 1884, the oyster harvest declined to just 168,000 bushels in 1992.

A handful of local environmentalists launched the initiative to save the Bay in the late 1960s. At that time, few people anticipated their efforts would blossom into a six-state, watershed-wide programme to restore the Chesapeake. Eventually, the effort would become a multimillion dollar restoration that would involve local, state and federal agencies and tens of thousands of people from all walks of life.

A non-profit membership organization, the Chesapeake Bay Foundation, was one of the key groups urging state governments to take a comprehensive watershed approach to the Bay's environmental problems. After a slow start in the early 1980s, the three key state governments—Maryland, Virginia and Pennsylvania—with help from the U.S. Environmental Protection Agency (EPA), agreed to launch an ambitious, integrated clean-up programme.

In 1987, when the EPA and the governors of the three main watershed states met at a major strategy conference, nothing on this scale had ever been attempted before in the U.S.A. The result was the Chesapeake Bay Agreement between the states and the federal government. The agreement provided solid political commitment from all watershed states for a 40 per cent reduction in nutrient loadings to the Bay by the year 2000, using 1985 as the base year.

"The year 2000 goal is a permanent cap on emissions of nitrogen and phosphorus," explained William Matuszeski, Director of EPA's Chesapeake Bay Programme in Annapolis, Maryland. It is, in essence, a non-degradation policy for the entire watershed, in which each major tributary of the Chesapeake will reduce nutrient pollution by 40 per cent.

In order to meet such an ambitious target, each state crafted its own pollution reduction strategy, working within the terms of the overall agreement. The Pennsylvania legislature even passed the first nutrient management law in U.S. history. Although neither Maryland nor Virginia took binding legislative steps, both states have encouraged farmers in the Chesapeake watershed to adopt 'best management practices,' which involve low-till or no-till agriculture, along with the reduced use of pesticides and a marked reduction in the application of chemical fertilizers, one of the main sources of nutrient pollution to the Bay.

The watershed states have made progress in reducing point sources of pollution—effluent from sewage treatment plants and industrial complexes. Maryland, Virginia, Pennsylvania, and the District of Columbia also have passed legislation to ban the use of phosphate detergents. These actions reduced phosphorus pollution to the Bay by 40 per cent.

"The main improvement," states Matuszeski, "is that we have halted the increase in nitrogen pollution to the Bay in spite of a growing population." This has been the result of building three-stage sewage treatment plants around the Bay and decreasing the amount of animal manure and fertilizers seeping into the region's surface waters.

According to the EPA, many farmers in Maryland, Pennsylvania, and Virginia have cut fertilizer use dramatically and some farmers use no commercial fertilizers at all, relying instead on animal manure and crop residues. The use of pesticides has dropped 20 per cent since 1985. The Bay is not free of problems, as evidenced by the 1997 outbreak of the toxic organism *Pfiesteria piscicida*, which kills marine life and degrades water quality. Still, Matuszeski thinks that progress in meeting watershed management goals will be faster "once we can get natural ecosystems to start working for us, like wetlands and sea-grasses." Progress has been slower than expected, but most trends are in the right direction.

Appendix IV

Price of Squandered Resources

Stockholm: As much as half the water used to grow food worldwide is lost due to wastage, experts said at a Stockholm conference, pointing out that the squandered resources are a major contributor to global water shortages.

"There is huge waste and loss of water through food that is produced, since roughly 50 per cent of the food that farmers grow is lost or wasted," said Jan Lundqvist, who heads the scientific programme at the Stockholm International Water Institute (SIWI). "There is a need for a mentality shift.... It would make a lot of sense for people to waste less."

According to SIWI, which hosted the annual World Water Week in the Swedish capital, tremendous amounts of food, and thus water, are discarded in the fields, during processing, in transport, in supermarkets, restaurants and in people's kitchens. In a new report on saving water the institute points out that in the United States, 30 per cent of food, worth $ 48.3 billion, is thrown away each year. "That corresponds to 40 trillion litres of irrigation water, enough water to meet the household needs of 500 million people," said the report, entitled *Saving Water: from Field to Folk – Curbing Losses and Wastage in the Food Chain.*

Societal Context

Food wastage depended largely on the society in which it was grown and consumed. In poor countries, most food was lost in the fields or due to lack of storage and cooling systems or poor transport mechanisms.

"In many areas of the world you simply cannot store food efficiently, because it is not handled well," said SIWI project director Jacob Granite.

In richer societies, most waste happened at the consumer level, while changing diets and an increased appetite for water-intensive foods like dairy products and meat, especially beef, in these regions amplified the water drainage according to experts.

"In urban settings, we have lost touch with realities. People do not know where food comes from, they do not know what it takes to produce food," Mr. Lundqvist said, pointing out that it takes between 10 and 15 tonnes of water to produce a single kilogram of beef. "Now, if you throw away half of that kilo that means you have thrown away 7.5 tonnes of water."

As the world struggles to feed and provide water to growing populations, it was essential that governments strived to reduce the amount of food wasted by at least 50 per cent by 2025, according to the SIWI report. "Unless we change our practices, water will be a key constraint to food production in the future," Pasquale Statute of the Food and Agriculture Organisation's Water Resources, Development and Management Service said in a statement.

For change to happen, economic incentives were essential, according to Mr. Granite. "The key incentive to make change is the price," he said, pointing out that in Sweden the consumption of beef had recently "gone down by 30 per cent because the price went up."

And in Kuwait, where water remained a free commodity, each person on average used 600 litres of water a day while in water-rich Sweden the average was just 150 litres, he said.

"We pay a price here for water that is not very high, but we also couple that with education and awareness so people know there is a cost to the environment to use that water," Mr. Granite said.

According to Mr. Lundqvist, today's massive food waste actually has a silver lining. "It means there is a huge potential for improvement," he said.—AFP (August 23, 2008).

Appendix V

Global Water Crisis

(***Mikhail Gorbachev's*** *essay written in 2000 was a prophetic warning of what the world is experiencing today. The solutions he suggested eight years ago are now finding favour with water technologists and governments*).

Water, like religion and ideology, has the power to move millions of people. Since the very birth of human civilization, people have moved to settle close to water. People move when there is too little of it. People move when there is too much of it. People journey down it. People write and sing and dance and dream about it. People fight over it. And all people, everywhere and every day, need it.

We need it for drinking, for cooking, for washing, for food, for industry, for energy, for transport, for rituals, for fun, for life. And it is not only we humans who need it; all life is dependent on water to survive.

But we stand today on the brink of a global water crisis. The two major legacies of the 20th century—the population and technological explosions—have taken their toll on our water supply. More people lack drinking water today than they did two decades ago. More and more freshwater sources are being used-up and contaminated. Modern technologies have allowed us to harness much of the world's water for energy, industry and irrigation—but often at a terrible social and environmental price—and many traditional water conservation practices have been discarded along the way.

Most of the solutions to the crisis must be developed and implemented locally, and always with the view that water is not to be taken for granted, or unjustly appropriated by particular groups for particular needs. Water is the most important single element needed in order for people to achieve the universal human right to 'a standard of living adequate for the health and well-being of himself and his family' (Article 25, Universal Declaration of Human Rights).

Without access to clean water, health and well-being are not only severely jeopardized, they are impossible: people without basic water supplies live greatly reduced and impoverished lives—with little opportunity to create better futures for their children.

Let us acknowledge that clean water is a universal human right, and in so doing accept that we have the corresponding universal responsibility to ensure that the forecast of a world where, in 25 years' time, two out of every three persons face water-stress is proven wrong. In this issue, United Nations' Secretary General Kofi Annan asks us to face up to the threat of a catastrophic water crisis and counter such bleak forecasts by adopting a new spirit of stewardship. To do otherwise would be nothing less than a crime and history will rightly judge current generations harshly for it.

The world's growing population should be seen not only as one of the causes of the water crisis, but also as the source of its solution as is stressed by former President of the Philippines, Fidel Ramos, using the example of the enormous potential of people-power in South East Asia. Human solidarity is the only force capable of facing a task of this magnitude. There must be solidarity in international and regional governance; there must be solidarity between sectors and stakeholders; and there must be political will amongst governments to work in good faith both with their neighbours and with their own people. These people, including often marginalized groups such as women and minorities, must have a voice, and the information and means necessary to use it.

Without water security, social, economic and national stability are imperilled. This is magnified where water flows across borders—and becomes crucial in regions of religious, territorial or ethnic tension. In some cases, as between India and Pakistan over the Indus River, successful cooperation over water resources can be cited as proof that even states with difficult relations can work together. In other cases, the opportunities to improve regional relations which a common watercourse presents have not yet been grasped. The Jordan Valley, shared by the people of Israel, Palestine, Jordan, Syria and Lebanon, is one such example.

Water has been a fundamental security matter in the arid Middle East since antiquity. The allocation, use and rights to the increasingly scarce water resources of this volatile region remain sensitive, and potentially explosive, issues. Water is also largely sidelined, or hidden, in the mainstream peace negotiations. Hanan Sher of *The Jerusalem Post* sheds light on the trials and tribulations encountered on the road towards achieving water for peace in the Middle East, a road which I myself have recently revisited. Earlier this year I met with Prime Minister Barak, Chairman Arafat and King Abdullah of Jordan, and obtained their commitment to work with my organization, Green Cross International, and our partners, the Centre for Middle East Peace and Economic Cooperation, to find solutions to the escalating regional water crisis.

These three leaders explicitly recognized that there can be no unilateral solutions to their essentially trans-boundary water problems. This is as true in the Middle East as it is regarding watercourses shared between the United States and its neighbours. In all of the world's 261 international basins, joint management should be built on a system of effective interdependence; a pooling rather than a restriction of each nation's sovereignty.

While armed, inter-state conflicts over water are unlikely, it must be remembered that these are not the only types of conflicts facing water-stressed societies. Internal conflicts between ethnic groups, regions, users and small communities can and do arise over water. Inter-state cooperation is essential to the search for regional water solutions. Where such solutions are not easily forthcoming, international mediation and support should be available. A movement to provide such support has been initiated by Secretary of State Madeleine Albright with the establishment of a Global Alliance for Water Security.

In most cases, however, the practical solutions required are local, reflecting the geographically and culturally specific nature of water-use. The Cold War era of 'the bigger the better', which prompted the construction of 45,000 large dams throughout the world, is over. This thoughtless tampering with nature has left a terrible legacy, not least in my own region where thousands of acres of fertile land have been lost, and man-made catastrophes such as in the Aral Sea region cause immeasurable suffering. The articles provided by Kader Asmal of the World Commission on Dams, and water expert Anil Agarwal, seek the path to a new era where social and environmental considerations are given precedence and the benefits of large constructs like dams are questioned. The United States, the second most 'dammed' nation, after China, is already breaching many of its dams; elsewhere, particularly in the developing world, the question is how to provide the services supplied by dam projects through other initiatives, like rainwater harvesting and demand management.

At the heart of the matter is the value which we assign to different uses of water. Again, there is no universal blueprint, but it is clear that neither of the two extreme stances, one advocating that water should be free for all, and the other promoting full cost pricing for all water supplies, are desirable. We must remember that the value and the price of water are two very different things; it is a substance which must be used efficiently, but must be available for the sustenance of all—including natural ecosystems. This makes the pricing of water a tricky business, as we gather further from World Commission on Water Chairman, Ismail Serageldin, and Douglas B. MacDonald's insights on the subject.

Thus, we are faced with a mighty challenge. Fortunately, we have a history of meeting great challenges using imagination and our irrepressible capacity to adapt. To ensure that we journey in the right direction, we must allow our knowledge, experience and institutions to catch up with the overwhelming progress of science and technology, and learn how to become both good neighbours for each other and good guests of the natural environment.

Just as we are moved by water, we must move quickly in order to save it.

Appendix VI

Water: Hot Investment Commodity?

YOU are reluctant to invest in oil since it doubled over the past year and you fear you have missed the boat with agricultural commodities after their 38 per cent gain, especially now that governments are talking about cracking down on biofuels. So what will be the next hot commodity?

Goldman Sachs, the investment bank that coined the term 'Bric' (Brazil, Russia, India and China) and was talking about $ 100 oil when everyone else was stuck at $ 40, thinks it has found the answer: water.

It has called the commodity the 'petroleum for the next century' and says it has been grossly undervalued for years. The story behind it is the same for every other commodity: demand is soaring while supply is tight.

In the United States, water demand has tripled in the past 30 years, while the population has grown just 50 per cent. Globally, water consumption is doubling every 20 years, more than twice population growth.

Expert View

> "The 'petroleum for the next century' has been grossly undervalued for years: demand is soaring while supply is tight."
>
> —Kathryn Cooper

Factor in the explosive growth in China, which has 21 per cent of the world's population, but only 7 per cent of its water supply, and you have a problem. As the Chinese get richer and eat more meat, the problem is going to get worse: it takes 15 cubic metres of water to produce 1 kg of beef, compared with just 1.5 cubic metres for corn. Given current trends, it is estimated that by 2025 about a third of the world will not have access to adequate drinking water.

On the flip side, supply is fixed. Only 2.5 per cent of all water is fit for human consumption and around two-thirds of that is locked away in icecaps and glaciers. That percentage is not about to change. Even if there were enough to go round, piping it to those who need it is getting harder. America desperately needs to upgrade its water infrastructure, a job that will cost between $ 300 billion and $ 1 trillion (two-thirds of which is for distribution through pipes and pumps). An estimated 60 per cent of America's water main pipes will be classified as substandard by 2020.

And the water supplied is deteriorating. American companies test for nearly 100 known contaminants and a disturbing number of new compounds are being found – a glass of water could contain aspirin, caffeine and even animal growth hormones from farm-water run-off.

One solution to the global problem is desalination, which is already popular in the Middle East. It is an expensive solution – 100 gallons of seawater produce just 50 gallons of desalinated water – though costs have fallen three to four times in the past 30 years.

The problem for investors is that the world leader in water and desalination, American giant GE, gets only 2 per cent of its revenues from this area, so it hardly offers pure exposure. Goldman tips smaller companies such as filtration specialists Clarcor and Pentair. They should benefit from the recent backlash against bottled water and are likely takeover targets as the $ 425 billion industry consolidates.

Both are listed on the New York Stock Exchange, but with many brokers charging as little to trade American shares as British ones, they are certainly worth a look. If you would prefer a fund, iShares, the exchange-traded fund arm of Barclays, recently launched the first water ETF in Europe – the iShares S&P Global Water Fund.

More established ETFs listed in New York include the Power-Shares Water Resources Portfolio tracking the Palisade Water index, up nearly 7 per cent over the past year, compared with a drop of 10 per cent in the FTSE 100. Alternatively, the First Trust ISE Water index fund is up 14.5 per cent.

The problem with these index trackers is that they give access to the big listed water companies rather than the smaller ones where the action is. For something more racy, try the offshore Pictet Water Fund—although this has barely bucked the down-turn with a fall of 11 per cent, against 17 per cent for the MSCI World index.

Alternatively, private bank Williams de Broë will soon launch an exchange-traded fund that will track six offshore water funds, because there is nothing in the U.K. for its clients. This dearth of funds suggests a genuine investment opportunity.

(This advisory to investors was recently issued in the U.S.A.)

Appendix VII

The Water Commons Approach

THE 'Water Commons' as a concept is easy to understand. And in a time when our planet is threatened by global warming, the importance of the idea is all-too-obvious.

Put simply, the water commons means that water is no one's property; it rightfully belongs to all of humanity and to the earth itself. It is our duty to protect the quality and availability of water for everyone around the planet. This ethic should be the foundation of all decisions made about use of this life-giving resource. Water is not a commodity to be sold or squandered or hoarded.

There are perhaps thousands of campaigns taking place around the planet that draw on shared principles and advance the water commons, although not using that label. The water commons (not always in common parlance) can be a powerful, unifying principle drawing together our diverse but inter-related efforts.

This is the firm conclusion made by a diverse group of leaders from many fields and nations who gathered in late spring at Blue Mountain Centre, amid the lake-dotted Adirondack Mountains of New York State, for a conversation exploring the theme of 'Water For All.' Brought together by On the Commons, the Blue Planet Project and Grassroots International, the group included a public health researcher, an economist, a filmmaker, lawyers, community organizers, authors, professors, NGO directors and foundation officers from the U.S.A., Canada, Mexico, Uruguay, Germany and India.

Maude Barlow, prominent Canadian social activist and author of the international bestseller *Blue Gold: The Fight to Stop Corporate Theft of the World's Water*, offered a wide-ranging overview of what is at stake from a paper she had specially prepared for the conference.

- It is a well-known fact that one-third of all Africans have no regular access to clean drinking water. However, what is not known is that this number is poised to rise to one-half due to increasing pollution and water privatization.
- In the United States, Pentagon officials are already being advised by defence contractors like Lockheed-Martin about securing new sources of water outside American borders – an eerie parallel to the oil politics that has driven U.S. foreign policy for decades.
- The stranglehold that multinational corporations hold on global water supplies has intensified since she published *Blue Gold* six years ago. General Electric is now the largest water company in the world and many others view the sale of water as a key growth industry for the 21st century. Bechtel Corporation went so far as to try to charge people in Bolivia for the rainwater that fell upon their roofs.
- The hydrological cycle – the natural process of precipitation and evaporation that governs ecosystems – is being permanently affected as we alter landscapes by damming, draining, paving, deforestation and other large-scale disruptions. This results in severe unintended consequences such as droughts, flood and desertification.
- The global warming crisis is tightly intertwined with water issues but rarely discussed by government panels and NGOs seeking climate change solutions.
- "Every human activity now needs to be measured by its impact on water and the water commons," Maude Barlow declared. "It is a flagrant violation of human rights when only the rich have access to clean water," she added.

  In her wide travels studying and speaking out on these issues, Barlow sees signs of an emerging water commons consciousness. The efforts at this point are largely local, but when added all together she sees potential for a global movement to press claims to water as a fundamental right for all.
- Uruguay amended its constitution to recognize the right to water free of charge as a basic principle. Colombia is considering a similar measure.
- A backlash against private operation of public water supplies is growing; it started in South America and has now spread to Africa

and even the United States. The World Bank and UN have both been forced to back off from their touting of privatized water as the only way to ensure safe drinking water.

- Norway has refused to fund any further World Bank project that promotes water privatization.

Rajendra Singh, founder of Tarun Bharat Sangh (TBS, or Young India Association), told a personal and at times very amusing story of his work in Rajasthan, India. Trained as a doctor in traditional Indian Ayurvedic medicine, he had always wanted to be a farmer and soon after university, he moved to the Alwar district to test some ideas he had long had in his head. The Arvari River had dried up during the 1940s when the surrounding hills had been stripped of trees. It flowed only during the monsoon season. This meant that over the decades, people had left the villages to seek their livelihood elsewhere and when Singh arrived in the early 1980s the area was populated by only the oldest and poorest residents.

Drawing on indigenous Indian knowledge of geology, hydrology and ecology, he began building tiny dams and johads (reservoirs) on streams flowing to the river in the hope of reviving the natural water flow. The local elders chuckled as they watched him do backbreaking work with very little results for two years. They then decided he was sincere in trying to help them so offered tips on the right spots to place dams and johads. It worked. Within four years the water captured in the johads during the monsoon season was rejuvenating natural vegetation and refilling the aquifers.

The Arvari River now runs all year and people who abandoned the district are now moving back. Villagers are creating their own 'river parliaments' to sustain this precious water commons; each is governed by two leaders—one who is responsible to the community, and one who is responsible solely to the water and nature.

"Water is a very emotional, spiritual thing," Singh explained, noting that the once-lost river is now as sacred to local people—many ask before they die that their ashes be sprinkled into the Arvari rather than the Ganga.

Johanna Miller, outreach director of the Vermont Natural Resources Council, recounted how environmentalists and water activists passed state legislation limiting the amount of groundwater that can be pumped for commercial uses. This was a noteworthy political victory in an era when 'property rights' and 'takings' still ring across the U.S.A. as a fierce rallying cry. Miller noted that the simple question, "Who owns the water?" sent an even more powerful message to many citizens, who showed their support for the bill.

Paula Garcia, executive director of the New Mexico Acequia Association, explained how this centuries-old example of cooperative water management works. Found throughout Latin America, *acequias* are communal irrigation systems shared by dozens or even hundreds of families living along the same stream. In New Mexico, they have been functioning for 400 years and survived many attempts at privatization. Garcia credits the ethic of *querencia*, expressed by many Hispanics and indigenous people in New Mexico, as key to the preservation of the *acequia* commons. *Querencia* means a deep love for the place where you feel most at home and safe. It is related to *quere*, the Spanish word for 'to want, to desire.'

Octavio Rosas Landa, an economics professor and activist from Mexico City, outlined how many Mexican peasants are losing longstanding water rights as the government aggressively pursues a strategy of clearing peasants from the land in the name of economic progress.

Twenty-two million of the country's 25 million campesinos are targeted, according to Rosas Landa. Control over who gets to use the water is one of the most effective tools wielded by the government and corporations to make this happen.

Cindy Parker, co-director of the Programme on Global Sustainability and Health at Johns Hopkins School of Public Health, noted how issues relating to the water commons, and environmental protection in general, get increased attention when discussed as health issues. "It's still easy for policymakers to distance themselves from a purely environmental issue. But it is much harder for them to ignore a public health issue." Health itself is a commons, she said, because everyone has a right to health.

V. Suresh—director of the Rights Research Centre of the Centre for Law, Policy and Human Rights Studies in Chennai, India—surveyed a world where even industrialized nations must respond to water shortages. Australia now places restrictions on washing cars with drinking water and last year London's mayor banned lawn sprinklers.

The World Bank and other agents of water privatization claim that their policies promote conservation of the water supply, ease the burden of women (who in traditional cultures often carry water long distances) and expand access to clean water. Yet in reality, the result of water privatization is that poor people are cut off from access to safe water.

Suresh declared there is absolutely no evidence to support claims that water privatization boosts conservation. Cooperative water sharing systems, on the other hand, like those used for generations in Latin America, have a proven record of accomplishment in preserving scarce water resources. He added that the recent emphasis on technological and free market solutions actually diminishes people's own creativity in addressing these problems. "Fifty years of development have wiped out local knowledge and skills about conserving and cooperating around water."

V. Suresh has effectively organized water utility workers—those often written off as spiritless bureaucrats—in radically reforming Chennai's water utility.

Harriet Barlow, director of Blue Mountain Centre—who convened the Water for All meeting with Anil Naidoo of the Blue Planet Project, Daniel Moss of Grassroots International and Julie Ristau of On the Commons—stressed that the point of the gathering was not to launch one more activist organization, but rather to explore something that might look more like a network of networks. "We're already part of many networks and campaigns. We've come here in a state of inquiry. How do we make a water commons revolution?" The stimulating conversation at Blue Mountain Centre marks the first step towards that goal.

A sampling of ideas about the commons and about water from the Blue Mountain Centre meeting:

- Every religion says water is the origin of life.
  Rajendra Singh – Founder, Tarun Bharat Sangh (Rajasthan, India).
- You can't simply look at one sector of the commons in isolation. All are interlocking and must be looked at holistically. The water commons relates to the public service commons, the tax commons, the public health commons, and the environment commons.
  Harriet Barlow, Senior Fellow, On the Common.
- The commons is a framework for reconstruction. Until now we have spent more time on resistance than on reconstruction.
  Alberto Villarreal, Co-founder, REDES (Social Ecology Network, Uruguay).
- Why is it so difficult to describe to the world something we know intuitively in our hearts? Commons poets and artists can help us do this.
  Juliette Majot, Consultant and former Executive Director of International Rivers.
- The World Bank and other international agencies know how to spend

$ 1 billion in one place, building a dam, but they do not know how to spend $ 1,000 in a million places that will make a positive difference by using local resources and knowledge.
Maude Barlow, Chairperson, Council of Canadians.

- In thinking about how legal frameworks can be used to protect the commons, it's worthwhile to consider the extent to which the law grew out of local commons and customs.
David Mears, Director, Environmental and Natural Resources Law Clinic at the Vermont Law School.

- The idea of pricing water did not originate with the environmental movement. It came out of right-wing think tanks in the 1970s. *Wenonah Hauter, Executive Director, Food and Water Watch.*

- Challenging the ownership of water was off the table as a credible mainstream issue for many years, but the framework of the commons is an opportunity to raise it again.
Alan Snitow, Director of the film Thirst *and author of the accompanying book* Thirst: Fighting the Corporate Theft of Our Water.

Appendix VIII

Irrigation Water Use per Country in the year 2000

	Total Renewable Water Resources	Irrigation Water Requirements (cubic km)	Water Requirement Ratio (%)	Water Withdrawal for Agriculture (cubic km)	Water withdrawal as percentage of Renewable Water Resources (%)
Afghanistan	65	8.78	38	22.84	35
Algeria	14.32	1.45	37	3.94	27
Angola	1.84	0.04	20	0.21	0
Argentina	6.14	3.43	16	21.52	3
Bangladesh	1210.644	19.09	25	76.35	6
Benin	24.8	0.06	30	0.19	1
Bolivia	622.533	0.26	23	1.16	0
Botswana	14.4	0.02	30	0.06	0
Brazil	8233	0.21	17	36.63	0
Burkina Faso	12.5	0.21	30	0.69	5
Burundi	3.6	0.06	30	0.19	5
Cambodia	476.11	1.20	30	4.00	1
Cameroon	285.5	0.22	30	0.73	0
Chad	43	0.07	35	0.19	0
Chile	922	1.59	20	7.97	1
China	2829.569	153.90	36	426.85	15
Colombia	2132	1.23	25	4.92	0
Congo, Republic of	832	0.00	30	0.00	0
Congo, Dem. Republic of	1283	0.03	30	0.11	0
Costa Rica	112.4	0.36	25	1.43	1
Cote d'ivoire	81	0.17	28	0.60	1

Continued...

Continued...

	Total Renewable Water Resources (cubic km)	Irrigation Water Requirements (cubic km)	Water Requirement Ratio (%)	Water Withdrawal for Agriculture (cubic km)	Water withdrawal as percentage of Renewable Water Resources (%)
Cuba	38.12	1.41	25	5.64	15
Dominican Republic	20.995	0.56	25	2.24	11
Ecuador	432	2.67	19	13.96	3
Egypt	58.3	28.43	53	53.85	92
El Salvador	25.23	0.19	25	0.76	3
Eritrea	6.3	0.09	32	0.29	5
Ethiopia	110	0.56	22	2.47	2
Gabon	164	0.02	30	0.05	0
Gambia	8	0.01	30	0.02	0
Ghana	53.2	0.06	26	0.25	0
Guatemala	111.27	0.40	25	1.61	1
Guinea	226	0.41	30	1.36	1
Guyana	241	0.45	28	1.60	1
Haiti	14.025	0.18	20	0.93	7
Honduras	95.929	0.17	25	0.69	1
India	1896.66	303.24	54	558.39	29
Indonesia	2838	21.49	28	75.60	3
Iran, Islamic Rep. of	137.51	21.06	32	66.23	48
Iraq	75.42	11.20	28	39.38	52
Jamaica	9.404	0.01	25	0.02	0
Jordan	0.88	0.29	39	0.76	86
Kenya	30.2	0.30	30	1.01	3
Korea, Dem. People's Rep.	77.135	1.49	30	4.96	6

Continued...

Continued...

	Total Renewable Water Resources (cubic km)	Irrigation Water Requirements (cubic km)	Water Requirement Ratio (%)	Water Withdrawal for Agriculture (cubic km)	Water withdrawal as percentage of Renewable Water Resources (%)
Korea, Republic of	69.7	2.67	30	8.92	13
Laos	333.55	0.81	30	2.70	1
Lebanon	4.407	0.37	40	0.92	21
Libyan Arab Jamahiriya	0.6	2.56	60	4.27	712
Madagascar	337	3.58	25	14.31	4
Malawi	17.28	0.20	25	0.81	5
Malaysia	580	1.68	30	5.60	1
Mali	100	2.06	30	6.87	7
Mauritania	11.4	0.44	29	1.50	13
Mexico	457.222	18.53	31	60.34	13
Morocco	29	4.28	37	11.48	40
Mozambique	216.11	0.22	39	0.55	0
Myanmar	1045.601	9.79	30	32.64	3
Namibia	17.94	0.07	40	0.17	1
Nepal	201.2	2.45	25	9.82	5
Nicaragua	196.69	0.30	27	1.08	1
Niger	33.65	0.62	30	2.08	6
Nigeria	286.2	1.65	30	5.51	2
Pakistan	222.67	72.14	44	162.65	73
Panama	147.98	0.05	20	0.23	0
Paraguay	336	0.08	23	0.35	0
Peru	1913	5.07	31	16.42	1
Philippines	479	6.33	30	21.10	4

Continued...

Continued...

	Total Renewable Water Resources (cubic km)	Irrigation Water Requirements (cubic km)	Water Requirement Ratio (%)	Water Withdrawal for Agriculture (cubic km)	Water withdrawal as percentage of Renewable Water Resources (%)
Rwanda	5.2	0.01	30	0.03	1
Saudi Arabia	2.4	6.68	43	15.42	643
Senegal	39.4	0.43	30	1.43	4
Siewrra Leone	160	0.12	33	0.35	0
Somalia	13.5	0.98	30	3.28	24
South Africa	50	2.34	21	11.12	22
Sri Lanka	50	2.92	24	12.00	24
Sudan	64.5	14.43	40	36.07	56
Suriname	122	0.18	30	0.62	1
Swaziland	4.51	0.12	16	0.76	17
Syrian Aram Republic	26.26	8.52	45	18.93	72
Tanzania, United Rep. of	91	0.56	30	1.85	2
Thailand	409.944	24.83	30	82.75	20
Togo	14.7	0.02	30	0.08	1
Tunisia	4.56	1.21	54	2.23	49
Turkey	229.3	11.27	40	27.86	12
Uganda	66	0.03	30	0.12	0
Uruguay	139	0.66	22	3.03	2
Venezuela, Boliv. Rep. of	1233.17	1.24	31	3.97	0
Viet Nam	891.21	15.18	31	48.62	5
Yemen	4.1	2.53	40	6.32	154
Zambia	105.2	0.26	19	1.32	1
Zimbabwe	20	0.67	30	2.24	11

Appendix IX

Glossary of Key Hydrological Terms

Aquifer: A layer or section of earth or rock that contains freshwater, known as groundwater (any water that is stored naturally underground or that flows through rock or soil, supplying springs and wells).

Hydrological (water) cycle: The natural cycle by which water evaporates from oceans and other water bodies, accumulates as water vapour in clouds and returns to oceans and other water bodies as precipitation. Precipitation over land has two components: runoff and moisture from evapo-transpiration.

Non-renewable water: Water in aquifers and other natural reservoirs that are not recharged by the hydrological cycle or are recharged so slowly that significant withdrawal for human use causes depletion. Fossil aquifers are in this category: They recharge so slowly over centuries that they are, in effect, a non-renewable resource.

Renewable water: Freshwater that is continuously replenished by the hydrological cycle for withdrawal within reasonable time limits, such as water in rivers, lakes or reservoirs that fill from precipitation or from runoff. The renewability of a water source depends both on its natural rate of replenishment and the rate at which the water is withdrawn for human use.

Runoff: Water originating as precipitation on land that then runs off the land into rivers, streams and lakes, eventually reaching the oceans, inland seas, or aquifers, unless it evaporates first. That portion of runoff that can be relied on year after year and easily used by human beings is known as stable runoff.

Water consumption: Use of water that results in its evaporation or transpiration (through plants) or that otherwise makes it unavailable for subsequent human use.

Water withdrawal: Removal of freshwater for human use from any natural source or reservoir, such as a lake, river or aquifer. If not consumed, the water may return to the environment and can be used again.

Water scarcity: According to a growing consensus among hydrologists, a country faces water scarcity when its annual supply of renewable freshwater is less than 1,000 cubic metres per person. Such countries can expect to experience chronic and widespread shortages of water that hinder their development.

Water stress: A country faces water stress when its annual supply of renewable freshwater is between 1,000 and 1,700 cubic metres per person. Such countries can expect to experience temporary or limited water shortages.

Bibliography

Abramovitz, J. 'Imperiled waters, impoverished future: The decline of freshwater ecosystems.' Worldwatch Institute. Washington, D.C., U.S.A., 1996, pp. 5–66.

Adams, W. M. 'Wasting the rain: Rivers, people and planning in Africa'. *Earthscan*, London, U.K., 1992.

Ainstein, L. 'Buenos Aires: A case of deepening social polarization.' In: (Ed.). Gilbert, A. *The Mega-city in Latin America*. United Nations University Press, New York, U.S.A., 1996. pp. 133–154.

Alam, N. 'Mother's personal and domestic hygiene and diarrhoea incidences in young children in rural Bangladesh.' *International Journal of Epidemiology*, 18: 242–247, 1989.

Alcamo, J., Döll, P., Kaspar, F. and Sieberg, S. *Global Change and Global Scenarios of Water Use and Availability: An Application of Water GAP*. Centre for Environmental System Research, University of Kassel, Kassel, Germany, 1998.

Ali, A. 'Water, sanitation and health: Role of NGOs.' In *Touch*. August 1992, pp. 1–2.

Allan, J. A. 'Water Security Policies and Global Systems for Water Scarce Regions.' *Sustainability of Irrigated Agriculture – Transactions*, Vol. 1-E. Special Session, The Future of Irrigation under Increased Demand From Competitive Uses of Water and Greater Needs for Food Supply. International Commission on Irrigation and Drainage, New Delhi, India, 1996.

Allaoui, K. 'Long-term finance for water projects: The IDB's approach.' Presented at the International Conference of Water and Sustainable Development, Paris, France. March 19–21, 1998.

Anker, R. and Knowles, J. C. 'An empirical analysis of morbidity differentials in Kenya at the macro- and micro-levels.' *Economics, Development and Cultural Change*, 29: 165–185, 1980.

Aung, M. H. and Thein, H. 'Prevention of diarrhoea and dysentery by handwashing.' *Transactions* of the Royal Society of Tropical Medicine and Hygiene, 83: 128–131, 1989.

Baltazar, J. 'Can the case-control method be used to assess the impact of water supply and sanitation on diarrhoea? A study in the Philippines.' *Bulletin* of the World Health Organization, 66: 627–635, 1988.

Basch, P. F. *Textbook of International Health.* New York, U.S.A.: Oxford University Press, 1990.

Bergkamp, G. and Acreman, M. 'Optimization of water resources management through maintaining the functioning of ecosystems.' Presented at the International Conference of Water and Sustainable Development, Paris, France, March 19–21, 1998.

Berrittella, M., Hoekstra, A. Y., Rehdanz, E., Roson, R. and Tol, R. S. J. 'The Economic Impact of Restricted Water Supply: A Computable General Equilibrium Analysis.' *Water Research,* 42, 1799–1813, 2007.

Billman-Golemme, L. 'Water resources protection—Government and civil society: necessary next steps.' Presented at the International Conference of Water and Sustainable Development, Paris, France, March 19–21, 1998.

Bos, E. and Bergkamp, G. 'Water and the Environment.' *Overcoming Water Scarcity and Quality Constraints,* 2020. (Eds.). Meinzen-Dick, R. S. and Rosegrant, M. W. International Food Policy Research Institute, Washington, D.C., U.S.A., 2001.

Bowman, J. 'Water is best: Would Pindar still think so?' In: (Ed.). Cartledge, B. *Health and the Environment: The Linacre Lectures 1992-93.* Oxford, U.K.: Oxford University Press, 1994.

Bradley, D. 'Health, Environment and Tropical Development.' In: (Ed.). Cartledge, B. *Health and the Environment: The Linacre Lectures 1992-93.* Oxford, U.K.: Oxford University Press, 1994.

Brismar, A. *Freshwater and Gender, a Policy Assessment.* Stockholm, Stockholm Environmental Institute, 1997.

Brown, L. and Halweil, B. 'China's water shortage could shake world food security.' *Worldwatch,* 11(4): 10–21, 1998.

Brunetto, R., Leon, A., Burguera, J. L. and Burguera, M. 'Levels of DDT residues in human milk of Venezuelan women from various rural populations.' *Science of the Total Environment,* 186(3): 203–207, 1996.

Bulloch, J. and Darwish, A. *Water Wars: Coming Conflicts in the Middle East.* London, U.K.: Victor Gollancz, 1993.

Burger, S. E. and Esrey, D. A. 'Water and sanitation: Health and nutrition benefits to children.' In: (Eds.). Pinstrup-Andersen, P., Pelletier, D. and Alderman, H. *Child Growth and Nutrition in Developing Countries: Priorities for Action.* Ithaca, New York, U.S.A.: Cornell University Press, 1995. pp. 153–175.

Burns, J. 'Sharing Ganges waters, India and Bangladesh test the depth of cooperation'. *New York Times,* May 25, 1997.

Cairncross, S. and Cliff, J. L. 'Water use and health in Mueda, Mozambique.' *Transactions* of the Royal Society of Tropical Medicine and Hygiene, 81: 51–54, 1987.

Caponera, D. A. 'The importance of water law and institutions for sustainable development.' Presented at the International Conference of Water and Sustainable Development, Paris, France, March 19–21, 1998.

Carpenter, B. and Watson, T. 'More people, more pollution.' *U.S. News & World Report,* 117(10): 63–65, 1994.

Carty, W. 'Towards an urban world.' *Earthwatch,* 43: 2–4. 1991.

Chapagain, A. K. and Hoekstra, A. Y. *Water Footprints of Nation's Value of Water.* Research Report Series, No.6, UNESCO-IHE, 2004.

Chapagain, A. K., Hoekstra, A. Y., Savenije, H. H. G. and Gautam, R. 'The water footprint of cotton consumption: An assessment of the impact of worldwide consumption of cotton products on the water resources in the cotton producing countries.' *Ecological Economics,* 60(1): 186–203, 2006.

Chatterjee, A. 'Communicating health.' *Health for the Millions.* July–August, 1995.

Chioccioli, E., Hamdy, A. and Lacirignoia, C. 'Institutional capacity building and integrated water resources management in the Mediterranean.' Presented at the International Conference of Water and Sustainable Development, Paris, France, March 19–21, 1998.

Cincotta, R. and Engelman, R. 'Economics and rapid change: The influence of population growth.' Population Action International, Washington, D.C., U.S.A., 1997.

Clapano, J. R. 'Water firm extends amnesty deadline.' *Philippine Star,* January 14, 1998.

Clarke, R. *Water: The International Crisis.* London, U.K.: Earthscan, 1991.

Cline, T. 'Sink or swim: Population pressures threaten the nation's water.' *ZPG Reporter,* September–October 1995.

Convention on Wetlands (Ramsar). 'The key role of wetlands in addressing the global water crisis.' Presented at the International Conference of Water and Sustainable Development, Paris, France, March 19–21, 1998.

Cosgrove, W. J. and Rijsberman, F. *World Water Vision: Making Water Everybody's Business.* World Water Council and World Water Vision and Earthscan, London, U. K., 2000.

Crossette, B. 'Severe water crisis ahead for poorest nations in next 2 decades.' *New York Times,* August 10, 1995.

Davidson, J. 'Women's relationship with the environment.' *Focus on Gender,* 1(1): 5–10. 1993.

Davidson, J., Myers, D. and Chakraborty, M. *No Time to Waste – Poverty and the Global Environment.* Oxford, U.K.: Oxfam, 1992.

Dillon, S. 'Capital's downfall caused by drinking...of water.' *New York Times*, January 29, 1998.

D'monte, D. 'Filthy flows the Ganga.' *People and the Planet*, 5(3): 20–22, 1996.

Dowdeswell, E. 'Editorial.' *Our Planet*, October, 1996.

Duddin, M. and Hendrie, A. *World Land and Water Resources*. London, U.K.: Hodder and Stoughton, 1988.

Dukhovny, V. and Sokolov, V. 'Water resources management strategy for the Aral Sea Basin: Problems in preparation.' Presented at the International Conference of Water and Sustainable Development, Paris, France, March 19–21, 1998.

Economist. 'Dirt poor: A survey of development and the environment.' *Economist*, March 21, 1998.

Economist. 'Valley of the dammed.' *Economist*, February 21, 1998.

Economist. 'Water in the Middle East: As thick as blood.' *Economist*, December 23, 1996.

Economist. 'Water, water, everywhere.' *Economist*, February 21, 1998.

Edungbola, L. D. 'The impact of a UNICEF-assisted rural water project on the prevalence of guinea worm disease in Asa, Kwara State, Nigeria'. *American Journal of Tropical Medicine and Hygiene*, 39: 79–85. 1988.

Edwards, R. 'Russia's real drink problem.' *New Scientist*, November 1, 1997.

El Quosy, D.E.D. 'Water scarcity and water security: Reasons and requirements.' Presented at the International Conference of Water and Sustainable Development, Paris, France, March 19–21, 1998.

Engelman, R. and Leroy, P. *Sustaining Water: An Update*. Washington, D.C., U.S.A.: Population Action International, 1995.

Engelman, R. and Leroy, P. *Sustaining Water: Population and the Future of Renewable Water Supplies*. Washington, D.C., U.S.A.: Population Action International, 1993.

Environmental Protection Agency (EPA). 'The quality of our nation's water: 1994.' Washington, D.C., U.S.A: *EPA*, December, 1995.

Esrey, S. A. and Habicht, J.-P. 'Epidemiologic evidence for health benefits from improved water and sanitation in developing countries.' *Epidemiologic Reviews*, 8: 117–128, 1986.

Esrey, S. A., Potash, J. B., Roberts, L. and Shiff, C. 'Effects of improved water supply and sanitation on ascariasis, diarrhoea, dracunculiasis, hookworm infection, schistosomiasis, and trachoma'. *Bulletin of the World Health Organization*, 69(5): 609–621, 1991

European Schoolbooks (ES). *The Battle for Water: Earth's Most Precious Resource*. Cheltenham, U.K.: ES, 1994.

Evans, A. and Stephenson, L. 'Not by drugs alone: The fight against parasitic helminths.' *World Health Forum*, 16(3): 258–261, 1995.

Falkenmark, M. 'Curing water scarcity blindness.' *Earthwatch,* 41: 9, 1991.

Falkenmark, M. 'Fresh water as a factor in strategic policy and action'. In: (Eds.). Davis, K., Bernstam, M. and Sellers, H. *Population And Resources In a Changing World.* Stanford, California, U.S.A.: Morrison Institute for Population and Resource Studies, 1989.

Falkenmark, M. 'Freshwater as shared between society and ecosystems: From divided approaches to integrated challenges.' *Philosophical Transactions* of the Royal Society of London, 2003.

Falkenmark, M. 'Landscape as life support provider: Water-related limitations.' In: (Ed.). Graham-Smith, F. *Population – The Complex Reality.* Golden, Colorado, U.S.A.: North American Press, 1994.

Falkenmark, M. 'Middle East hydro-politics: Water scarcity and conflicts in the Middle East.' *Ambio,* 18(6): 350–352, 1989.

Falkenmark, M. 'Population growth and water supplies: An emerging crisis.' *People,* 17(1): 18–20, 1990.

Falkenmark, M. 'Population, environment and development: A water perspective.' In: Population, Environment and Development. Proceedings of the United Nations Expert Group Meeting on Population, Environment and Development. [January 20–24, 1994] New York, U.S. A., 1994.

Falkenmark, M. 'Rapid population growth and water scarcity: The predicament of tomorrow's Africa.' In: (Eds.). Davis, K. and Bernstam, M. *Resources, Environment, and Population: Present Knowledge and Future Options.* New York, U.S.A.: Oxford University Press, 1991.

Falkenmark, M. 'Water scarcity: Time for realism.' *Populi,* 20(6): 11–12, 1993.

Falkenmark, M. and Lindh, G. 'Water and economic development.' In: (Ed.). Gleick, P., *Water in Crisis.* New York, U.S.A.: Oxford University Press, 1993.

Falkenmark, M. and Lundqvist, J. *World Freshwater Problems – Call for a New Realism.* Stockholm: Stockholm Environmental Institute, 1997.

Falkenmark, M. and Widstrand, C. 'Population and water resources: A delicate balance.' *Population Bulletin,* 47(3): 1–36, 1992.

Falkenmark, M., Lundqvist, J. and Widstrand, C. 'Macro-scale water scarcity requires micro-scale approaches: Aspects of vulnerability in semi-arid development.' *Natural Resources Forum,* 13(4): 258–267, 1989.

Feldmann, L. 'Water, water everywhere, but not enough to drink.' *Christian Science Monitor,* November 9, 1993.

Garcia, L. 'A role for river basin organizations within an integrated water resources management strategy.' Presented at the International Conference of Water and Sustainable Development, Paris, France, March 19–21, 1998.

Gardner, R. and Blackburn, R. 'People who move: New reproductive health focus.' *Population Reports,* Series J, No. 45. Baltimore, U.S.A.: Johns

Hopkins School of Public Health, Population Information Programme, November 1996.

Gardner-Outlaw, T. and Engleman, R. 'Sustaining water, easing scarcity: A second update'. Washington, D.C., U.S.A.: Population Action International, 1997.

Garrett, L. *The Coming Plague: Newly Emerging Diseases in a World Out of Balance.* New York, U.S.A.: Farrar, Straus and Giroux, 1994.

Gathiram, V. and Ravdin, J. I. 'Amoebiasis and other enteric protozoan infections.' In: (Eds.). Lankinen, K. S., Berström, S., Mäkelä, P. H. and Peltomaa, M. *Health and Disease in Developing Countries.* London, U.K., Macmillan Press, 1994.

Gazdag, I. and Remai, J. 'Hungarian national wastewater programme.' Presented at the International Conference of Water and Sustainable Development, Paris, France, March 19–21, 1998.

Gleick, P. 'An introduction to global fresh water issues.' In: (Ed.). Gleick, P. *Water in Crisis.* New York, U.S.A.: Oxford University Press, 1993.

Gleick, P. 'Basic water requirements for human activities: Meeting basic needs.' *International Water,* 21(2): 83–92, 1996.

Gleick, P. 'Water and conflict: Fresh water resources and international security.' *International Security,* 18(1): 79–112, 1993.

Goldenstein, S. 'Sustainable management and the water resources system in São Paulo State.' Presented at the International Conference of Water and Sustainable Development, Paris, France, March, 19–21, 1998.

Green, C. P. 'The environment and population growth: Decade for action.' *Population Reports,* Series M, No. 10. Baltimore, U.S.A.: Johns Hopkins School of Public Health, Population Information Programme, 1992.

Haines, M. R. and Avery, R. C. 'Differential infant and child mortality in Costa Rica: 1968–1973.' *Population Studies,* 36: 31–43, 1982.

Hall, A. W. and Walmsley, N. 'Case studies of water resource planning in developing countries: Lessons learned.' Presented at the International Conference of Water and Sustainable Development, Paris, France, March, 19–21, 1998.

Halstead, S. B. 'Dengue, yellow fever and rabies.' In: (Eds.). Lankinen, K. S., Bergstöm, S., Mäkelä, P. H. and Peltomaa, M. *Health and Disease in Developing Countries.* London, U.K.: Macmillan Press, 1994.

Harrison, P. *The Third Revolution: Environment, Population and a Sustainable World.* London, U.K.: I. B. Tauris, 1992.

Haub, C. 'New UN projections depict a variety of demographic futures.' *Population Today,* 25(4): 1–3, 1997.

Havas-Szilagyi, E. 'National groundwater protection programme in Hungary.' Presented at the International Conference of Water and Sustainable Development, Paris, France, March, 19–21, 1998.

Helmer, R. 'News from the waterfront.' *World Health*, July-August 1992.

Helmer, R. 'Water quality.' Presented at the International Conference of Water and Sustainable Development, Paris, France, March 19-21, 1998.

Henry, F. J. 'Environmental sanitation infection and nutritional status of infants in rural St. Lucia, West Indies.' *Transactions* of the Royal Society of Tropical Medicine and Hygiene, 75: 507-513, 1981.

Hinrichsen, D. 'Acid rain and forest decline.' In: (Eds.). Goldsmith, E. and Hildyard, N. *The Earth Report: Monitoring the Battle of our Environment*. London, U.K.: Mitchell Beazley, 1988.

Hinrichsen, D. 'Aral yesterday and now: Problems and perspectives of Aral's crisis.' Almaty, Kazakhstan: International Fund for the Aral Sea, 1997.

Hinrichsen, D. 'The world's water woes.' *International Wildlife* 26(4): 22-27, July-August 1996.

Hinrichsen, D. 'Winning the food race.' *Population Reports*, Series M, No. 13. Baltimore, U.S.A. Johns Hopkins School of Public Health, Population Information Programme, November 1997.

Hinrichsen, D. *Coastal Waters of the World: Trends, Threats and Strategies*. Washington, D.C., U.S.A.: Island Press, 1998.

Hoekstra, A. Y. and Chapagain, A. K. 'Water footprints of nations: water use by people as a function of their consumption pattern.' *Water Resources Management*, 21(1): 35-48, 2007.

Holmes, B. 'Water, water everywhere....'. *New Scientist*, February 17, 1996.

Holmes, B. 'Don't ignore nature's bottom line.' *New Scientist*, May 17, 1997.

Hovi, U. T. and John, T. J. 'Poliomyelitis.' In: (Eds.). Lankinen, K. S., Berström, S., Mäkelä, P. H. and Peltomaa, M. *Health and Disease in Developing Countries*. London, U.K.: Macmillan Press, 1994.

Hunter, J. M., Rey, L., Chu, K. Y., Adekolu-John, E. O. and Mott, K. E. *Parasitic Diseases in Water Resources Development: The Need for Inter-sectoral Negotiation*. Geneva, Switzerland: World Health Organization, 1993.

International Herald Tribune. 'The world's freshwater supplies: The crunch is here.' *International Herald Tribune*, September 30, 1997.

Jauro, A. 'Lake Chad basin commission (LCBC) perspectives.' Presented at the International Conference of Water and Sustainable Development, Paris, France, March 19-21, 1998.

Juma, C. 'The CBD and the biological diversity of inland waters.' Presented at the International Conference of Water and Sustainable Development, Paris, France, March 19-21, 1998.

Khan, A. H. 'The sanitation gap: Development's deadly menace.' In: *The Progress of Nations*. New York, U.S.A.: UNICEF, 1997.

Khan, M. U. 'Interruption of shigellosis by hand-washing'. *Transactions* of the Royal Society of Tropical Medicine and Hygiene, 76: 164-168, 1982.

Kiernan, V. 'Wealthy nations face drinking water crisis.' *New Scientist*, June 1, 1996.

Kjellén, M. and Mcgranahan G. *Urban Water – Towards Health and Sustainability.* Stockholm: Stockholm Environmental Institute, 1997.

Klohn, W. and Wolter, W. 'Perspectives on food and water.' Presented at the International Conference of Water and Sustainable Development, Paris, March 19–21, 1998.

Kohen, S. 'A thirsty Syria may make Turkey's water price of peace.' *Christian Science Monitor*, January 9, 1996.

Koopman, J. S. 'Diarrhoea and school toilet hygiene in Cali, Colombia.' *American Journal of Epidemiology*, 107: 412–420, 1978.

Kraemer, D. 'Integrated information management and the utilization of hydrological data.' Presented at the International Conference of Water and Sustainable Development, Paris, France, March 19–21, 1998.

Kristof, N. 'For third world, water is still a deadly drink.' *New York Times*, January 9, 1997.

Kuylenstierna, J. L., Björklund, G. and Najlis, P. 'Sustainable water future with global implications: Everyone's responsibility.' *Natural Resources Forum*, 21(3): 181–190, 1997.

Lean, G. and Hinrichsen, D. *Atlas of the Environment*. New York, U.S.A.: Harper Perennial, 1994.

Lefort, R. 'Down to the last drop.' *UNESCO Sources*, No. 84: 7, 1996.

Lenzen, M. and Foran, B. 'An Input-Output analysis of Australian water usage'. *Water Policy*, 3: 321–340, 2001.

Livernash, R. 'The future of populous economies: China and India shape their destinies.' *Environment*, July–August, 1995.

Livernash, R. and Rodenburg, E. 'Population change, resources, and the environment.' *Population Bulletin*, 53(1): 1–40, 1998.

Lundqvist, J. and Gleick, P. *Sustaining our Waters into the 21st Century.* Stockholm: Stockholm Environmental Institute, 1997.

Marcoux, A. *Population and Water Resources*. Rome, Italy: United Nations Food and Agriculture Organization (FAO), 1994.

Maywald, A., Zeschmar-Lahl, B., and Lahl, U. 'Water fit to drink?' In: (Eds.). Goldsmith, E. and Hildyard, N. *The Earth Report: Monitoring the Battle for our Environment*. London, U.K.: Mitchell Beazley, 1988.

McCormack, M. S., Treloar, G. J., Palmowski, L. and Crawford, R. H. 'Modelling direct and indirect water consumption associated with construction.' *Building Research and Information*, 35[2], 156–162, 2007.

Mckibben, B. 'A special moment in history.' *Atlantic Monthly*, May 1998.

Merla, A. A. 'Commitment to the global environment: The role of GEF and international waters.' Presented at the International Conference of Water and Sustainable Development, Paris, France, March, 19–21, 1998.

Misch, A. 'Sanitation in the time of cholera.' *World Watch*, July–August 1999,. pp. 37–38.

Misra, K. K. 'Safe water in rural areas.' *International Journal of Health Education*, 18: 53–59, 1975.

Mitchell, J. 'Before the next doubling.' *World Watch*, January–February 1998.

Moncayo, A., Kuzoe, F. and Modabber, F. 'Trypanosomiases and leishmaniases.' In: (Eds.). Lankinen, K. S., Berström, S., Mäkelä, P. H. and Peltomaa, M. *Health and Disease in Developing Countries*. London, U.K.: Macmillan Press, 1994, pp. 211–220.

Muller, R. and Morera, P. 'Helminthoses.' In: (Eds.). Lankinen, K. S., Berström, S., Mäkelä, P. H. and Peltomaa, M. *Health and Disease in Developing Countries*. London, U.K.: Macmillan Press, 1994.

Murphy, C. 'Middle East faces major water woes.' *Washington Post*, March 10, 1990.

Nash, L. 'Water quality and health.' In: (Ed.). Gleick, P. *Water in Crisis*. New York, U.S.A.: Oxford University Press, 1993.

Nelson, L. and Sandell, C. 'Population and water resources.' *National Audubon Society*, New York, U.S.A., 1990.

Niemczynowicz, J. 'Megacities in water perspective.' *Water International*, 21(4): 198–205, 1996.

Niemczynowicz, J. 'Wasted waters.' UNESCO Sources, No. 84, p. 8, November 1996.

Olshansky, S. J., Carnes, B., Rogers, R. and Smith, L. 'Infectious diseases—New and ancient threats to world health.' *Population Bulletin* 52(2): 2–43, July 1997.

Organization for Economic Cooperation and Development (OECD). 'Water management performance and challenges in OECD countries.' Presented at the International Conference of Water and Sustainable Development, Paris, France, March 19–21, 1998.

Parmar, B. J. and Gulati, O. T. 'Sustainable water resources development through integrated river basin management on Sabarmati river basin of India.' Presented at the International Conference of Water and Sustainable Development, Paris, France, March 19–21, 1998.

Patel, T. 'India faces chaos over water rights.' *New Scientist*, April 26, 1997.

Philippine Legislators' Committee on Population and Development. 'Of all the planet's renewable resources, fresh water.' *People Count*, January 1994.

Pimentel, D. and Pimentel, M. 'Land, energy and water: The constraints governing ideal U.S. population size.' In: (Ed.). Grant, L. *Elephants in the Volkswagen: Facing the Tough Questions about our Overcrowded Country*. New York, U.S.A.: W. H. Freeman and Company, 1992.

Population Reference Bureau (PRB). *Population and Environment Dynamics*. Washington, D.C., U.S.A.: PRB, 1997.

Population Reference Bureau (PRB). *World Population Data Sheet, 1998.* Washington, D.C., U.S.A.: PRB, 1998.

Postel, S. 'Changing the course of trans-boundary water management.' *Natural Resources Forum*, 21(2): 85–90, 1997.

Postel, S. 'Dividing the waters: Food security, ecosystem health, and the new politics of scarcity.' Washington, D.C., U.S.A.: *World Watch Institute*, September 1996.

Postel, S. 'Sharing the rivers.' *People and the Planet*, 5(3): 6–9, 1996.

Postel, S. 'The politics of water.' *World Watch*, July–August 1993.

Postel, S. 'Trouble on tap.' *World Watch*, September–October 1989.

Postel, S. 'Water and agriculture'. In: (Ed.). Gleick, P. *Water in Crisis.* New York, U.S.A.: Oxford University Press, 1993.

Postel, S. 'Water tight.' *World Watch*, January–February 1993.

Postel, S. 'Where have all the rivers gone?' *World Watch*, May–June, 1995.

Postel, S. *Last Oasis: Facing Water Scarcity.* New York, U.S.A.: Norton, 1997.

Postel, S., Daily, G. and Ehrlich, P. 'Human appropriation of renewable fresh water.' *Science*, 271(5250): 785–788, 1996.

Prakash, R. 'Tapping mountains for freshwater as global resources dwindle.' *Earth Times News Service/Environment*, May 1, 1998.

Pullen, S. and Hurst, P. 'Marine pollution prevention.' WWF background report. Gland, Switzerland, *World Wide Fund for Nature*, July 1993.

Purdum, T. 'U.S. acts to meet water needs in the West.' *New York Times*, December 19, 1997.

Rahaman, M. M. 'The Teknaf health impact study: Methods and results.' Presented at the International Workshop on Measuring Health Impacts of Water and Sanitation Programmes, Cox's Bazaar, Bangladesh, November 21–25, 1983.

Rahman, A. 'Groundwater contamination in rapidly growing Asian cities.' Stockholm Water Front, June 1, 1995.

Rahman, M. 'Impact of environmental sanitation and crowding on infant mortality in rural Bangladesh.' *Lancet*, 8445(2): 28–31, 1985.

Raskin, P., Gleick, P., Kirshen, P., Pontius, R. G., and Strzepek, K. Water Futures: Assessment of Long-Range Patterns and Problems. Stockholm: Stockholm Environmental Institute, 1997.

Ray, K. and Kakabeeke, W. J. 'Community participation in urban water and sanitation: The missing link in public-private partnership.' Presented at the International Conference of Water and Sustainable Development, Paris, France, March 19–21, 1998.

Reisner, M. *The American West and its Disappearing Water.* New York, U.S.A.: Penguin Books, 1986.

Revkin, A. 'Billion-dollar plan to clean New York City water at its source.' *New York Times*, August 31, 1997.

Riviere, J. W. M. 'Threats to the world's water.' *Scientific American,* 261(9): 80–94, September 1989.

Robey, B., Ross, J. and Bhushan, I. 'Meeting unmet need: New strategies.' *Population Reports,* Series J, No. 43. Baltimore, U.S.A.: Johns Hopkins School of Public Health, Population Information Programme, October 1996.

Robey, B., Rutstein, S. O., Morris, L. and Blackburn, R. 'The reproductive revolution: New survey findings.' *Population Reports,* Series M, No. 11. Baltimore, U.S.A.: Johns Hopkins School of Public Health, Population Information Programme, December 1992.

Rodda, J. *The Depths of our Knowledge. UNESCO Sources.* No. 84, November 1996.

Rowley, J. 'Linking population to conservation—special report on Pakistan.' *Earthwatch* 40: 3–5, 1990.

Safina, C. *Song for the Blue Ocean: Encounters along the World's Coasts and Beneath the Seas.* New York, U.S.A.: Henry Holt and Co., 1997.

Sampat, P. 'The river Ganges' long decline.' *World Watch,* 9(4): 24–32, July–August 1996.

Seabright, P. *Water: Commodity or Social Institution*? Stockholm: Stockholm Environmental Institute, 1997.

Seckler, D., Amarasinghe, U., Molden, D., Rhadika, S. and Barker, R. *World Water Demand and Supply, 1990 to 2025: Scenarios and Issues.* Research Report Number 19. International Water Management Institute, Colombo, Sri Lanka, 1998.

Serageldin, I. 'Water resources management: New policies for a sustainable future.' *Stockholm Water Front,* June 1, 1995.

Serageldin, I. 'Water supply, sanitation, and environmental sustainability: The financing challenge'. Washington, D.C., U.S.A.: World Bank, 1994.

Serageldin, I. *Toward Sustainable Management of Water Resources.* Washington, D.C., U.S.A.: World Bank, 1995.

Sherbinin, A. *Water and Population: The Urgent Need for Action.* New York, U.S.A: Inter-American Parliamentary Group on Population and Development, 1997.

Shiklomanov, A. 'Electronic Data Provided to the Scenario Development Panel, World Commission on Water for the 21st Century.' State Hydrological Institute, St. Petersburg, Russia, 1999.

Shiklomanov, I. 'World fresh water resources.' In: (Ed.). Gleick, P. *Water in Crisis.* New York, U.S.A.: Oxford University Press, 1993.

Shiklomanov, I.. A. *Assessment of Water Resources and Water Availability in the World.* Stockholm: Stockholm Environmental Institute, 1997.

Silfverberg, P. 'Environmental health hazards.' In: (Eds.). Lankinen, K.S.,

Berström, S., Mäkelä, P. H. and Peltomaa, M. *Health and Disease in Developing Countries*. London, U.K.: Macmillan Press, 1994.

Suresh, V. 'Strategies for sustainable water supply for all: Indian experience.' Presented at the International Conference of Water and Sustainable Development, Paris, France, March 19–21, 1998.

Torun, B. 'Environmental and educational interventions against diarrhoea in Guatemala.' In: (Eds.). Chen, L. C. and Scrimshaw, N. S. *Diarrhoea and Malnutrition: Interactions, Mechanisms, and Interventions*. New York, U.S.A.: Plenum Press, 1982.

Tyler, P. 'China's fickle rivers: Dry farms, needy industry bring a water crisis.' *New York Times*, May 23, 1996.

Tyler, P. 'Huge water project would supply Beijing by 860-mile aqueduct.' *New York Times*, July 19, 1994.

United Nations (UN) Commission on Sustainable Development. 'Comprehensive assessment of the freshwater resources of the world.' *Report* of the Secretary General. New York, U.S.A: United Nations, 1997.

United Nations (UN) Commission on Sustainable Development. 'Strategic approaches to freshwater management.' *Report* of the Secretary General. New York, U.S.A.: United Nations, 1998.

United Nations (UN) Department for Economic and Social Information and Policy Analysis. *Population Growth and Policies in Mega-cities*. São Paulo. New York, U.S.A.: United Nations, 1993.

United Nations (UN) Department for Policy Coordination and Sustainable Development. *Critical Trends – Global Change and Sustainable Development*. New York, U.S.A.: United Nations, 1997.

United Nations Children's Fund. *Facts and Figures 1997*. Online:http://www.unicef.org/factx/facright.htm

United Nations Children's Fund. *Water and Sanitation Progress and Disparity*. Online: http://www.unicef.org/pon97/p12b.htm

United Nations Development Programme (UNDP). *Urban Agriculture – Food, Jobs and Sustainable Cities*. New York, U.S.A.: UNDP, 1996.

United Nations Environment Programme (UNEP). *Global Environment Outlook*. New York, U.S.A.: Oxford University Press, 1997.

United Nations Food and Agriculture Organization (FAO). *Dimensions of Need: An Atlas of Food and Agriculture*. Rome, Italy: FAO, 1995.

United Nations Food and Agriculture Organization (FAO). *Food for All*. Rome, Italy: FAO, 1996.

United Nations Food and Agriculture Organization (FAO). *Water for Life*. Rome, Italy: FAO, 1990.

United Nations Population Fund (UNFPA). *Food for the Future: Women, Population and Food Security*. New York, U.S.A.: UNFPA, 1996.

United Nations Population Fund (UNFPA). *India: Towards Population and Development Goals.* New Delhi, India: Oxford University Press, 1997.

United Nations Population Fund (UNFPA). *Population and Sustainable Development – Five Years after Rio.* New York, U.S.A.: UNFPA, 1997.

United Nations Population Fund (UNFPA). *The State of World Population.* New York, U.S.A., 1996.

United Nations Educational, Scientific and Cultural Organization (UNESCO). Ground Water: Managing the 'Invisible' Resource. *Environment and Development Briefs,* No. 2, 1997.

United Nations Educational, Scientific and Cultural Organization (UNESCO). *The Makings of a Water Crisis – Can Supply Keep up with Demand?* UNESCO Sources, No. 84: 12–13, November 1996.

United States Agency for International Development (USAID). *Strategies for Linking Water and Sanitation Programs to Child Survival.* Washington, D.C., U.S.A.: USAID, September 1990.

United States Centre for Disease Control and Prevention (CDC). 'Update: Dracunculiasis eradicationá á Pakistan, 1994.' *Morbidity and Mortality Weekly Report* 44(6): 117–119, February 17, 1995.

Vanderslice, J. and Briscoe, J. 'Environment interventions in developing countries: Interactions and their implications.' *American Journal of Epidemiology,* 141(2): 135–144.

Varma, A. 'Will water soon be too expensive for the poor of the world?' *Earth Times News Service/*Economic Development, May 4, 1998.

Vesikari, T. and Torun, B. 'Diarrheal diseases.' In: (Eds.). Lankinen, K. S., Berström, S., Mäkelä, P. H. and Peltomaa, M. *Health and Disease in Developing Countries.* London, U.K.: Macmillan Press, 1994.

Wallensteen, P. and Swain, A. *International Fresh Water Resources: Conflict or Cooperation?* Stockholm: Stockholm Environmental Institute, 1997.

Warner, D. 'Drinking water supply and environmental sanitation for health.' Presented at the International Conference of Water and Sustainable Development, Paris, France, March 19–21, 1998.

Whittle, H. and Van Hemsbroek, M. B. 'Malaria.' In: (Eds.). Lankinen, K. S., Bergström, S., Mäkelä, P. H. and Peltomaa, M. *Health and Disease in Developing Countries.* London, U.K.: Macmillan Press, 1994.

World Bank (WB). *African Water Resources: Challenges and Opportunities for Sustainable Development.* Washington, D.C., U.S.A.: World Bank, 1996.

World Bank (WB). *Water Resources Management.* A World Bank policy paper. Washington, D.C., U.S.A: World Bank, 1993.

World Conservation Union (IUCN) and Population Reference Bureau (PRB) and U.S. Agency for International Development (USAID). *Water and Population Dynamics: Local Approaches to a Global Challenge.* Washington, D.C., U.S.A.: PRB and USAID, 1996.

World Health Organization (WHO). 'First countries certified as free of guinea worm disease.' Press release WHO/7, January 24, 1997.

World Health Organization (WHO). *Division of Control of Tropical Disease homepage*. Online: http://www.who.ch/ctd/. February 25, 1998.

World Health Organization (WHO). *Health and Environment in Sustainable Development Five Years after the Earth Summit*. Geneva, Switzerland: World Health Organisation, 1997.

World Health Organization (WHO). *Our planet, our Health*—Report of the WHO Commission on Health and Environment. Geneva, Switzerland: World Health Organization, 1992.

World Health Organization (WHO). *Rich-poor Gap Remains in Death*. Reuters News Service, May 11, 1998.

World Health Organization (WHO). *The World Health Report 1996*: Fighting disease, fostering development. Geneva, Switzerland: World Health Organisation, 1996.

World Resources Institute (WRI), 2nd United Nations Environment Programme (UNEP), United Nations Development Programme (UNDP) and World Bank (WB). *World Resources 1996–97*. New York, U.S.A.: Oxford University Press, 1996.

World Resources Institute (WRI), United Nations Environment Programme (UNEP) and United Nations Development Programme (UNDP). *World Resources 1992–93*. New York, U.S.A.: Oxford University Press, 1992.

World Resources Institute (WRI). *World Resources, 1987*. Washington, D.C., U.S.A: WRI, 1987.

World Wildlife Fund Canada (WWFC) and World Wildlife Fund U.S.(WWF). *Resolving the DDT Dilemma*. Toronto, Canada and Washington, D.C., U.S.A.: World Wildlife Fund Canada and World Wildlife Fund, June 1998.

Xinhua Chinese News Agency. 'Rampant use of DDT pollutes Bangladesh's underground.' Dhaka, Bangladesh, June 7, 1998.

Yacoob, M., Brieger, W. and Watts, S. 'Primary health care: Why has water been neglected?' *Health Policy and Planning*, 4(4): 328–333, December 1989.

Young, B. and Briscoe, J.A. 'Case-Control Study of the Effect of Environmental Sanitation on Diarrhea Morbidity in Malawi.' *Journal of Epidemiology and Community Health*, 42: 83–88, 1987.

Zakharova, N. *The Role of Rural Women in Food Security*. New York, U.S.A.: United Nations Division for the Advancement of Women, October 1995.

Index

O

P

R

S

T

U

V

W